Politics of the Maya Court

Politics of the Maya Court

Hierarchy and Change in the Late Classic Period

Sarah E. Jackson

UNIVERSITY OF OKLAHOMA PRESS : NORMAN

Library of Congress Cataloging-in-Publication Data

Jackson, Sarah E., 1976–
Politics of the Maya court : hierarchy and change in the late classic period / Sarah E. Jackson.—1st ed.
p. cm.
Includes bibliographical references and index.
ISBN 978-0-8061-4341-5 (hardcover : alk. paper)
1. Mayas—Kings and rulers.
2. Mayas—Politics and government.
3. Courts and courtiers—Mexico—History.
4. Courts and courtiers—Central America—History.
I. Title.
F1435.3.K55J33 2013
972'.6—dc23

2012037302

The paper in this book meets the guidelines for permanence and durability of the Committee on Production Guidelines for Book Longevity of the Council on Library Resources, Inc. ∞

1 2 3 4 5 6 7 8 9 10

For Matthew

A book in the Latin American and Caribbean
Arts and Culture initiative.
Latin American and Caribbean Arts and Culture is
supported by the Andrew W. Mellon Foundation.

LATIN AMERICAN
AND CARIBBEAN
ARTS AND CULTURE

Contents

Illustrations

Figures

Maps

Charts and Tables

Charts

Tables

Figure 1. Photograph of hieroglyphic bench, Structure 9N-82, Copán, in excavated context: a monument that provoked thought about interpreting hierarchical organization from textual records. Photograph by William Fash.

Preface

A Visit to the Court

Setting Out

Several afternoons in the summer of 1997, spent in the half-darkened town archaeological museum in Copán Ruinas, Honduras, woke me to the possibilities of reading ancient texts in multiple ways. I was sitting uncomfortably on a borrowed folding campstool, drawing the hieroglyphic text on the front of the carved bench from Structure 9N-82 at Copán (figure 1). This task was undertaken not because no such drawing existed but rather to get to know the images in a way that only a pencil in hand and the copying of lines and shapes can yield. The resulting drawing was imperfect, but it still captured a sense of the intricate imagery of the glyphs carved into the stone. As I replicated words and images set down over a thousand years ago by a Maya scribe—words and images that documented distinctive political structures of the time—I began to think about how this monument represented more than a simple written record of a past event or political institution. Reading it carefully revealed that the stone seat also conveyed larger cultural ideas about hierarchical inequality and processes of change and, in turn, served as a materialization of these concepts.

This hieroglyphic bench belonged to an individual named Mak'an Chanal who lived during the eighth century and was an official in the court of Yax Pasaj, the sixteenth ruler of Copán. Mak'an Chanal lived in Las Sepulturas, a pleasant residential enclave east of the Copán city center. He was a fortunate individual in the attention his ruler bestowed on him, attention that included the privilege of displaying an elaborate carved text in his home. Textual evidence indicates that Mak'an Chanal's involvement with Copán's court provided him with formal recognition and status within his community. We can imagine him walking to and from the central meeting places of the city, treading one of Copán's *sacbeob*, or roads, contemplating the pressing religious and political news of the day. As I drew the elaborate images that graced his bench, I began to wonder about political organization in the Classic Maya world and how hierarchical differences between individuals were conceptualized and acted out. How could we read the hieroglyphic record—directly and indirectly—in order to think about these topics?

My own imaginings of Mak'an Chanal and his Late Classic compatriots occurred as I, too, walked the causeways and entered the ancient buildings of Copán, abustle now not with homage payers from distant Classic-era polities but with tourists from near and far, there to pay respects and be dazzled by the city in a different way. My training to approach the past through both material and textual records left me acutely aware of the power of text and its materialized forms at a site like Copán.

Mak'an Chanal's bench is a monument not only in its solid form, impressive size, and elaborate decoration but also in its ability to mark identity and differentiation in ways that would have been legible to members of a Classic Maya community. Mak'an Chanal's high standing, as indicated by his bench, is further significant for being part of the change sweeping through many Late Classic Maya polities (A.D. 600–900). The long-held position of the *k'uhul ajaw*, or "holy lord," as the singular charismatic ruler was modified to make way for strategies of power sharing with certain members of the court, such as Mak'an Chanal.

My meditations on one particular monument led to ongoing interest in the possibilities for a nuanced understanding of Classic Maya political organization, illuminated by individuals and offices newly accessible from hieroglyphic evidence. Many field seasons, written pages, thoughtful exchanges, contemplative moments, and miles from Copán later, this book emerges as the result of ongoing engagement with the topic.

Destinations

This is a book about the Classic Maya royal court and its members. It addresses the composition of the Classic Maya court, examines the officials of that institution and their roles, and grapples with the question of why the court matters. Far from representing a static and reified framework, the study reveals a dynamic and variable political structure, one that was responsive to particular temporal and spatial contexts. A fine-grained focus on the court also brings our level of analysis to the unit of the individual. Such a perspective allows a fruitful and fascinating glimpse of particular agents and their life stories as a way of humanizing Late Classic period processes and understanding its historical trajectories as the results of individuals' choices and actions.

Despite the focus on elite individuals as members of the court, the topics examined in this work also help to shed light on individuals beyond, and outside of, the space of the court. The reciprocal nature of relationships both inside the court and beyond is an important idea here. Even in situations of radical hierarchical disparity, we see the significance to ancient Maya elites of the reception and replication of ways of being and acting by other individuals. This would have involved an ongoing interplay between what happened in the charged central space of the court and what was then discussed, imitated, and even resisted beyond that core space. Leaders and followers in the Classic Maya political world were involved in an intricate dance. Figuring out the steps of one of the partners in turn allows the delineation of the other's footwork.

This book illuminates more than Maya politics of a certain era. Thematically, the evidence and discussion speak to questions of identity differentiation and how hierarchy is constructed and expressed. The development of a full-fledged courtly institution within the context of the at-times tumultuous years of the Late Classic allows for identity issues to be examined through the lens of change, providing an important comparative template for the study of strategically adopted, dynamic identities in other times and places. The interrelationships between change and variation, illuminated through the textually derived data that I examine, emerge as an important theme; locally produced cultural metaphors couch the experience and understanding of these processes. In turn, examination of metaphor allows for the exploration of the meanings of cultural structures and the incorporation of these perspectives into our interpretations.

The questions that began to emerge for me in the Copán museum over a decade ago, and which will be explored in the chapters of this text, rest upon this basic query: what was the nature of the Classic Maya political community? Delving into the topic necessitates a clear understanding of courtly roles and positions, the sources and meaning of hierarchically oriented status within the court, and how these variables changed over time. Throughout my research, I have been curious to see what can be illuminated or accessed of particular experiences, and even mind-sets, through the close reading of textual evidence. Ultimately, the book provides an understanding of the institution of the Classic Maya court as a productive locus of influence and power, suggesting new perspectives on concepts of leadership and strategic adaptations in the face of changing conditions.

Acknowledgments

I count myself extremely fortunate to be a member of multiple generous and stimulating scholarly communities: ideas, discussion, and valuable feedback that helped to mold and influence this book came from a variety of sources. I want to acknowledge the contributions of close friends and academic peers, conversations with whom fueled my thinking, as well as those of fellow scholars whom I have not met but whose writings I referred to again and again as I worked through my own ideas and argument; it is a privilege to share the resulting work with you.

In particular, for their direct or indirect contributions to this project, I want to single out David Stuart, William Fash, Stephen Houston, Joanne Pillsbury, Vernon Scarborough, Megan O'Neil, Linda Brown, and Charles Golden for thanks. Sylvia Sellers-García and Isaac Campos-Costero were compatriots in a stellar writing group that improved this manuscript significantly. My thanks also go to Meredith Coats, Lindsay Argo, Holly Dorning, Angela Hood, and Emily Culver, who were my graduate student research assistants at UC at various times and were of great help with myriad small details. Finally, numerous undergraduate and graduate students in my classes on the Maya and on Royal Courts at the University of New Hampshire, the University of Toronto, and the University of Cincinnati have been wonderful sources of inspiration and founts of challenging and thought-provoking questions; I am appreciative of all their enthusiasm and curiosity.

Support in the form of funding and time was critical in the successful completion of this book. First, I am very grateful to the Mellon Foundation for its generous support of this project as part of the Latin American and Caribbean Arts and Culture Mellon Initiative. Key support for the project was provided by the Taft Research Center of the University of Cincinnati, the University Research Council of the University of Cincinnati, the Department of Anthropology at the University of Cincinnati, and a Mellon Foundation Postdoctoral Fellowship at the University of Toronto.

This book grows out of my dissertation work, conducted in the Department of Anthropology at Harvard University. While I will not reiterate the lengthy thank-yous that accompanied the completion of that project, I do wish to mention a few important individuals who helped guide and shape earlier versions of this one: Dave Stuart, Bill Fash, Steve Houston, Gary Urton, and Arthur Demarest. My thanks to them for their mentorship. The incomparable collections and staff at Tozzer Library and at Dumbarton Oaks were treasured resources for the duration of the undertaking; I feel very fortunate to have had access to them.

I am grateful for kind assistance with illustrations, images, and permissions from Barbara Fash, David Greene, Nikolai Grube, Stephen Houston, Barbara and Justin Kerr, Peter Mathews, Juan Carlos Meléndez, Megan O'Neil, Diane Griffiths Peck, David Stuart, Alexandre Tokovinine, David Webster, the Cleveland Museum of Art, Dumbarton Oaks, FAMSI, the Peabody Museum, the Ministerio de Cultura y Deportes de Guatemala and the Museo Nacional de Arqueología y Etnología de Guatemala. Alessandra Tamulevich, at the University of Oklahoma Press, deserves special recognition for her belief in this book and her thoughtful guidance of its shaping; my future writing no doubt will be influenced by thinking back to her kind and incisive advice. I appreciate Emmy Ezzell's hard work on the beautiful illustrations in this volume. Kevin Cain and his team at INSIGHT also worked on the illustrations to ensure optimal clarity of reproduction. Alice Stanton, with assistance from Margery Tippie, shepherded the manuscript to completion—I thank them for their careful readings and attention to detail. I am grateful for all of the support at the press. Insightful comments, suggestions, and criticisms from two anonymous readers substantially strengthened my arguments. Any errors or shortcomings in what follows are my own.

Last but never least, warmest thanks go to my family. My parents, Susan and Howard Jackson, are relentlessly supportive of my pursuits. My husband, Matthew Peattie, and my daughter, Clara, both regularly perform miracles, and my son, Benjamin, arrived just in time to witness the book's completion. This work would not have been possible without you.

Politics of the Maya Court

CHAPTER ONE

Entering the Classic Maya Royal Court

For ancient Maya citizens, entering the court involved walking decorously up plastered masonry stairs and into cool, secluded rooms decorated with textiles, or gathering in a sunny and hot temple courtyard to sit attentively and watch a ritual presentation, depending on the level of access they had to the social and spatial components of the royal court. For the modern visitor or reader attempting to imagine and cross the threshold of this ancient Maya institution, some intellectual travel and orientation are necessary.

Geographically, let us situate ourselves in southern Mexico and Central America, the heartland of the ancient Maya world. Treading the ground of a royal court means that we are located in one of the many polities or city-states that dotted the landscape of the Maya region. This was not a unified empire but rather a loosely aggregated culture area, sharing many traits but composed of independent kingdoms. Royal courts were found at large, central communities ranging from Chiapas to Yucatán to the highlands of Guatemala to western Honduras. Each major polity was ruled by a *k'uhul ajaw*, or "holy lord," who embodied intertwined aspects of religious and political authority.

Temporally, the modern visitor has time traveled back to the Classic period, dating from approximately A.D. 250 to 900, seen as the apogee of Maya culture. The heyday of the institution of the court is specifically associated with the Late Classic period (ca. A.D. 600–900). Its development represents important changes in political structure, as well as larger cultural adjustments to some of the challenges facing Maya culture in advance of its eventual collapse in the Terminal Classic period.

As we stand on the threshold of the court and look around us in wonder—awed by the impressive trappings of the space—we can observe the materials that provide Maya scholars in the present day with the data to reconstruct key components of this governmental institution. Architecture and physical remains of objects, as well as the human skeletal remains of courtiers lingering in the hallways, provide modern archaeologists with insight into both the built and social environments of this world. The hieroglyphic texts that adorn walls, furniture, and portable items are especially critical for illuminating ancient Maya perspectives on their own political hierarchy and organization. These texts provide specific information that helps to untangle the positions, roles, and meanings of the Classic Maya court. Understanding Classic Maya political organization and, specifically, the institution of the royal court, using the primary source documentation recorded by ancient Maya scribes themselves is the central focus of this book.

In this introductory chapter, we situate ourselves with an overview of recent research related to the Maya court, after which we come to a discussion of how modern scholars access information about the court, through the hieroglyphic texts mentioned above. Thus, a critical understanding of these texts as an evidentiary source is necessary. We then meet the courtly players who are identified with specific offices in the hieroglyphic texts and review aspects of the data set discussed in this book. Finally, we take a broader perspective, considering conceptions of the institution of the court in terms of comparative perspectives and relevant models. This view is important for placing work on the Classic Maya in the larger context of connected topics in other times and places.

Courtly Contexts: Scholarly Approaches to the Court

The topic of Classic Maya political organization has only recently been examined through the lens of the royal court. While research in the field of Maya studies has long included issues of differentiation and discussion of Maya elites, exploration of a governing institution that might reveal how the Maya themselves conceptualized hierarchy within their society is relatively new. A 1998 symposium at Yale University, organized by Takeshi Inomata and Stephen Houston, led the way in proposing a new framework for approaching governance and recognizing the contribution of individuals beyond the ruler to political processes in the Maya world. This conference led to the publication of two seminal edited volumes, *Royal Courts of the Ancient Maya,* Volumes 1 and 2 (Inomata and Houston 2001a, 2001b). Significantly, the contributions in these two books represent scholarship that draws on diverse sets of evidence (including hieroglyphic, archaeological, iconographic, and ethnohistoric data) and perspectives from multiple temporal and geographical spaces. These multievidentiary and comparative approaches are a hallmark of this era of investigation—insights into royal courts are forthcoming, in part, because of the broader data sets of information now available.

While this conference and the associated volumes represent the beginning of focused consideration of the topic of royal courts in the Maya world, two other scholarly developments are also directly related. The first of these is the recognition of changing forms of governmental organization in the Late Classic. Archaeological, iconographic, and epigraphic work on the council house at Copán (Structure 10L-22A, also referred to as the Popol Nah or Mat House) set the stage for discussion of shifting strategies of Late Classic rulers (Fash et al. 1992). In particular, the presence and use of council houses during the Late Classic period suggests a more inclusive form of rule, in which other voices and individuals became part of the process of governance. Research at Copán resulted in a notably well investigated example of a council house, drawing upon detailed archaeological and iconographic evidence at the site, and underlines the necessity of examining analogous structures at other sites.

Second, in a related advance, epigraphic work in the 1980s and 1990s recognized the presence of titles beyond that of the *k'uhul ajaw*, or central ruler, which indicated the existence of other official elite positions (e.g., Houston 1993:127–36; Lacadena 1996; Ringle 1988; Schele 1991b; Schele and Miller 1986:136–38; Stuart 1992). Attention was focused particularly on the *sajal* and the *ajk'uhuun* titles, the latter often referred to as the "God C title." These titles were correlated with iconographic depictions of elite individuals accompanying rulers, such as those seen on carved stone panels at Piedras Negras and Yaxchilán, and with residential spaces occupied by titled elites, such as Group 9N-8, Las Sepulturas, at Copán. With a new awareness of hieroglyphic titles, both artistic and archaeological data could be interpreted in ways that illuminated the roles and affiliations of these elite individuals. Like the recognition of the Late Classic use of council houses, the ability to identify individuals bearing titles contributed to the conception of Late Classic political organization as including multiple individuals, and as becoming diversified beyond the personage of the *k'uhul ajaw*.

Since then, the exhibition and volume *Courtly Art of the Ancient Maya* (Miller and Martin 2004) reinforced the identification of the royal court as a creative location in which special materials were produced and knowledge curated. The objects that were the focus of the exhibition, and that were highlighted in the catalog, served to emphasize the ways in which courtly status and identity were materially marked. Similarly, the space of the court came into focus with the volumes *Palaces of the Ancient New World* (Evans and Pillsbury 2004) and *Maya Palaces and Elite Residences* (Christie 2003).

While these steps toward recognizing and studying the royal court were important for the exploration of the diversified political structure of the Late Classic period, they lacked the ability to reliably describe the boundaries of the institution. Defining the court has always presented a problem, in that Maya texts do not actually employ a collective word to refer to it. This is not surprising. The hieroglyphic texts do not record terms for other collective, societal institutions like family or government or community, either. Rather, for all of these examples, specific constituent components or roles are named. Courtly titles function in the same way, acting as a textual proxy for the communal entity of the court. While Late Classic evidence supports the presence of a collective ruling body, describing or defining it in recent scholarship has been a challenge, and scholars have frequently used loose, differing, or poorly defined criteria to delineate what we mean by a "royal court" in Maya contexts.

Discussion of bounded segments of Classic-era society and sociopolitical organization to date has primarily focused on topics related to class-based hierarchy. Over the years, Mayanists have argued for two-class models, three-class models, or more complex systems of social organization. The two-class model (e.g., Farriss 1984:167; Marcus 1992:221; Sanders and Price 1968:160; Sharer 1993:93; Thompson 1954:81) is based upon a primary division between nobles or elites and commoners, setting up a marked/unmarked dichotomy and a gulf between two oppositional status groups.

Proponents of the three-class model emphasize the addition of a middle class (Chase 1992:42, 47; Chase and Chase 1992:9). They assert that supposed material markers of eliteness identify too large a portion of the population for it to be considered "elite" (i.e., restricted). This model suggests that an elite class category, by definition, must represent a small percentage of the community's population. However, such concerns may also belie a static perspective, rather than one that incorporates social change as experienced in real-world polities. In considering the Maya scenario, demographic processes of expansion, as well as fissioning of lineages, might reasonably result in a bloated elite group by the Late Classic period (Houston and Inomata 2009:171).

Other interpretations of class structure have included multiclass models, featuring more than three proposed class divisions, and describing a more complex hierarchy (e.g., Adams 1970; Borhegyi 1956:349–50; Culbert 1974:67; Hammond 1982:197; Kidder 1950:8; Morley 1947:168). Many of these models represent a fundamentally different take on Classic Maya hierarchy. Specifically, they discuss ranked groups composed of specialized positions and particular functional occupations, such as craft specialists or priests. The different models of class organization demonstrate the multiple modes of organization for any group; contrasting these models indicates differing—or at times confused—results, depending on which organizational structures (from an emic point of view) or modes of analytical categorization (from an etic perspective) are used.

Scholarly fixation on class structure presages our ability to study the court by recognizing the necessity of thinking about group organization and differentiation. Class-oriented investigations have largely lacked the vocabulary, however, to discuss internal divisions in ways that mesh with Maya experience or the evidence left behind that reflects on these topics. Using hieroglyphic data allows the possibility of understanding ideas of differentiation and official organizations in terms that reflect an ancient reality. While glyphic texts related to the royal court do not speak directly to the number of classes present in Maya society, they do help to identify the locations of meaningful social divisions or boundaries.

One of the aims of the present work is to provide a rationale, rooted in textual data, for defining official membership within the court. By examining the suite of hieroglyphic titles used to describe elites, I identify five such titles (*ajk'uhuun*, *sajal*, *ti'huun* or *ti'sakhuun*, *yajaw k'ahk'*, and "banded bird"—discussed in greater detail below) that are set apart from other honorifics by involving an accession event parallel to that undergone by the ruler. These positions thus form a foundation of the official courtly hierarchy. While other individuals—we can think here of captives, visitors, attendants, dwarves, and others who are vividly pictured in images of the court on painted ceramic vessels—certainly shared the social and physical space of the court, a recognition of courtly offices provides a basis for discussing the institutions's core. As will be discussed, studying these titles also allows for consideration of what sociopolitical boundaries were enacted by the Maya as particularly salient. Using hieroglyphic data as public and official records of Maya political structure opens the door for future work on understanding court structure through archaeological, iconographic, and ethnohistoric evidence as well.

With this book, we enter a new phase of our ability to talk about Maya political organization and the Late Classic emergence of the royal court, using the Maya's own conception of this institution. Armed with a clearer sense of the membership of the court, we are now positioned to address pressing questions about the court itself. These include the nature of courtly organization and hierarchy, the ways that courtly positions functioned and their affiliated responsibilities, and culturally informed understandings of how difference was conceptualized within this official framework. With the data that I discuss in the following chapters, we are poised to answer these questions and, in a larger sense, to emerge with a sharper view of the hierarchical organization and political changes that characterized Maya polities during the Late Classic period.

Maya Written Records as an Evidentiary Source

Since the information found in hieroglyphic texts, written by Maya individuals during the Classic period, provides the basis in this volume for understanding the royal court, a short overview of Maya hieroglyphic writing will provide necessary context for the investigations and data that follow. Scholars of ancient Maya culture are fortunate to have primary source documentation that has survived, providing the possibility of internal cultural perspectives on topics discussed in ancient Maya voices. Even such primary sources must be read with a critical eye, however. Understanding the nature of the script, the media in which it is preserved, the contexts of production, and topics recorded provides an informed perspective on the strengths and weaknesses of this data set, which is critical to modern scholars for gaining access to the Maya institution of the court. My aim is to provide such background for the reader in the section that follows, so that he or she can appreciate and critically understand the data discussed here, and follow how hieroglyphic texts are used in the service of an argument about Classic-era political organization. Detailed histories of particular decipherments, as well as guidance in reading the glyphs, are beyond the scope of this text. Readers who are interested in learning more about the mechanics and operation of this writing system, as well as the process of decipherment, may find it useful to consult such recent publications as *Reading the Maya Glyphs* (Coe and Van Stone 2001), *The Decipherment of Ancient Maya Writing* (Houston et al. 2001), and *Breaking the Maya Code* (Coe 1999).

Let us turn now to some important hieroglyphic background that will contextualize the data of this book for those unfamiliar with Maya writing. Maya hieroglyphic writing is logosyllabic in nature; that is, it is composed both of signs that stand for entire words (logograms) and signs that signal particular phonetic values (syllables). After a variety of breakthroughs in decipherment during the twentieth century, including the key recognitions that the script had a phonetic component (Knorosov 1956) and that it records historical events (Proskouriakoff 1960), epigraphers of Maya writing are now at a stage in which the vast majority of this writing system can be read and understood. The hieroglyphic writing system is closely related to the modern Ch'orti' Mayan language spoken in eastern Guatemala (Houston et al. 2000) and typically reflects a verb-object-subject reading order (Coe and Van Stone 2001:27; Houston 1989:43).

Hieroglyphic texts are found written on a variety of types of media (see overview in Houston 1989:27–30). These include different forms of carved stone monuments—for example, freestanding erect stelae, altars, and integrated architectural elements such as panels, lintels, and stairways. Portable objects, particularly such items as painted ceramic vessels as well as personal items—carved shells, bones, jewelry—were adorned with shorter texts. In contrast to these formal textual expressions, a few examples of graffiti or hasty sketches represent a less-mediated format for text and image recorded in this era. Additionally, the tropical environment of much of the Maya region means that scholars must confront the probable loss of perishable materials, including important media for writing such as bark-paper books, examples of which are preserved from later periods and neighboring culture areas. This lacuna may represent not only a loss of particular types of textual objects, but also the distinct genres of writing that were recorded on them.

Topics recorded in the textual records that remain address several areas of preoccupation for Classic Maya individuals. As noted, the hieroglyphic texts engage substantively with the historical record of Maya polities (per Proskouriakoff's observation [1960]). The rise and fall of particular cities, rulers, individuals, relationships, and the events in which polities and personages took part are written down with pleasing specificity of personal names, places, and dates. The ability to comprehend the majority of the phonetic system used (typically composed of consonant-vowel, or CV, syllables, as Knorosov identified [1956]) allows for these ancient terms to be uttered by the modern reader.

The calendrical details that anchor recorded historical events are also used to frame cosmological and religious observances that were important to Maya citizens. Dates notated in the calendar system frequently provide structure within longer texts, serving both to introduce action and to relate multiple events through recognition of passing time (recorded as "distance numbers"). Two main calendar systems were employed: the Long Count, which represents a count of days elapsed since a mythical creation date in 3114 B.C., thus marking a unique temporal location, and the Calendar Round, which itself combines two cyclical calendars (a 365-day solar calendar and a 260-day ritual calendar) in order to form a cycle that repeats once every 52 years. The Calendar Round, then, provides "local" temporal locations but must be contextualized or correlated with a Long Count date or other relevant historical information in order to yield an absolute date. (Summaries of the structure of the Maya calendar may be found in sources that include Coe and Van Stone [2001:37–48], Houston [1989:48–50], Marcus [1976:39–41], and Rice [2008:282–84].)

Texts addressing historical or religious matters are typically found in the lengthier passages recorded on stone monuments. Other genres are more commonly found on other objects. Ceramic vessels, for example, often display a formulaic text wrapped around the rim of the vessel. This type of text, referred to as a Primary Standard Sequence (Coe 1973:26; Houston et al. 1989:720; MacLeod 1990; Stuart 1989a:149–55), obeys a common pattern of specifying the pot's owner, the object form or type, and its contents. So-called name-tagging texts, which appear on portable personal items and name the items and its owner (Stuart 1989a:154–55), are similar to ceramic texts in serving to locate individuals and their material goods within social spheres. These types of texts are all different from each other, but all work to organize and document the world of the Maya in ways large and small.

One other type of text—captions—might similarly be considered orientational or locational. Captions are found on large stone monuments and small portable ceramic vessels alike. These brief texts mediate between longer written passages and the vivid visual imagery that frequently accompanied them by labeling individuals pictured in particular scenes. These people are typically identified with a name and relevant title or other appellation and serve as reminders that artistic depictions of events or individuals are often historically specific and represent close attention to the attendees or participants in such activities. Sometimes these captions may also refer to an invisible hand—that of the artist, who at times signed his work with a caption specifying himself as the carver, painter, or creator of a particular piece (Stuart 1989a:156–58).

Both longer and shorter texts can be read at multiple levels: as literal narrations of happenings that were sufficiently important to the Maya to write down, and also as metatexts that shed light on how realities were constructed and how text was used to order complex sociopolitical and material realities.

There are some types of records that do not exist within the corpus of Maya hieroglyphic texts—whether because of the destruction (natural or human) of certain types of records or because of a disinclination on the part of the Maya to record certain types of information. In a particularly striking example, economic records—something frequently found in the records of the Aztecs, neighbors to the north—are notably absent among Maya writing. Despite the fact that the Maya archaeological record indicates the presence of trade routes and exchange of valued goods, as well as the payment of tribute (documented in painted scenes on ceramic vessels), hieroglyphs do little to illuminate these activities. Also lacking are records that involve multiple voices or that record differing perspectives—a gap that is especially important to acknowledge in investigating systems of governance. Hieroglyphic texts, and the ability to read them, were the purview of a particular segment of society; even within this upper class, we see evidence of control of public texts, in particular, by a very limited set of individuals.

This control of textual information is also reflected in the production of hieroglyphic texts. These texts were carved or painted by scribes and artists who were affiliated with the royal court. The specialized knowledge and talent necessary to create textual objects represents one of the types of limited resources associated with the upper echelons of society. Evidence from sites like Aguateca, a rapidly abandoned Late Classic polity in the Petexbatún area with remarkable preservation of elite craft production areas (Inomata 2001b, 2008; Inomata et al. 2002), provides particularly useful data for identifying specialized craft production, including creation of monuments, occurring in close physical and social proximity to the royal palace.

The circumscription of production is echoed in the limitation of literacy to members of the upper class as well (Houston 1994:35–39). However, it is important to bear in mind that literacy in Classic Maya contexts was not a black-and-white issue. Even individuals without extensive training in hieroglyphic writing might have been able to recognize key signs—such as the emblem glyph that referred to their home polity. The close integration of text and iconography would also have allowed for messages to be more accessible to a range of viewers, even if not directly or completely decipherable. In terms of detailed readings of Maya writing (such as those referred to in this volume), however, we must recall that hieroglyphic texts topically reflect the concerns of a small slice of Maya society and were also primarily produced and consumed by the elite.

How do the parameters of the Classic Maya hieroglyphic writing system impact what we can learn about members of the royal court? The advanced state of hieroglyphic decipherment means that the titles of court members—which serve as basic units of analysis for the present study—are readily accessible to modern readers, as are the outlines of the temporal, spatial, and historical frames in which these individuals operated. However, hieroglyphic texts are a threatened resource and a fragmentary record, due to both environmental pressures and looting. Important efforts at documenting hieroglyphic texts by a variety of scholars and institutions,

Figure 2. An image of the court on a ceramic vessel (rollout image). Such depictions readily show the multiple individuals who attend the court and frame the central figure of the ruler, who is pictured here on an elevated bench or throne and interacting with several of these individuals. Drawing by Diane Griffiths Peck. Courtesy of Diane Griffiths Peck.

and especially the Corpus of Maya Hieroglyphic Inscriptions Program at the Peabody Museum of Harvard University, mean that the set of texts available for analysis through photographs and drawings is ever increasing and represents a large set of evidence from across the Maya world.

Hieroglyphic style dictates the use, with very few exceptions, of formal and third-person accounts of largely public and structured occasions. The accounts we read about court members are thereby shaped by an expected writing style. Furthermore, the process of text production, in which specialist scribes encoded information presumably given to them, means that courtly elites were not always in control of the creation of the written documents that concerned them. While this trope is limiting for finding out about the personalities and idiosyncrasies of courtly players (or other Maya folk), or identifying resistance to an official story, it does provide—as a public representation of elite individuals—an excellent idea of how such an identity was publicly presented and what its most salient characteristics were. Even in such potentially formulaic and mediated fora, the presence of a surprisingly wide degree of variability in depictions and descriptions of elites reveals that these textual records do encode individual experiences to some extent; this suggests the possibility of examining the interplay between individual courtly actors and cultural institutions and identities, even for this ancient period.

An Introduction to Maya Courtly Titles

Five Formal Titles

A focus on the individual members of the courtly elite relies upon the tantalizing, and at times frustratingly fragmented, first-hand accounts recorded in the hieroglyphic record. In order to understand the court members who are the focus of this book,

A

B

C

Figure 3. *A:* Accession verb, describing a court member taking his office: *chum* (seating) of a “banded bird,” from a wooden box from Tortuguero. Drawing by Diane Griffiths Peck. Courtesy of Diane Griffiths Peck. *B:* Accession verb, describing a court member taking his office: *k'alhuun* (headband tying) of a *yajaw k'ahk'*, from Tablet of the Slaves, Palenque. Drawing by Linda Schele, © David Schele, courtesy of the Foundation for the Advancement of Mesoamerican Studies, Inc., www.famsi.org. *C:* Accession verb, describing a court member taking his office: *joy* (encirclement) of a *sajal* from wall panel, Dumbarton Oaks. Drawing by Stephen Houston and Alexandre Tokovinine. Courtesy of Dumbarton Oaks, Stephen Houston, and Alexandre Tokovinine.

we must first look carefully at the titles or offices that identify them. These titles have proven notoriously difficult to decipher; nonetheless, contextual study of their usage reveals a wealth of information about the identities, actions, and meanings of these critical positions.

Like many institutions of power, the Maya court was organized through the use of titled positions. The ruler, or *k'uhul ajaw* (Houston and Stuart 1996:295; Schele and Freidel 1990:58, 419), was attended by numerous elites—as seen on many a painted vessel from the Classic period (figure 2); some of these elites bore the privilege of a courtly title. These official titles, which include the positions *sajal*, *ajk'uhuun*, *yajaw k'ahk'*, *ti'huun* or *ti'sakhuun*, and the enigmatic “banded bird” (which remains undeciphered) provide a grammatically defined parallel to the ruler through the shared description of the ritual of ascending to office. That is, just like the ruler (Houston and Inomata 2009:142–43; Stuart 1996:156–57), titled elites were inducted into their new positions through an accession process described as seating (indicated by the term *chum*) (figure 3a), headband tying (*k'alhuun*) (figure 3b), or encircling (*joy*) (figure 3c). These shared descriptors of accession, recorded in the hieroglyphic texts, indicate the strength of the bond between kingly and nonroyal offices through the use of common language, highlighting the importance of these offices and providing indications of the ways in which high offices were formally marked. This distinguishing characteristic of formal accession into office defines the parameters of my own investigation into courtly elite individuals, yielding a focus on five particular positions that were especially important to, and formally incorporated into, the court.

The accession verbs themselves yield some insight into sources and markers of power for these positions. As is supported through text, image, and the material record, the physical seat of the ruler—as well as of other elites—served to define the space and authority of his office. Deceased individuals are frequently found buried under their benches, thereby profoundly marking the association between bodily location, official seat, and power. The accession verb *chum* references these meanings. The headband—seen most frequently in iconographic depictions, though sometimes implied in the archaeological record, such as at Aguateca (Eberl and Inomata 2001:134)—is not only a decorative marker, identifying the ruler or other elite in his office. Rather, it also acts to encircle the “tied” elite in a ritual binding or knotting that we see enacted in Mesoamerican religion on both sentient creatures and on aspects of the built environment, such as stelae and altars (Stuart 1996:155–58). These meanings connect with *k'alhuun*, another designation of accession; the concept of wrapping is echoed in the third term of accession, *joy*, which denotes encirclement (tying and ritually containing) in a similar vein.

The decipherment of the meaning of the five formal elite titles mentioned above has remained surprisingly cloudy, despite the advances in understanding of the Maya script in recent years. Efforts to attach a particular meaning to each title have yielded mixed results and have done relatively little to illuminate the functional significance or role of each of these posts. Focusing, instead, on both individual life stories recorded in the hieroglyphs, as well as on aggregate information available from textual discussion of courtly elites, provides a useful portrait of the activities, roles, and functions of these members of the political hierarchy.

The nitty-gritty of hieroglyphic decipherment is not the focus of the present work; instead, I emphasize investigation of the gestalt of elite lives and their participation in larger social structures. Nonetheless, the ongoing obscurity of these five courtly titles—specifically, their resistance over time to precise or meaningful decipherment—means that a brief overview of what we do know about these words, from a hieroglyphic perspective, is helpful. Those interested in additional detail as well as a historical discussion of the progression of decipherments of these titles will find more exhaustive information in the references cited. A few published sources include discussions of multiple titles and may be of particular interest (see, in particular, Coe and Van Stone 2001; Houston 1993; Houston and Inomata 2009; Houston and Stuart 2001; Jackson 2005; Villela 1993; Zender 2004).

The *sajal* title (figure 4), the most common of the courtly titles (Houston and Stuart 2001:61–64; Houston and Inomata 2009:175–76) and one of the earliest identified by modern scholars, has been read variously as "regional governor" (Schele 1991a:7; Stuart 1985b:17–18), "war captain" (Schele 1991a:10), and "feared one" (Grube and Nahm 1991). The first two readings describe contextual interpretations of this title's meaning, rather than representing actual decipherments of the linguistic basis of the title. The third suggestion is a more literal reading, hypothesizing that the title is based on the Mayan root *sah* (the first part of the word *sajal*), meaning "to fear" (Grube and Nahm 1991).

Figure 4. Images of title glyphs: *sajal*. *Left:* A version of the title from Lintel 54, Yaxchilán. Drawing by Ian Graham, Courtesy of the Corpus of Maya Hieroglyphic Inscriptions, Peabody Museum of Archaeology and Ethnology, © President and Fellows of Harvard College, 2004.15.6.6.28. *Right:* A version of the title from Lintel 2, Laxtunich. Drawing by Peter Mathews. Courtesy of Peter Mathews.

The *ajk'uhuun* title (figure 5), often referred to as the "God C title," has undergone considerable scrutiny and debate over time, including differences in grammatical understanding, parsing, and interpretation. It was long considered to be a scribal title via the logographic reading of *aj-k'uh-huun* (Coe and Kerr 1998:91–96; Houston 1993:130–34; Schele et al. 1998). This interpretation suggests that the title is made up of three distinct logographs (signs that stand for entire words). *Aj* is an agentive prefix meaning "he of," *k'uh* means "holy," and *huun* means "book or paper," thus yielding a decipherment of "he of the holy books."

Figure 5. Images of title glyphs: *ajk'uhuun*. *Left:* A version of the title from Tableritos, Palenque. Drawing by Linda Schele, © David Schele, courtesy of the Foundation for the Advancement of Mesoamerican Studies, Inc., www.famsi.org. *Right:* A version of the title from Lintel 4, Site R. Drawing by Nikolai Grube. Courtesy of Nikolai Grube.

Recent rereadings of the title have focused on its grammatical structure. In particular, scholars have recognized variants over time of the title in which the *huun* logogram appears, or does not appear, in different versions, apparently as an elision of the two signs *k'uh* and *na* (combining the end sound of *k'uh* with the beginning sound of *na*) (Jackson and Stuart 2001:223; Lacadena 1996:46). Such analyses suggest that the title might better be read as *aj-k'uh-na*, or a variation thereof, an interpretation yielding a reading of something like "he who guards" or "he who venerates" (Jackson and Stuart 2001:224–25). Most recently, Zender has suggested that this title may describe a "worshipper," lending a priestly function to the position (2004:180–95). It has also been interpreted over the years with a variety of other functional meanings, which have not been widely accepted, illustrating the ongoing complexities of deciphering these titular terms. Such previously proposed interpretations include, among others, "he of the temple" (Ringle 1988), "architect" (Schele 1992:45), and "political mediator" (Stuart 1992). While headway has been made on interpreting this title, it seems that we have not yet arrived at fixed or firm readings of either its glyphic components or associated meanings.

The other three titles, each of which is used significantly less frequently than *sajal* and *ajk'uhuun*, remain less clearly understood. *Yajaw k'ahk'* (figure 6) yields an easy literal reading—"lord of fire" (Stuart 2005b:18). *Yajaw* is the possessed version of "lord" (*ajaw*), and the word *k'ahk'* means "fire." Despite this unambiguous literal

Figure 6. Images of title glyphs: *yajaw k'ahk'*. *Left:* A version of the title from Temple XIX platform, Palenque. Drawing by David Stuart. Courtesy of David Stuart. *Right:* A version of the title from Tablet of the Slaves, Palenque. Drawing by Linda Schele, © David Schele, courtesy of the Foundation for the Advancement of Mesoamerican Studies, Inc., www.famsi.org.

Figure 7. Images of title glyphs: *ti'huun/ti'sakhuun*. *Left*: A version of the *ti'huun* title from Monument 140, Toniná. Drawing by Ian Graham, Courtesy of the Corpus of Maya Hieroglyphic Inscriptions, Peabody Museum of Archaeology and Ethnology, © President and Fellows of Harvard College, 2004.15.6.16.30. *Right*: A version of the *ti'sakhuun* title from Panel 1, Pomoná. Drawing by Linda Schele, © David Schele, courtesy of the Foundation for the Advancement of Mesoamerican Studies, Inc., www.famsi.org.

reading, the functional meaning or specialization of the office remains obscure. Stuart has hypothesized, based on Palenque's Temple XIX inscriptions, that this title could have military, or possibly religious, connotations (2005:18); the title may be associated with incense or fire rituals, which could indicate religious duties associated with the position (Zender 2004:205, 210). The relatively limited regional distribution of the title, and the small number of examples recorded in the texts, suggests that this was a highly specialized office.

Ti'huun and *ti'sakhuun* (figure 7) seem to be related titles, meaning, when read literally, "the edge/mouth of the (white) paper." *Ti'* means "edge" or "mouth," and *huun* (also seen above in the title *ajk'uhuun*) means "paper." I treat *ti'huun* and *ti'sakhuun* as the same title; the significance of the addition of *sak* (white) in the longer version is uncertain. A possible clue to the meaning of *ti'huun/ti'sakhuun* is its relationship to the so-called Glyph F of the supplementary series (part of the calendrical/astronomical references found in Maya texts) (Coe and Van Stone 2001:49-50); Glyph F is visually identical to the *ti'huun* form of the title. Without getting bogged down in the complexities of the Maya calendrical system, we may learn something about the meaning of the *ti'huun* title through a quick look at its parallel with Glyph F. A summary of the relevant segment of the lunar series reads: "Glyph G [one of the Nine Lords of the Night—a cycle of nine divinities] is the Glyph F [or *ti'huun*] of the day sign." Thus a particular day (indicated in the previous sentence by the day sign) is understood as having a *ti'huun*, which is also one of the Nine Lords of the Night. Glyph F seems to function as a title even in its supplementary series role. A functional parallel, which may suggest the religious importance of this title, is thus set up between "an underworldly title loyal to a calendrical day" and "an elite loyal to a ruler."

A relevant association for understanding this title may be Stuart's interpretation of Glyph F (read as "the edge of the paper") as referring to marginalia, and especially the practice in central Mexican contexts of painting the Nine Lords of the Night along the edges of the page (2005:63). It seems that these elites could have been in charge of the movement of time, or possibly impersonation of temporal or underworld deities. At Toniná, the connection between *ti'huun*s and paddler gods, who are often linked with period endings, may also highlight the connection between this title and the ritual passage of time. Additionally, the use of the term *sak huun* ("white paper") to refer to the paper headbands worn by Maya rulers may indicate a play on words in this title, recognizing both the cosmological position of the office and the relationship of these office holders to the headband as a symbol of office and metonym for the ruler. Related to this observation, Zender has suggested that this officeholder might literally have been a "mouth," or spokesperson, for the ruler himself, as epitomized by his headband (2004:220).

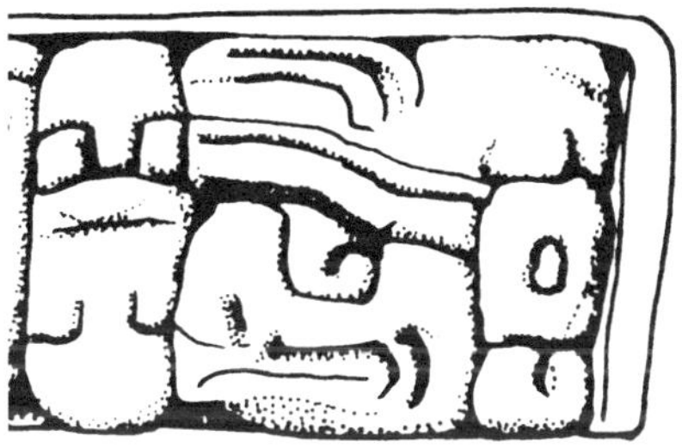

Figure 8. Images of title glyphs: "banded bird." A version of the title from a wooden box at Tortuguero. Drawing by Diane Griffiths Peck. Courtesy of Diane Griffiths Peck.

Finally, the "banded bird" title (figure 8) remains undeciphered. Visually, it is an image of a raptorial bird with a band around the head, possibly a headband of rulership. One proposal has been to read this title as a variant of *itz'at*, meaning "scribe" or "artisan" (Coe and Kerr 1998:135; Freidel et al. 1993:94–95), but others have rejected this reading on the basis of insufficient resemblance and lack of evidence of substitution (Stuart 2005b:133–36).

Despite the lingering vagueness of the decipherments of these titles, they do not represent dead ends in approaching the Late Classic courtly community. Rather, as the coming pages will reveal, rich contextual evidence allows the titles to serve as entryways into the space of the court.

A More Inclusive View of the Courtly Community

The five courtly titles mentioned above are set apart from a variety of other designations used by those present in the court by codified rituals of accession. Before embarking on a discussion of Classic period *sajal*s, *ajk'uhuun*s, *yajaw k'ahk*s, *ti'huun*s or *ti'sakhuun*s, and "banded birds," it is worth mentioning that people present at the court and recorded in the hieroglyphic texts are also named with other appellatives. Some of these are likely toponymic designations, indicating a place of origin or geographical affiliation; others are descriptive of achievement (such as *aj chan baak*, or "he of four captives"—a designation for someone who has experienced this success in war); and some are general evocations of role or position such as *ajaw* ("lord") or the less clearly understood *anab*. These more informal descriptors were no doubt important to the individuals who held them and helped to mark the variegated hierarchical social landscape of the court. They are of less interest to the project of contextualizing individuals within the formalized institution of the court, however, because they are not typically used extensively over multiple areas, nor are they associated with the official investiture that the titles under discussion here involve.

One must remember that, in the larger scheme of the court, the individuals who held one of the five formalized titles were relatively few. Nontitled individuals who were part of both the physical and social space of the court included other elites, as well as individuals not typically considered to be high status, such as entertainers, dwarfs, war captives, and servants (Houston and Stuart 2001:61, 68–69; Inomata 2001a:40). Thus, while titles help to illuminate the formal structures of the court, they by no means describe the boundaries of membership in, or access to, that institution.

In fact, textual examples in which elites are mentioned on multiple monuments indicate that even those who carried formal titles did not always use them in all contexts. The elevation to the more generalized rank of "officeholder" was perhaps more significant than the possession of a particular title. One may therefore recognize the importance of the collective courtly body, composed of a variety of constituent parts, while simultaneously favoring the titled members as the most textually "vocal" and the most strongly marked in terms of their standing within a courtly hierarchy.

Even further outside the court, commoners and others without immediate access to the ruler were nonetheless active agents in the constitution of a Maya identity. To suggest that they were not is to ignore the realities of Classic Maya existence, in which, in many cases, the meeting of basic subsistence needs for privileged members of society was provided wholly or in part by others. The court could not have operated independently of the masses outside of it. Simultaneously, the lives of those outside of the court would have been very different without the presence of this institution that served as a mouthpiece for the gods, as a broadcaster of social and religious norms, and as a mediator with neighboring polities. As will be discussed later in the book, the work of commoners in providing an agricultural base for the members of the court is neatly mirrored in the Maya conception of elites performing metaphorical agricultural duties that sustained their community via their political service. Through this feedback loop, in which nourishments of different types (physical, politico-religious) are provided by different sectors of the population, we see a binding together of concerns that might otherwise seem disparate or removed from each other.

Commoners were also implicated in the courtly community in their critical role as audience for the public performances of the court, which served to articulate shared cultural values and confirm locally formed senses of identity. The current study focuses on only a section of the population within Classic-era Maya cities—officially titled members of the court, determined in part by the circumscribed nature of textual content. This partial view represents an important node of identity production within Maya culture and may thus be used to access ways in which cultural coherence is produced and reproduced using the resources and public space of the court.

A Data Set for Understanding Membership in the Court

The formalized titles, representing courtly offices, that were introduced above provide a logical starting point for looking at the Classic Maya court and its membership. These offices formed the officially acknowledged building blocks upon which the political hierarchy was based. The data I track in subsequent chapters depend on titles as individual units of analysis, forming parts of an elaborate and elaborated courtly institution. Analysis of the usage of these specific titles over time and across space allows for insight into the development and implementation of a distinctively Late Classic–style royal court.

In order to comment on communities of Late Classic Maya elites, I have compiled examples of textually recorded elite titles (specifically, the five formalized positions: *sajal*, *ajk'uhuun*, *yajaw k'ahk'*, *ti'huun/ti'sakhuun*, and "banded bird") from both published and unpublished sources, representing sites throughout the Maya area (see appendix; see also Jackson 2005 for additional detailed listings). I have attempted to be exhaustive in documenting these titles, and my efforts have yielded a database of 221 examples of records of titled courtly elite individuals. Despite my thorough combing of the known and recorded hieroglyphic texts, I am certain that this number will grow as new examples are discovered and examples that I failed to record are added. Nonetheless, this database represents the vast majority of examples of titled elites recorded in the corpus of known texts, and as such it provides a meaningful sample to use as a basis for analysis.

Before discussing these data, let me explain a little more about what exactly I recorded in my data collection. My compilation consisted of records of *every* instance and event in which a titled elite is mentioned, even when mentioned multiple times on the same monument. It is worth noting that a prominent elite at a site (such as several of the individuals discussed in chapter 2) may receive a significant amount of textual attention. Additionally, elites who hold multiple titles will be recorded more frequently in the database. Thus it must be emphasized that this is not a record of 221 *different* titled elite individuals.

The records were cross referenced in a way, however, that allowed the majority of such repeated records of individuals to be identified. The approximate number of individuals recorded is identifiable by eliminating multiple examples of individuals with the same personal name, multiple examples of individuals named more than once on the same monument, and individuals who carry multiple titles. Eliminating these identified overlaps, the database includes approximately 160 different elite individuals.

In addition to documenting the written record of a particular title and the individual named with it, I also collected other contextual information. For example, I noted adjectival modifiers of titles, which are useful for understanding relative ranking and construction of status. I documented co-occurrence of multiple titles with a single individual, thereby helping to clarify the way particular positions were used. Textual specifications of action or event were noted as well, in order to provide a framing for elite activity. I was also interested in association with other, fellow courtly elites, as part of investigating the peer relationships that helped to structure the court. Finally, I paid attention to highlighted connections between courtly elites and the rulers under which they served (in contrast to instances in which such elites were discussed on their own monuments, as primary actors). All of this information allows for a tracking of important trends, such as temporal and spatial usage, as well as an understanding of what frameworks were employed, or emphasized, in public records of the court and official constructions of elite identity.

These data will be discussed in the chapters that follow, in the context of topics that highlight particular aspects of the institution of the court. To set the stage for examinations of the court, let me say a few words about the relative distribution of the five courtly offices. As was mentioned in the initial discussion of these titles, these positions are not equally common. In fact, two of them are wildly more popular in usage than the others. This information begins to illuminate these offices as distinctive and used in differing ways within the court.

Not surprising to those accustomed to hearing of *sajal*s and *ajk'uhuun*s in the literature on Maya studies, these two offices are significantly more common than any of the other positions. Of the entire number of records of elites, the office of *sajal* yields a notable 50 percent of all titles recorded. *Ajk'uhuuns* come next in popularity, with 32 percent of the total. Together, these two positions represent the overwhelming majority of courtly elite positions and are dominant in terms of their widespread usage within the court.

The other positions that also involve formal accession—*yajaw k'ahk'*, *ti'huun/ti'sakhuun*, and "banded bird,"—are represented, respectively, by 8, 5, and 5 percent of the total known corpus of titular records. In contrast to *sajal* and *ajk'uhuun*, these three positions represent a very small portion of the records of titled courtly elites. There are several possible interpretations for this infrequent use. The pattern may indicate that these offices were specialized, and thus less commonly represented—in reality, or in the textual record. Along these lines, the duties associated with the positions may have been more esoteric and thus more rarely filled by qualified practitioners. Such specialization of duty or role might also have meant that the positions were less critical to the structure of the court and could be omitted, as opposed to the more central offices of *sajal* and *ajk'uhuun*. Such lack of centrality to the court might also have meant that such positions were viewed as less important and thus less likely to be privileged with representation in text and image.

In chapter 2 we will meet individual historic figures who were members of Late Classic period Maya courts and who carried these titles. First, however, this more particularistic focus on specific courtiers must be contextualized within a larger understanding of courtly institutions.

Viewing the Court through a Wider Lens

Thus far in this chapter we have situated ourselves within the institution of the Maya royal court in several ways. We have reviewed important previous scholarship that provides an intellectual foundation for the current project. We have examined Maya written records as a key evidentiary source for investigating the court. And we have looked at how the Classic Maya court is textually documented through a series of five formal titles, or positions. All of this information sets the stage for discussion of the membership and functioning of the Maya royal court in the chapters that follow. Before moving on to these topics, however, it is important to position this specific study of the Classic Maya court within a broader sphere, in order to identify possible intersections with other contexts, to think thematically about the significance of the Maya court, and to establish the relevance of this study beyond the Maya realm.

Moving outward from an exclusively Maya perspective, what do we mean by a court, a type of formalized hierarchical organization found in a variety of places and times? We can posit that most courts are experienced as spaces of identity negotiation and performance. They are inhabited by individuals marked by the privilege of access to scarce resources; such resources take many forms, including material wealth, spatial and personal access, knowledge (including literacy), and behavioral prerogatives. Their responsibilities usually combine official duties with the social reproduction of certain behaviors and styles. In the context of the court, the ruler himself may be simultaneously regarded as central (the *axis mundi* and the leader of the polity) and external (deified, otherworldly, and distanced) to a society. So may the court be understood as an open and vital performative institution that reproduces governmental structures and also serves as an exemplar for the other members of the society. Simultaneously, however, it is a socially (and sometimes spatially) closed and inwardly turned body that is defined by a cycle of producing and reproducing a way of life that is, by definition, restricted and inaccessible to most. This dichotomy characterizes the way in which courts manage and retain their power by balancing opposing forces. These paired strategies also indicate how the court may have deliberately functioned in notably diverse ways, differentially emphasizing these orientations in response to changing contexts.

With these general observations about courtly institutions in mind, we are positioned to seek broader connections for the present study through two perspectives: one comparative, the emphasis here on two other ancient New World contexts, and one thematic, framed through three models for characterizing the influence and impact of courts.

Comparative Perspectives

The royal court, as an institution, is hardly unique to the Classic Maya world. Analogous spaces of power are found in a variety of times and places. Within the ancient New World, courts or courtlike institutions were found among the complex cultures of both the Aztec and Inca. Neighboring examples such as these illustrate common elements of the court, while also indicating the variety of forms that this institution can take.

Within the Aztec empire, located to the north in central Mexico and dating to the fifteenth and sixteenth centuries, courts were quite similar to those of the Maya (Evans 2001:273). They were located within the royal palace, or *tecpan* (Evans 2001:240), and like Maya examples, they were filled with both titled courtiers and throngs of "palace people." In the Aztec court, this encompassed a surprisingly diverse group of people, including both ranked elites and others connected to the court (family, servants, visitors, skilled specialists), who, as recorded by Cortés, arrived at the court each morning and numbered as many as six hundred (Evans 2001:252). Nobility within the court were members of the restricted rank of *pipiltin* (López Austin 1961:56–58), a clearly defined class group. At the apex of the *pipiltin*, and the heart of the court, was the supreme council, composed of four titled positions: the *tlacatéccatl*, the *tlacochcácatl*, the *ezhuahuácatl*, and the *tlillancalqui* (López Austin 1961:90), below which were titled lords of less exalted positions (Zorita 1994:89). The members of the supreme council served in an advisory role to the *tlatoani*, or ruler, and were also in charge of determining his successor (López Austin 1961:90, 95). Descriptions of Aztec courtly work and activity indicate that their attentions were divided between conducting governmental business and taking in the pleasures and prerogatives of elite status (Evans 2001:252), the latter ranging from enjoyment of chocolate, alcohol, and psychoactive mushrooms to the recitation of poetry (Evans 2001:247, 248; López Austin 1961:67). Like the Maya court, change in the composition of the Aztec court occurred over time, with the elite population increasing substantially in number (Evans 2001:239–40)—much like the Late Classic "boom" that we will observe among the Maya. In short, the Aztec royal court exhibits many similarities to the analogous Maya institution, despite obvious differences in place, time, and cultural milieu.

To the south, the Inca represent a different political setting, and a rather different form of courtly institution. Nonetheless, some intriguing structural similarities are present. In this setting (the western coast of South America, also in the fifteenth and sixteenth centuries), the royal court, as a formalized institution, is not frequently referred to in Inca scholarship. However, elite individuals, organized into a complex hierarchy and playing an integral role in the government, formed themselves into groups called *panacas* (Zuidema 1964:15), which provide a useful courtly parallel. These groups were composed of the ruler's descendants and other relatives, an indication that kinship was an emphasized and organizing aspect of the *panacas*. The groups acted as an advisory body to the ruler and were the source of officials who formulated government policy (D'Altroy 2002:99). Their dual connection with everyday administrative duties and the organization of the ritual landscape (D'Altroy 2002:155–59; Moseley 2001:82; Zuidema 1964:11) supports the idea of such institutions being intertwined with both governmental/literal and cosmological/metaphorical structures of the state or polity. This is an idea that we will encounter among the Maya as well.

Within the *panacas*, there are no known specific roles or offices. However, this is likely due to the lack of a historical record, not because of a lack of internal structure to these groups. (In the Sican culture in northern Peru, for example, late sixteenth-century ethnohistoric documents name "officials" and a "retinue," including individuals designated as Blower of the Shell Trumpet, Master of the Litter and Throne, Royal Cook, Steward of the Face Paint, Master of the Bath, and others [Donnan 1990:243–44]. These specific offices indicate a tradition of courtly-type positions in this culture area.) Notably, multiple *panacas*—connected to both the current and past rulers—operated simultaneously, yielding a complex and dynamic political landscape within Cuzco, the Inca capital. The overt similarities with the Maya case are less obvious in the Inca courts, yet even with their distinctive and different form, analogous thematic elements are identifiable. The Inca example also underlines the adaptation of circumscribed, ranked institutions like courts to particular social and political circumstances—in this case, related to rulership and succession.

Courtly institutions are not limited to the ancient New World, of course. Many of the courts that are most immediately familiar to the reader are likely from England and other parts of Europe, for example. Indeed, scholarly discussion of courts ranges from Europe to Asia to Africa. While it is not my purpose to undertake a cross-cultural survey of courts, it is useful to be aware that illuminating comparisons for the Maya court are located both near and far. Identifiable similarities indicate that these types of institutions represent useful adaptations within complex cultural settings. Imagine: Ruler 4 of Late Classic Piedras Negras presiding, from his ornate throne, over a gathering of courtiers, relatives, and visitors; Queen Elizabeth II inspecting her regiments outside of Buckingham Palace during Trooping the Colour; the College of Cardinals in Vatican City, sequestered, sending up puffs of smoke to herald the election of a new pope. Even with their varied trappings, motivations, cultural contexts, and degrees and spheres of influence, all of these recognize the effectiveness of, and cultural work accomplished by, certain types of political configurations. Furthermore, while there is great variability in the forms that hierarchical, bounded political institutions take across the world, recognizing common elements provides vocabulary for talking about how people organize themselves and offers perspectives on the range of cultural choices available. Additionally, comparative perspectives lend themselves to identifying general models that describe the role of the court. Three such models are discussed below. This bigger-picture view of the court sheds light on why this institution mattered and the impact that it had.

Modeling the Court

Three conceptual models prove useful in describing the institution of the court, not only in thinking about the political organization of the Late Classic Maya but also of courts in other times and places: the court may be understood as a theater, as a school, and as a household. The three frameworks provide language to describe the work, and the impact, of the royal court and serve to identify key characteristics of courtly bodies.

The model of the court as theater is found in a variety of cultures, representing a critical way in which activities and ideas that are located within the circumscribed space of the court propagate outward to impact other members of a polity, thus helping to establish the relevance of the institution as more than a restricted and esoteric island of privilege. Specifically, courtly performances, taking the form of rituals or other public events, provide a communicative moment in which not only the specific event is conveyed (e.g., the accession of a ruler) but cultural ideals, mores, or restrictions are enacted in a way that clarifies cultural identities, enacts boundaries, and inspires imitation by the viewer. The theater state of Bali, as discussed by Geertz, provides a compelling example of the power of the court as theater (1980). Geertz argues that for the Balinese state, political structure was actually equivalent to (not just dramatized by) court ceremonialism and mass ritual, imparting a particular power to these performative activities (1980:13).

Within Maya contexts, the formal staging of elite dramas using the backdrop of the royal court provides a public context for the exercising and display of elite identity. The idea of the court as a stage or a theater has been productively explored in recent works (e.g., Inomata and Coben 2006) as representing a structured performance and a choreographed type of elite practice. Long-acknowledged components of elite activity support this framework for the royal court. For example, the use of masks and costumes as part of a process of dramatic transformation between identities is a key feature of theatrical performance as well as an important part of Maya belief in co-presence and movement between identities and planes (Houston 2006:145–49; Houston and Stuart 1996:297–300). Similarly, architectural settings for courtly events at the center of Maya polities frequently feature spatial arrangements that include stages for performers (i.e., architectural configurations that allow for the appearance and disappearance of players) as well as seating or viewing spaces that would accommodate an audience for the performance (Inomata 2006:197–201). Ritual or political events were planned and enacted in ways that served to broadcast messages and may be aptly described as fitting a model of a theater.

One of the key features of the theater model is dissemination of ideas important to the community, emanating outward from the authoritative space of the court. In this sense, the model of court as a theater or stage overlaps with that of court as school. The court-as-school represents a space in which elites become conversant in idealized forms. These forms are demonstrated for the edification of, impression on, and imitation by noncourtly—or, to continue the metaphor, uneducated—audiences. A tension emerges, then, between the restriction of information and skill to courtly corridors (in the scholastic model) and the demonstration and enactment of some of these behaviors before much larger crowds, with the knowledge that they may be—in fact, may be intended to be—subsequently imitated at other times and in other places (as in a theatrical model). Innes, in discussing Carolingian courts (2003), talks about them as living communities, reminding us that they operated through "imitation and discipline" rather than through formal schooling or instruction (2003:75).

Among the Maya, the role of the court as an educational institution may at times have been literal and formal. The example of a high-ranking young man from the region of La Corona who went, or was sent, to the powerful city of Calakmul for a few years before returning to the smaller center of La Corona after his father's death to assume rulership (Houston and Stuart 2001:67–68) illustrates a situation in which courts used knowledge, and possibly indoctrination, as a means of both education and control. Children are seen depicted in imagery of courts on stone monuments and painted ceramic vessels, indicating their presence and participation in this institution from a young age (Houston 2009). We can imagine that they would have been taught, explicitly or implicitly, several types of specialized information during their formative years. These types of knowledge would have ranged from skills such as literacy or ritual fluency to shared understandings of bodily practice, including gestural positioning and emotional restraint (Houston 2001:67–68), yielding a trained and knowledgeable noble (Houston and Inomata 2009:187). The goal of the teaching and learning that occurred within courtly contexts was to reproduce sets of acceptable or desirable behaviors, and to mobilize knowledge as a resource and boundary marker that helped to define membership within a restricted organization.

The third model of the court is that of a household, in which the court served as an ideal and exemplary domestic space, to be stylistically imitated by individuals of lower status. This model recognizes the daily functionality of the court beyond its ritual or ceremonial aspects. It acknowledges the multiple activities of the court and provides a structural framework for inclusion of the court's diverse members. Additionally, the household model emphasizes the idea of human and cultural reproduction as part of the reinforcement of cultural norms, with the court acting as an exemplary household that is replicated and imitated at multiple levels of society. Charlemagne's court provides an example of the court as an expansive and flexibly constituted household, of which he was the head. Nelson describes Charlemagne's courtly household as attracting and including "clients, litigants, seekers of justice, beggars, whores," individuals who observed and then replicated the roles and meanings found within this hyperdomestic space (2003:40–41).

Among the Maya, the household model of the court connects with recent application of house society models to Maya contexts (Gillespie 2000). Whether or not Lévi-Strauss's idea (1984) is fully relevant to the ancient Maya world (Houston and McAnany 2003; Watanabe 2004), the conception of scaled domestic entities—ranging from grand to humble—with certain shared forms or characteristics, resonates with ideas of Maya structural replication that are recognized in both ancient and modern contexts (Houston and Inomata 2009:154; Vogt 1969:571–81). Archaeological work on courtly spaces supports this model through evidence of quotidian activities, including food preparation, use of private domestic quarters, and inclusion of extended families, that took place within those spaces. One of the important elements of the Lévi-Straussian model of the household for understanding courts is the inclusion of a set of individuals extending beyond an immediate kin group. This idea of a more inclusive, integrated community within the household (or court) is supported strongly by representations of the court on painted ceramic vessels, where the royal family is joined not only by other elites but by a variety of supporting personnel (including entertainers, servants, captives, and others).

These three courtly models can be used to describe royal courts in a variety of contexts, including those of the Maya. In light of the available data on Maya courts, the models should not be seen as mutually exclusive, or contradictory. Rather, each has elements that serve to illuminate parts of the Maya royal court. Trying on these models or frames provides vocabulary and useful comparisons for the types of work that courts do and the influence that they exercise.

We have now entered the court, looked around us, and made some immediate, important observations. Like any good traveler, we have quickly gained a sense of time and place and are beginning to familiarize ourselves with the preoccupations of the culture and context in which we find ourselves. By necessity, we bring a critical and comparative eye but also attempt to try on the worldview of our hosts. And, of course, we are eager to meet the locals. Pull up a bench. They are arriving now.

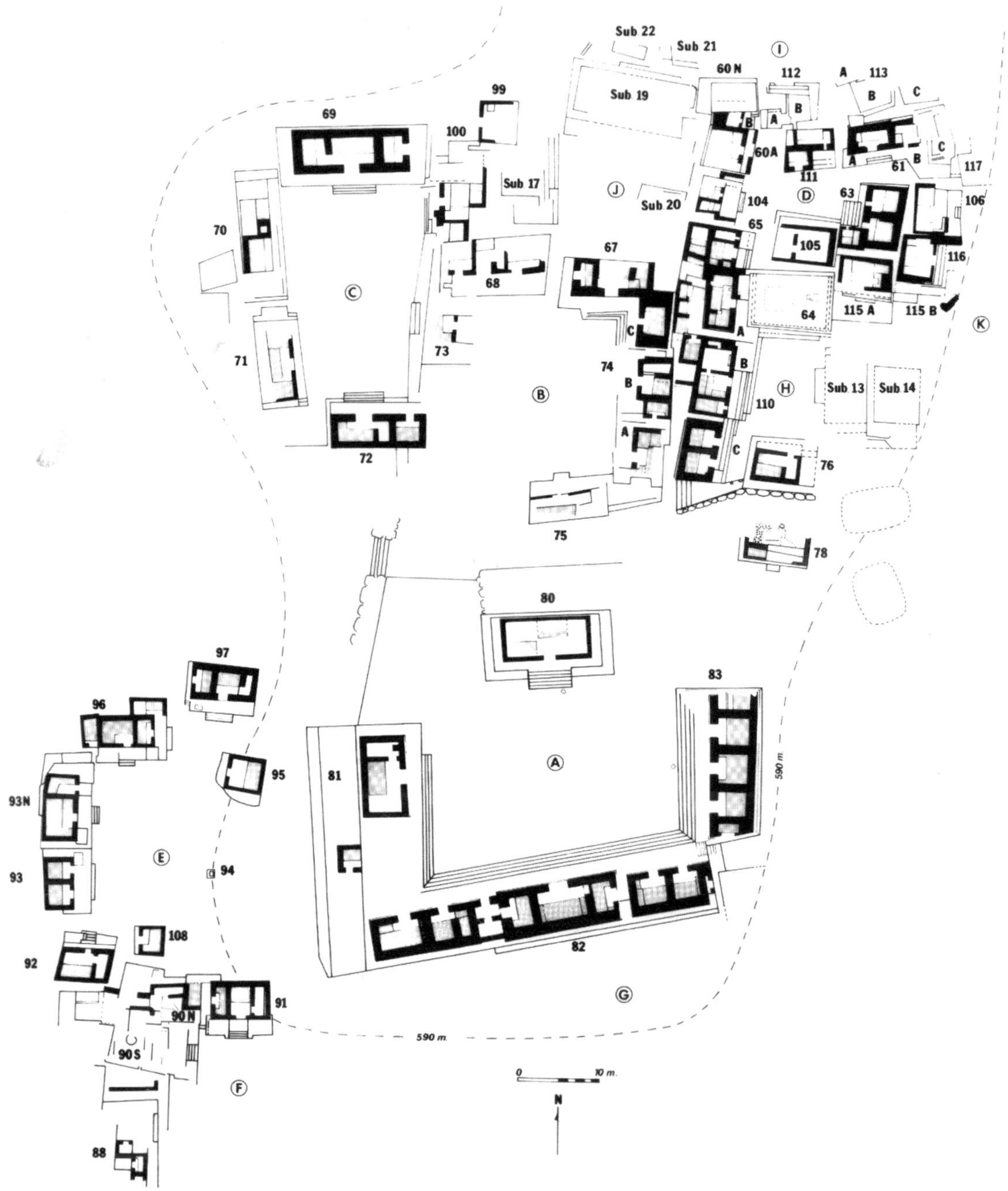

Map 1. Map of residential group 9N-8, Copán. Structure 9N-82 represents Mak'an Chanal's home. Courtesy of David Webster and Dumbarton Oaks.

CHAPTER TWO

Profiles of Courtly Officials

Individual Histories and Political Positions

Stories about Classic Maya courtly elites can be pieced together and read in sometimes astonishing detail from the hieroglyphic texts. Information about elite lives appears both in contexts in which these individuals are featured on their own monuments and in ones in which they appear as characters in narratives featuring rulers. Many instances in which elites are clearly mentioned are too brief or fragmentary to conclude much about the individual's political trajectory or courtly identity. In some instances, however, we can construct a partial narrative of particular elites' lives through detailed texts dedicated to certain courtly individuals or through multiple appearances of certain individuals in texts dedicated to others. These cases provide vital information on the functioning of elite offices and their position within the court. Some of the challenges of literal decipherment of courtly titles fade in prominence in the face of extensive contextual information. From this we can derive synthesized understandings of the nature of courtly roles.

Bringing such life stories to light allows us to study individuals in the past. The court itself is, of course, composed of individuals, and a focus on individuals is critical for understanding how variations, adjustments, and local responses played a part in the court's management of change during the Late Classic. The life stories discussed below provide a critical understanding of the Maya royal court and the changing political landscape of the Late Classic period, through the lens of the court's members. We see here the ways in which particular lives intersected with, and were described in the context of, the court. What follows are nine elite profiles of Late Classic Maya individuals, drawn from hieroglyphic texts from a variety of ancient polities in the Maya lowlands. The texts allow us to get to know the individuals a little bit and give a sense of what official courtly portraits looked like. I have chosen these profiles out of a larger pool of possibilities because each of them reveals important points about the functioning of elite positions within the court.

Mak'an Chanal of Copán: Man with a Monument

Mak'an Chanal, whom we met on the first page of this book, was an *ajk'uhuun* at the site of Copán. He served under Yax Pasaj Chan Yopat, the sixteenth ruler, who ruled from approximately A.D. 763 to 810 (Martin and Grube 2000:206). Mak'an Chanal lived in Structure 9N-82, part of Group 9N-8 (map 1), located east of the main group of Copán and separated from the site center by a distance of about a kilometer (Webster 1989a:11, Webster 1989b). Mak'an Chanal represents one of the very few instances

Figure 9. Drawing of the hieroglyphic bench from Structure 9N-82, Copán. This is the hieroglyphic seat in Mak'an Chanal's home and names him as an *ajk'uhuun*. His title is highlighted. Drawing by David Webster and Ann Dowd. Courtesy of David Webster and Dumbarton Oaks.

in which textually identified courtly elites may be definitively associated with a known residence or architectural space. The other unequivocal instances are at Copán, El Cayo, Palenque, and Xcalumkín and will be touched upon in chapter 3. Mak'an Chanal's home, of the known examples, is particularly well investigated.

At Copán Mak'an Chanal was the head of a compound that housed other elites—including his extended family—as well as individuals of lower rank (Sanders 1989; Webster 1989a). The residents of the group included craft specialists, whose presence is indicated via material evidence in sections of the complex that were devoted to shell working and weaving (Webster 1989a:13). These individuals would have contributed to the diversity of the people that occupied this residential group. Localized special-purpose spaces within Patio A of Group 9N-8, where Mak'an Chanal's residence was itself located, included Structure 80, a likely shrine or temple, as well as Structure 81, a space associated with the ritually significant Maya ballgame and related paraphernalia (Webster 1989a:20–22). Structure 82, Mak'an Chanal's home, was a multiroomed masonry structure that contained a carved bench that was partially visible from outside the building. This beautiful hieroglyphic bench named Mak'an Chanal and provided context for his elevated position (figure 9).

The association between Mak'an Chanal and the ruler he served—Yax Pasaj—was a close one, perhaps explaining why Mak'an Chanal was awarded the privilege of erecting a hieroglyphic bench within his home. Furthermore, the relationship between the ruler and his courtier was highlighted on the bench through the use of a possessive grammatical construction, *yajk'uhuun*, or "his *ajk'uhuun*," which frames Mak'an Chanal as belonging to Yax Pasaj. Mak'an Chanal's official role of *ajk'uhuun* was combined on this sculptured seat with the honorific designation *koxop ajaw*, or "lord of *koxop*," a local title and possibly a toponym referring to a particular place.

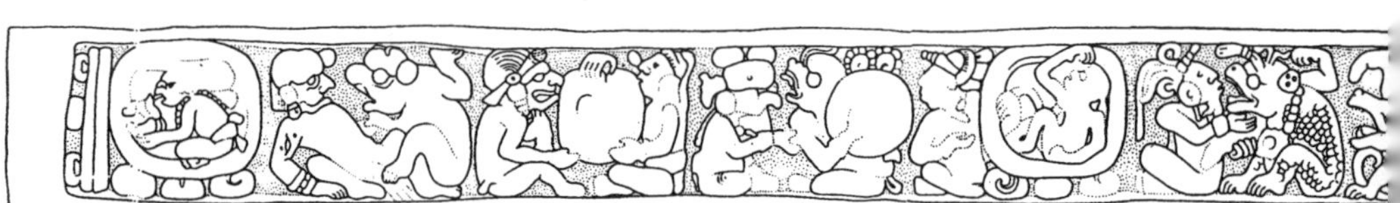

The same term also appears on Altar W', found in the same group. The awarding of elaborate hieroglyphic benches to elites is seen in several contexts at Copán: in addition to Mak'an Chanal's bench, the bench in Structure A of Group 9M-18 is carved with a text, as is the bench designated CPN 999 from Structure 10K-15. Carved thrones are known to be symbols of authority, and to represent a literal and metaphorical seat of rulership. The presence of these hieroglyphic benches in elite compounds indicates the widening of previously royal prerogatives, as part of a change in the nature of status and political hierarchy in the Late Classic.

The event most centrally highlighted in the Structure 9N-82 bench text is the erection and dedication of Mak'an Chanal's house, which archaeological investigations indicate was an expansion and elaboration of earlier versions in the same spot (Webster 1989a:22–24). This elaboration on past space or precedent, a familiar trope in Maya architecture and ideology, is textually reinforced through genealogical references. In the text, Mak'an Chanal identifies his mother, father, and grandfather and names himself as his father's successor (literally, the "completion" of his father). Thus, both architecturally and textually, Mak'an Chanal recognizes and builds upon the legacy of his forebearers. Whether or not such courtly positions were passed directly from generation to generation, lineage played a part in Mak'an Chanal's public assertion of his authority.

Mak'an Chanal likely was not alone in his official duties within the court at Copán. Another *ajk'uhuun*, whose name is too eroded to read, was also awarded a hieroglyphic bench by the sixteenth ruler, Yax Pasaj. This *ajk'uhuun* lived in Group 9M-18 (Leventhal 1979), not far from Mak'an Chanal. The bench text tells us that Yax Pasaj even visited to perform a scattering rite at Structure A's dedication (figure 10). This second *ajk'uhuun*'s bench uses the same possessive construction seen on the bench from Structure 9N-82 to specify that he was associated with K'ak' Yipyaj Chan K'awiil ("Smoke Shell"), the fifteenth ruler of Copán. This assertion contrasts with Mak'an Chanal's explicit association with the current, or sixteenth, ruler, raising the possibility that the connection between a ruler and his courtiers was one that persisted after the death of the ruler. The *ajk'uhuun*-without-a-name may thus have been senior to Mak'an Chanal or may have held an "emeritus" position. The ongoing privilege of Ruler 15's *ajk'uhuun* in this instance suggests that such "emeritus" elites would nonetheless still have had special and honored positions in the court of subsequent rulers. Another interpretation of these Copán examples is that this

Figure 10. *(Below and opposite)* Hieroglyphic bench from Group 9M-18, Copán. This bench belonged to an *ajk'uhuun* neighbor of Mak'an Chanal. His title is highlighted. Drawing by Barbara Fash. Courtesy of Barbara Fash.

conceit was an effort on the part of the ruler to make clear which was his favored or appointed courtier, in contrast with the courtier, appointed by the previous ruler, whom he had inherited. For both of these *ajk'uhuuns*, it was important to explicitly articulate personal affiliation and social relationships. Such details helped to locate them within the sociopolitical landscape of the city, just as their elegant hieroglyphic benches helped to "seat" their authority within the realms of their homes and residential groups.

In actuality, the emphasis on personal connection between particular rulers and the members of their court at Copán may be anomalous and not a pattern shared across the Maya lowlands. In other contexts, textual evidence points to a separate, and concurrent, cycle of ruling dynasties and elite successions. The hieroglyphic texts unmistakably indicate that Maya polities shared an understanding of the nature of the institution of the court. However, as this example regarding two Copán *ajk'uhuuns* and their associations with particular rulers may illustrate, Maya centers in various regions differed in ways small and large in the implementation and operation of the courtly hierarchy.

K'an Nik Te' of Piedras Negras: Member of a Populous Court

K'an Nik Te' of Piedras Negras was a *sajal* who served under both Ruler 3 (Yopnal Ahk II, ruled A.D. 687–729) and Ruler 4 (ruled A.D. 729–57) (Martin and Grube 2000:142, 148). K'an Nik Te' 's portrait provides an intriguing foil to the story of personal ties with a ruler that Mak'an Chanal's profile illustrated. K'an Nik Te' appears on two monuments at Piedras Negras. On Stela 5 (figure 11) he is depicted in conjunction with Ruler 3 in an image that prominently features the ruler and includes K'an Nik Te' as a visually subsidiary figure. On Panel 3 (figure 12), a remarkable representation of Ruler 4's royal court, K'an Nik Te' is shown together with a variety of other high-ranking individuals.

The affiliation of K'an Nik Te' with sequential rulers provides a clue, echoed elsewhere, that many titled courtly elites functioned somewhat independently of their rulers, despite their obvious reliance on and connection to the *k'uhul ajaw*'s favor and political cachet. The model of a governmental cabinet, in which deputies to a leader are completely replaced with each transfer in power, is not one that applies to the Maya court. Even in the case of the Copán *ajk'uhuun* who was appointed under Ruler 15, and whose bench highlighted that relationship, his ongoing relationship with the present ruling power is indicated by the dedication of his house under Ruler 16.

In fact, multiple examples in which titled elites weathered the transition between rulers suggest that not only were these courtiers not in the pocket of a given ruler but that they may actually have served as an important stabilizing device during times of transition. In this way, courtly officials lent continuity to a political system that would have involved considerable tumult during the liminal time of change between rulers. Examples such as that of K'an Nik Te' suggest that stability in the form of elite support contributed to maintaining a secure rulership.

K'an Nik Te''s importance is also emphasized in other ways. He is graced with the flattering modifier *baah* when named as a *baah sajal* on Piedras Negras Panel 3, in the company of Ruler 4. This term indicates primacy of an individual and is usually translated as "head" or "first" (Houston and Inomata 2009:174–75; Houston

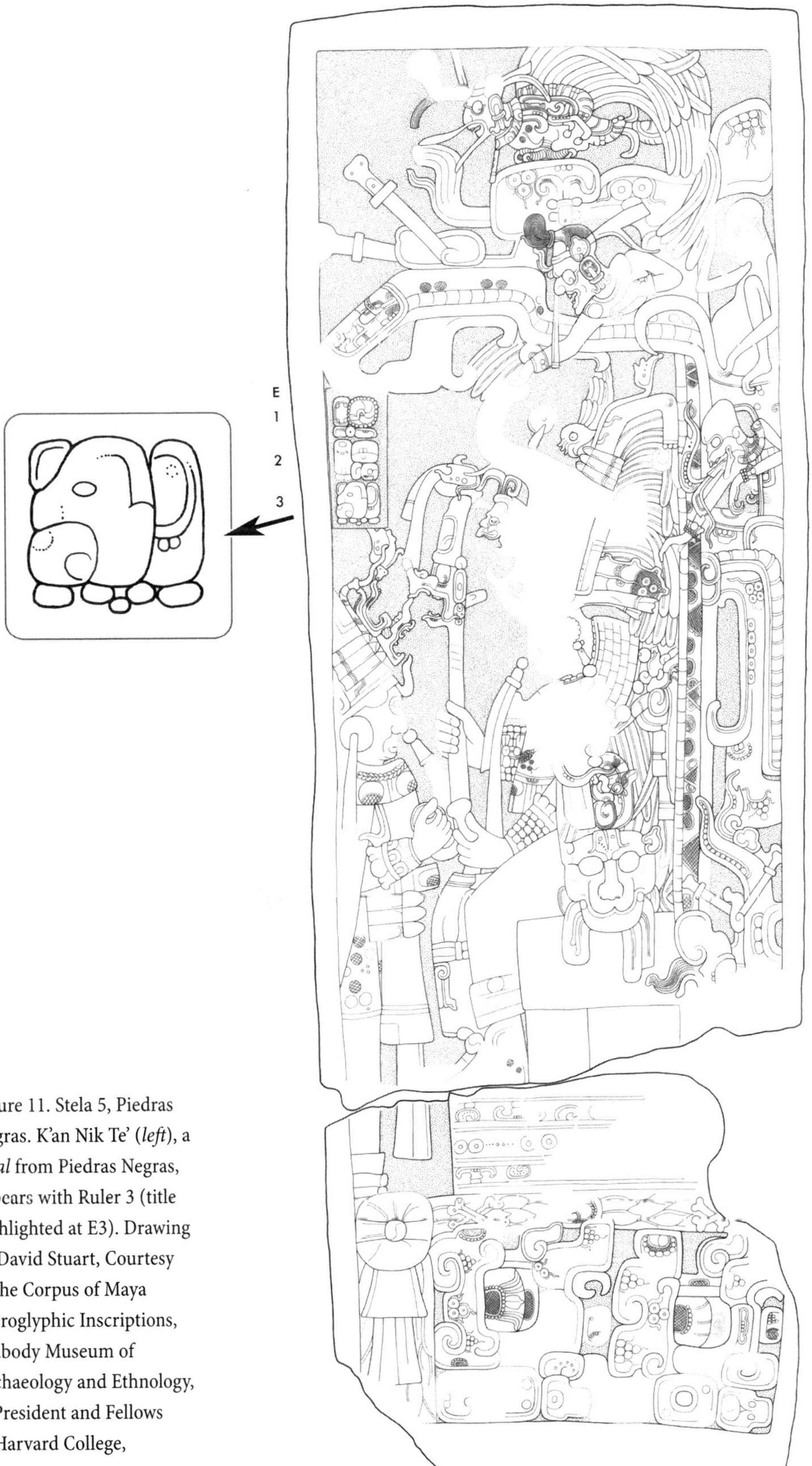

Figure 11. Stela 5, Piedras Negras. K'an Nik Te' (*left*), a *sajal* from Piedras Negras, appears with Ruler 3 (title highlighted at E3). Drawing by David Stuart, Courtesy of the Corpus of Maya Hieroglyphic Inscriptions, Peabody Museum of Archaeology and Ethnology, © President and Fellows of Harvard College, 2004.15.6.19.14.

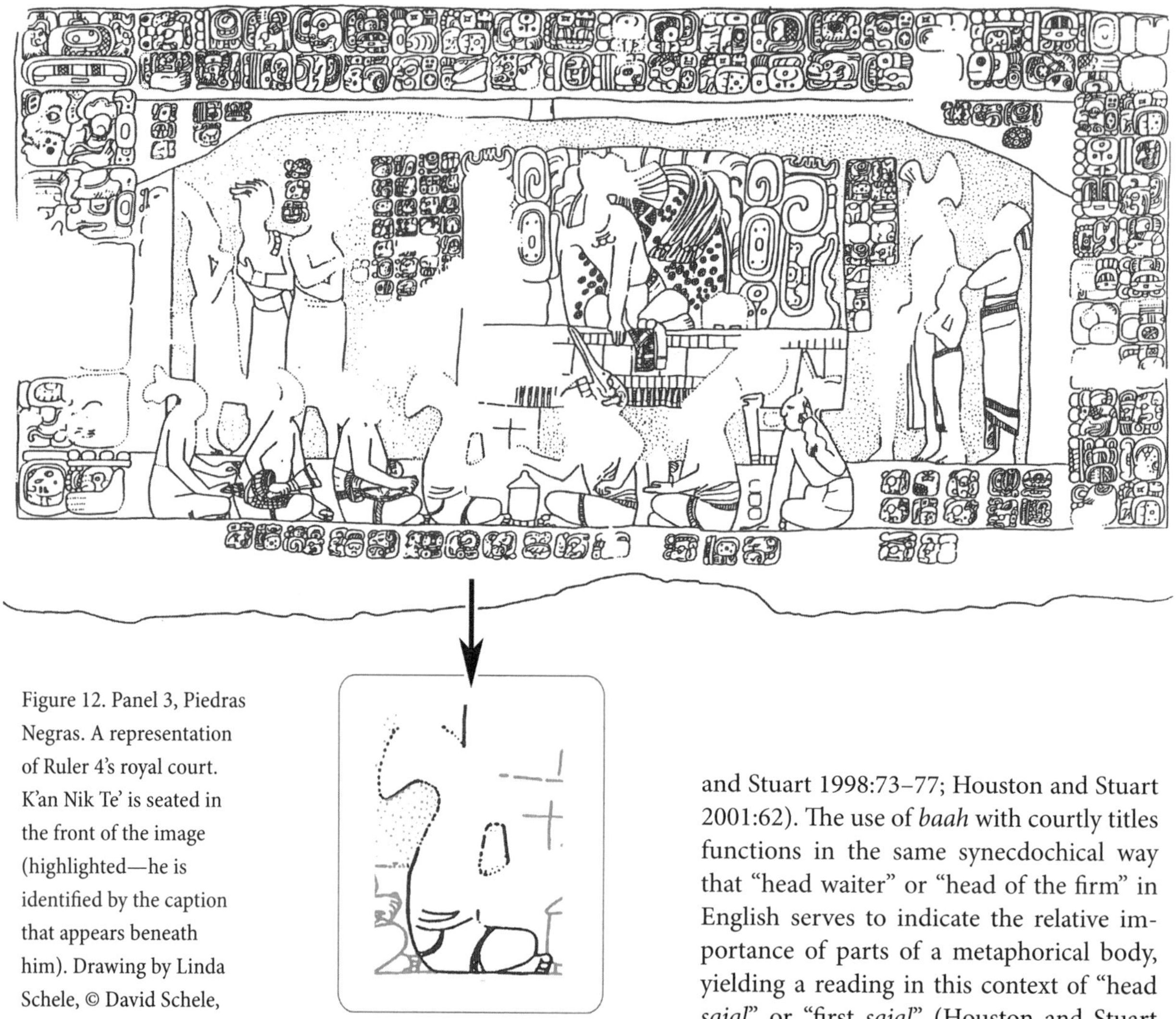

Figure 12. Panel 3, Piedras Negras. A representation of Ruler 4's royal court. K'an Nik Te' is seated in the front of the image (highlighted—he is identified by the caption that appears beneath him). Drawing by Linda Schele, © David Schele, courtesy of the Foundation for the Advancement of Mesoamerican Studies, Inc., www.famsi.org.

and Stuart 1998:73–77; Houston and Stuart 2001:62). The use of *baah* with courtly titles functions in the same synecdochical way that "head waiter" or "head of the firm" in English serves to indicate the relative importance of parts of a metaphorical body, yielding a reading in this context of "head *sajal*" or "first *sajal*" (Houston and Stuart 2001:62). In contrast, when K'an Nik Te' appeared some years earlier with Ruler 3 on Stela 5, he was named only as a *sajal*. The use of *baah sajal* to describe K'an Nik Te' on the later monument could suggest that *baah* was an elevated rank obtained over time and through years of service. Alternatively, the term may have been contextually driven, describing an individual in contexts where multiple officers were present and rank status had to be clarified, such as the group scene portrayed on Panel 3. Certainly, the use of this modifier indicates gradations of rank even within a single office, as well as the precedent for multiple individuals holding the same office simultaneously—a situation that would necessitate a clarification of relative status within a multipart hierarchy.

A hierarchy composed of multiple court members assembled together is shown in the stunning scene on Piedras Negras Panel 3. The detailed and naturalistic depiction on this monument contrasts with many representations of courtiers and rulers that seem stylized or formulaic. Instead, Panel 3 provides a snapshot of Ruler 4's court, convening to celebrate the anniversary of the ruler's accession to power (Houston and Stuart 2001:69–73). K'an Nik Te', joined by six other seated court members, appears in the front row of elites. In comparison with the static impression of the past that fragmentary textual evidence can often yield, this monument is a reminder of the liveliness of the court, as seen in the presence of numerous elite individuals surrounding the king, animated in their finery. Along with K'an Nik Te', labeled as *baah sajal*, other courtly officials shown here include two additional *sajal*s, a person who is both a *baah ajaw* (head or first lord) and *anab* (a little-understood honorific title), and two other seated individuals whose captions are unreadable. Members of the Yaxchilán and Piedras Negras royal families stand on either side of the throne. Both K'an Nik Te', located at the front of the line of elites on the viewer's left, and the last person in the right-hand line sit in front of the supporting legs of Ruler 4's throne. The overlap of their vertical bodies and the legs of the throne provides a visual metaphor for the roles of these elites as pillars of support for their ruler.

While this striking tableau may be mined for a variety of kinds of information about the court and the relationships that structured it, the spatial hierarchy that governed the placement of individuals is especially visibly notable. The panel's composition revolves around Ruler 4, who, animated, leans out from his ornate throne. The spaces to the sides of the ruler are dedicated to his family, on the left, and honored visitors, on the right (Houston and Stuart 2001:63). Additionally, the lines of elites in the foreground are arranged in an orderly manner (Houston and Stuart 2001:72–73), suggesting a formality in their assembly and an understanding of "seating" that underlines the profound connection between power and place among the Maya.

The captions that identify these two lines of court members also tell us something about the internal composition of the court. Most of the individuals are named with both a personal name and a title of some sort, but not all of them. In fact, the seated individual farthest to the viewer's right has no conventional caption at all. Instead, he leans forward and says to the ruler, "*a-winak-en*," or "I am your servant" (Stuart et al. 1999:42). What can we make of this apparent inconsistency in captioning? One wonders if these individuals were known figures in the Piedras Negras community, perhaps even local celebrities. Perhaps it was not necessary to thoroughly caption all of them, as their identities were common knowledge. Such a query is complicated in this case, as this depiction of Ruler 4's court was not carved until the era of Ruler 7 (Houston and Stuart 2001:69). (Ruler 4 reigned from A.D. 729 to 757, whereas Ruler 7 was in power from A.D. 781 until approximately 808 [Martin and Grube 2000:148].) Additionally, the ruler himself would have been well known and yet is named in the text. Nonetheless, the apparent shorthand in some of these examples may be evidence of a close social community, with relationships and mutual knowledge among the courtly elites as important as their connection to their ruler.

If we examine the courtiers pictured at the front of the image, we will see that captions indicate further complexities in courtly identification and organization. Of the seven seated individuals, three are named as *sajal*s, but the two others that are not badly eroded are not named with one of the formalized courtly titles. Even two of the *sajal*s who are named also sport other, less recognizable appellations. Thus a variety of other titles—ones that did not apparently involve an official accession and perhaps were locally defined—are acknowledged and at play within the courtly hierarchy. These positions or honorifics served as complements or alternatives to more formally recognized and widely used offices.

The social world of the court is powerfully illustrated on this monument. The material setting of the court is also richly depicted. On Panel 3, K'an Nik Te' sits at the head of one of the two implicitly parallel lines of courtiers, lined up in front of their ruler (Houston and Stuart 2001:72). Directly in front of him is a ceramic vessel with a lid, of the type often used to contain chocolate (Houston and Stuart 2001:72). An individual in the facing line holds a cup, and Ruler 4 has a bowl—perhaps of tamales—by his right knee. Whatever the official business being undertaken at this meeting was, food offerings and consumption must have played a part, and courtly elites may have been in charge of key practices such as the pouring and serving of chocolate. In addition to the ceramic vessels depicted, the material trappings of the court are seen in this image through the beautifully detailed architectural framing, including the throne, walls, and curtains that helped to define the physical space of this gathering. This definition of setting provides an important reminder of the specific material contextualization of courtly performances and the lives of courtly elites.

Aj Sik'ab of Palenque: Superior of a Fellow Courtier

Aj Sik'ab of Palenque, whose story is recorded on the Group IV incensario stand (figure 13), was at different times a *ti'sakhuun* and a *sajal*. During his years of service at the court, Aj Sik'ab served under both Janab Pakal, the preaccession "ruler" who preceded K'inich Janab Pakal I, and K'inich Janab Pakal I, who ruled from A.D. 615 to 683 (Martin and Grube 2000:160–62). His story indicates that courtiers imparted resiliency and stability in passing from one regime to the next. At Palenque this was important, given the shadowy circumstances surrounding Janab Pakal's leadership at the site (epigraphers remain uncertain about his precise relationship within the Palenque royal family, and he seems never to have officially acceded to the throne [Martin and Grube 2000:160–61]).

Aj Sik'ab was seated as a *ti'sakhuun* under Janab Pakal in A.D. 608, then was described as a *sajal* at the time of his death in A.D. 654, during the reign of K'inich Janab Pakal I. Aj Sik'ab's story, of different titles being used at different times, may suggest that movement between courtly offices over one's life was possible. This supports the idea that a general elevation in status, accomplished when one is seated into one's initial title, is more salient to courtly identity than the particular title held. Supporting this idea in turn is the fact that multiple accession events do not occur over an individual's lifetime, even if he eventually holds multiple titles.

Aj Sik'ab's story differs, however, from those of the other individuals we have examined so far in the way we can understand his place among his fellow courtiers. On the Group IV incensario stand, Aj Sik'ab is named as a *sajal* under K'inich Janab Pakal I, as is another fellow, who is named Yukmakabte'. Incidentally, Yukmakabte' also began his service in the court during the period of Janab Pakal's apparent power. There is nothing surprising here. Previous profiles of court members have revealed multiple individuals holding the same title at the same time, or under the same ruler. We have wondered what the relationship was among these office holders. Recall the observation about K'an Nik Te' of Piedras Negras: is he called *baah sajal* ("head or first *sajal*") on Panel 3 because his position must be distinguished within the ranks of multiple *sajals* present at this event? Aj Sik'ab's case provides evidence for noticeably articulated ranking within the court, as well as a sense of how such differential sta-

Figure 13. Group IV incensario stand, Palenque. The text records the story of Aj Sik'ab of Palenque, a *ti'sakhuun* and *sajal* (his titles are highlighted). Drawing by Linda Schele, inked by Mark Van Stone, © David Schele, courtesy of the Foundation for the Advancement of Mesoamerican Studies, Inc., www.famsi.org.

tus was conceptualized. On the incensario stand Aj Sik'ab is described as grammatically possessing the other *sajal*—Yukmakabte' is "his *sajal*." This phrasing is a direct parallel to the relationship usually specified between a *k'uhul ajaw* and members of his court, as seen on Mak'an Chanal's bench in Copán.

Aj Sik'ab's apparent dominance or superiority over Yukmakabte' suggests even more complex levels and nesting of hierarchy within the court. Such internal ranking between titled courtly elites is recorded rarely. The only other example known to this author is also from Palenque and involves Chak Suutz', who was seated into office in A.D. 723, 115 years after Aj Sik'ab's accession. Chak Suutz' was known as a *yajaw k'ahk'* and *sajal*, and he is recorded as grammatically possessing an *ajk'uhuun* ("his *ajk'uhuun*"). In the case of Aj Sik'ab, the fact that he and Yukmakabte' shared the title of *sajal* may have necessitated the clarification of relative rank. The contextual use of *baah* at other sites to indicate "first-ness" may be a similar practice, but the trope of grammatical possession indicates a more specific differential relationship between two courtiers. Aj Sik'ab's dominance over his fellow *sajal* indicates that relationships among courtiers were obviously not egalitarian, and it also suggests that the disparate, hierarchical relationships that were enacted by the ruler, who "possessed" his courtiers, also extended downward to involve various members of the court, reflecting additional nuance within the ranks of the broader court.

Kelen Hix of Toniná: Loyal to Rulers and Gods Alike

Whereas K'an Nik Te' of Piedras Negras was depicted in the social context of the court, and as an aide to Ruler 3, Kelen Hix of Toniná had the distinguished honor of appearing solo on his own monument, Monument 165 (figure 14). At Toniná Kelen Hix was a fixture of the courtly stage. For over thirty-five years and over the reigns of three Toniná rulers, he was depicted on hieroglyphic monuments, reflecting the ongoing role he played in the court at that site. Kelen Hix's career demonstrates a number of important facets of courtly offices. He illuminates the way in which the acquisition and holding of these offices, as indicated by formal titles, represented an important change in status or state within the sociopolitical hierarchy of the court. Additionally, his story indicates the twin spiritual and political elements that contributed to courtly roles.

Beyond his official longevity, Kelen Hix is notable for holding multiple titles and for sharing his positions with other courtly officials during his life. On Toniná Monument 165, the monument that recorded his death, Kelen Hix is named as both an *ajk'uhuun* and a *ti'huun*. This contrasts with Aj Sik'ab of Palenque, who was not named with both of his known titles at the time of his death. This difference may indicate that death records did not necessitate a full recounting of all titles held, and thus the titles mentioned in such a context represent those which were actively in play at the time of death. Alternatively, the acknowledged variations in courtly practice may mean that the description of an individual at time of death simply followed different norms in different polities. Whether or not the naming of multiple simultaneous titles is connected to a final accounting at the time of his demise, Kelen Hix's identity as a court member was not tied too closely to a single titular sphere. Others at Toniná, such as Aj Chaanah, one of Kelen Hix's compatriots, more clearly hold two positions at the same time.

In fact, in surveying the monuments that record Kelen Hix (Monument 8, Monument 140, Monument 162, and Monument 165), one sees fluidity in terms of which title or titles are used when. Such variation might be chronological, representing processes of maturation or advancement. Or this variation could be contextually driven, determined by the demands of a particular event. Either way, Kelen Hix's record suggests a measure of looseness by which individuals who were qualified, by status and/or knowledge, to take part in the courtly community could respond to official responsibilities from a variety of functional assignments or positions. This

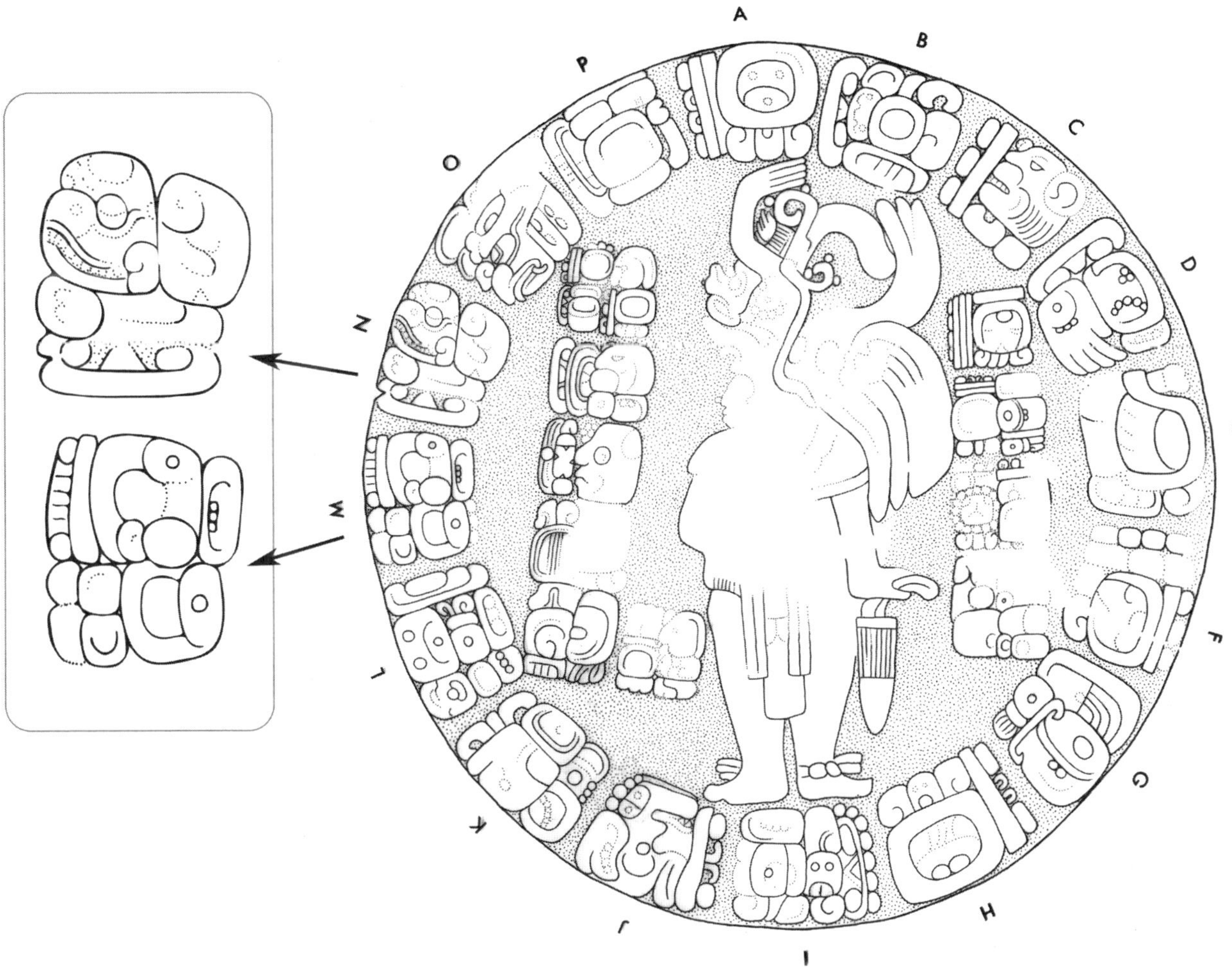

Figure 14. Monument 165, Toniná. This monument features Kelen Hix of Toniná, an *ajk'uhuun* and *ti'huun*. His titles are highlighted at M and N. Drawing by Lucia Henderson, Courtesy of the Corpus of Maya Hieroglyphic Inscriptions, Peabody Museum of Archaeology and Ethnology, © President and Fellows of Harvard College, 2004.15.6.20.25.

observation is supported by a lack of absolute functional mapping of particular activities or responsibilities onto the different formalized titles, a topic that will be further explored in chapter 3. An initial elevation, through an accession ceremony, is ultimately the most marked change of state for these courtly elites and seems to represent their entrance into a bounded elite echelon. Subsequent movement between positions did not carry the same significance in terms of changing status or identity.

Indeed, Kelen Hix is not named with any title on Monument 8, where he is described as witnessing a scattering ritual performed by Ruler 2 (who ruled from A.D. 668 to 687 [Martin and Grube 2000:180]). This is the earliest record of Kelen Hix, so perhaps he had not yet acceded to office. We do not have a record of the date of his accession to status as a courtly official, but it seems unlikely that he was not yet elevated in stature, given the record of his presence at a ritually significant moment. After all, he seemingly had access to important people and events at this point. As on Piedras Negras Panel 3, perhaps he was a known figure, and thus it was not critical to list his title or titles. Or he may have already experienced the rite of passage to courtly position-ship, representing the critical change in status, but was not holding a particular office at the time of Monument 8.

Kelen Hix can also be seen as a collegial official, sharing his courtly duties throughout his career with a fellow courtier named Aj Chaanah. Kelen Hix and Aj Chaanah appear together on two monuments (Monuments 140 and 162) and form a kind of couplet, analogous to the noted linguistic pairings found in the Maya hieroglyphic script (Bricker 2007:2). As they work together at ritual events, such as period endings (Monument 140), or political events, such as accessions (Monument 162), the complementary nature of their official roles is highlighted. They are named with a variety of titles when they appear together. On Monument 140 Kelen Hix is called *ti'huun*, as well as a likely second title that is effaced, and Aj Chaanah, *ajk'uhuun* and *yajaw k'ahk'*. On Monument 162, Kelen Hix is a *ti'sakhuun* and Aj Chaanah is called *yajaw k'ahk'*. As a team, Kelen Hix and Aj Chaanah in their official roles made an important whole or unit, composed of complementary parts, that assisted the ruler in moments of temporal and political transition.

The positions and partnership of Kelen Hix and Aj Chaanah were sufficiently stable and politically useful to weather the shift from Ruler 3 to Ruler 4, marking the ability of titled elites to maintain position and conserve their power even during times of profound change. Aj Chaanah provided continuity of another sort after Kelen Hix's death in A.D. 717 (as recorded on Monument 165) by forming half of a new elite duo, this time with a courtier called "Bird Jaguar." While Bird Jaguar seems to have taken Kelen Hix's place, his pairing with Aj Chaanah at the period ending in A.D. 721 (Monument 110) features both elites being named as *ajk'uhuuns*. On this monument, Bird Jaguar and Aj Chaanah are each named with only a single title. Just as the team of Kelen Hix and Aj Chaanah served as a bridge between rulers, Aj Chaanah himself provided a link during a period of transition within the hierarchy of nonroyal courtly officials.

In addition to his prominence at Toniná in conjunction with the ruler and with fellow courtiers, Kelen Hix also derived standing from his connections with otherworldly authorities. On Monument 165, his death monument, Kelen Hix is linked to the paddler gods. He is named here as a *ti'huun* or, more specifically, with the unusual designation of *k'uhul*, or "holy," *ti'huun* of the paddler gods. This description suggests a parallel between his obligations as a worldly *ti'huun* to the ruler and his duties as a holy *ti'huun* to the gods. In imagining the nature of his connection to both human and supernatural authorities, Zender's suggestion of "mouth" or "mouthpiece" as a reading of this title is particularly intriguing (2004:210–21). Kelen Hix's story helps to frame these courtly positions in light of both earthly and otherworldly access and suggests the possibility of dual kinds of authority and allegiance. The constancy of courtly elite offices across political transitions, as seen in Kelen Hix's story and other stories recounted here, was anchored by the cosmological ties maintained by court members, independent of their immediate political loyalties.

Ahkmo' of Site R: Leader of a Subsidiary Site

The *sajal* Ahkmo' was active as a courtier at Site R at the same time that Kelen Hix was a court member at Toniná, though they likely never met. Ahkmo' called Site R, one of the satellite sites of Yaxchilán that has yet to be located, his home during the reigns at Yaxchilán of Itsamnah Balam II (A.D. 681–742) and Bird Jaguar IV (A.D. 752–68) (Martin and Grube 2000:122, 128). The position of Site R as a satellite of Yaxchilán presents a different context for understanding the significance of courtly elite positions. Such satellite sites were closely affiliated with a central city and did not possess their own emblem glyph or *k'uhul ajaw* (Golden 2003, 2010; Mathews 1988:378–79).[1] Thus, *sajals* in such contexts may have acted as overseers of settlements with a close allegiance to a larger power (Houston 1993:128–30; Houston and Inomata 2009:180–81; Stuart 1985b:4–10)—perhaps in the role of regional governor, as in the interpretation suggested by Stuart (1985b). This role for *sajals* suggests a different mode of operation than for *sajals* like K'an Nik Te' of Piedras Negras or Chak Jol of Yaxchilán (whom we will meet below), who were closely affiliated with the ruler and kept close at hand. Despite the lack of clear functional differentiation among the different formalized courtly titles, *sajal* does stand out in examples from multiple sites as being the one position that seems to employ two distinctive modes of operation. The nature of this office seems to have differed depending on whether the officeholder was located within the central polity or whether he was based at a settlement further afield, in which case his leadership role was more singular than in the local context.

Like both K'an Nik Te' and Kelen Hix, Ahkmo' also bridged multiple rulers at Yaxchilán: Itsamnah Balam II and Bird Jaguar IV. This is a particularly notable feat in the context of Yaxchilán politics, as a cloudy ten-year interregnum period separated the rules of these two kings (Martin and Grube 2000:127). Ahkmo''s affiliation with the rulers on either side of what must have been a tumultuous era suggests his own savvy. This also further demonstrates the importance of courtly elites in providing continuity across the liminal times of change of rule, both in instances extreme, like this one, or more routine, such as seen at Piedras Negras and Toniná.

Like Kelen Hix, Ahkmo' fulfilled more than one courtly office over his career, occupying not only the role of *sajal* but also that of *ajk'uhuun*. On Site R Lintel 1 (figure 15), which is undated, Ahkmo' appears with Itsamnah Balam in a ritual dance. On this monument, Ahkmo' is named as the captor of four captives, *ch'ok*, *sajal*, and the *yajawte'* of Itsamnah Balam II. His designation as *ch'ok*, meaning "young" or

1. Site R, Laxtunich, and La Pasadita are all names used to refer to satellite sites of Yaxchilán. While La Pasadita is a known site, Site R and Laxtunich are less useful designations. Site R is an epigraphic designation based on textual information but is not yet associated with an identified location. Laxtunich, also known as the "Lamb site," was explored by Dana and Ginger Lamb (1951), but it has not, to my knowledge, been located again since then. It is, in fact, possible that these various site names refer to the same place; all three designations are used to refer to a similar and related set of textual material. Despite this confusion, I continue to use the nomenclature of the three sites in order to use the same primary designations by which these monuments have previously been called.

Figure 15. Lintel 1, Site R. Ahkmo' (*left*), a *sajal*, is depicted here with Itsamnah Balam. His title (here *ch'ok sajal*) is highlighted at B3 and B4. Drawing by Peter Mathews. Courtesy of Peter Mathews.

"unripe" (Houston and Stuart 2001:67, 72; Pérez Martínez et al. 1996:58), correlates nicely with this being the earliest monument on which he is mentioned, based on the affiliation with Itsamnah Balam II, and may indicate the presence of stages through which officials pass as they grow into their roles, from an initial junior rank. This is not a conclusive observation, however, as he is not named as a *sajal* on the two other monuments on which he appears, disallowing a parallel comparison. Later, during Bird Jaguar IV's reign, Ahkmo' appears on Lintels 4 and 3 (figures 16 and 17); in both images he appears with the ruler. On Lintel 4 Ahkmo' is named as an *ajk'uhuun*, with no mention of his identity as a *sajal*. On Lintel 3 he is named as the *yajawte'*—a less formalized elite designation—of Bird Jaguar IV.

Figure 16. Lintel 4, Site R. Here, Ahkmo' (*left*) is shown dancing with the ruler Bird Jaguar IV; on this monument he is described as an *ajk'uhuun*. His title is highlighted. Drawing by Nikolai Grube. Courtesy of Nikolai Grube.

These portraits are notable in part because of the visual prominence given to Ahkmo'. On these monuments he repeatedly shares the space of the lintel with a ruler, and on Lintels 1 and 4 he is portrayed as nearly equal in stature to the ruler, acting as a symmetrical part of the balanced composition of two figures. Clearly, a privilege of portrayal is demonstrated here. Perhaps the parallel set up between courtly official and ruler in these images reflects Ahkmo's role as the governor of a satellite site rather than as one of many elites operating within the sphere of the court.

Despite Ahkmo''s ongoing prominence in the Yaxchilán sphere over the reigns of multiple rulers, his place in the court apparently changed over time, as indicated by the use of different titles (i.e., *sajal* versus *ajk'uhuun*) in conjunction with his appear-

Figure 17. *(Opposite)* Lintel 3, Site R. Ahkmo' (right) again appears with Bird Jaguar IV; here he is not named with an official court position. Photograph courtesy of www.mayavase.com.

ances with Itsamnah Balam II and Bird Jaguar IV. While he maintains ongoing importance in the political sphere, his position may have been modified by Bird Jaguar IV, perhaps removing Ahkmo''s local power as a regional *sajal*.

These monuments, though they provide relatively limited information on Ahkmo''s political career, could serve as support for the idea that courtly elites moved from one titled position to another over the course of their public lives—in Ahkmo''s case from *sajal* to *ajk'uhuun*. Certainly there is no contextual reason from these monuments to provide a functional explanation of why he would be named with one title in one case and another in the other case; in both situations he is dancing with the ruler. Such a hypothesis of official movement is plausible (though not provable), but it does not hold for all Classic Maya courts. Kelen Hix and his compatriots at Toniná, for example, are recorded as holding multiple titles simultaneously. This possible contradiction should not be seen as troubling, however, given the recognizable variations seen throughout the Maya area in the functioning and structure of the court. The court of the Late Classic Maya should in no way be seen as a static or homogeneous institution. Rather, even as understood through the inherently partial perspective of textual evidence, the court seems to have been flexible and sensitive to change. These characteristics allowed for the incorporation of shifting number of individuals in a small constellation of positions and through a variety of political trajectories. The result imparted stability to the court through reliance on more broadly elite-derived, versus solely royal, power and authority.

The K'utims of El Cayo: A Family of Influence

At the site of El Cayo, one can see other kinds of intriguing relationships among members of the court. At El Cayo the narrative focuses on family. The office of *sajal* seems to have been particularly prominent at this site. The polity of El Cayo was a satellite site to the separate center of Piedras Negras (Chinchilla and Houston 2003; Golden 2010:378–79; Martin and Grube 2000:150; Schele 1991b:84; Zender 2002:167–69), like the relationship discussed above between Site R and Yaxchilán. Thus, the *sajal*s at El Cayo operated with some degree of independence from the central administration at Piedras Negras.

In the case of the *sajal*s of El Cayo, between at least A.D. 731 and 795 this office seems to have remained in the hands of one family. Multiple generations of *sajal*s, representing six distinct officeholders of the position, are documented on El Cayo Altar 4 (figure 18), El Cayo Lintel 1, and the Cleveland Panel (figure 19). They almost all share a common final name element—akin to a surname—of K'utim. The one exception is specified as being the son of a K'utim.

These monuments make this family connection explicit in several cases by articulating the father-son relationship that characterized multiple generations of K'utims. On Altar 4, for example, Aj Chak Wayib K'utim, a "four *k'atun*" *sajal* (a designation

Figure 18. Altar 4, El Cayo. This monument depicts Aj Chak Wayib K'utim, one of the many *sajal*s at the site of El Cayo (additional text on the sides and legs of this altar is not pictured). Drawing by Peter Mathews. Courtesy of Peter Mathews.

indicating his advanced age), is recorded as celebrating the period ending 9.15.0.0.0 (A.D. 731) with a scattering ceremony; his father is specified as also carrying the K'utim name. Similarly, Lintel 1 connects father and son *sajal*s. The text here opens with the birth, in A.D. 763, of Ch'ok Chan Panak Wayib, who later in life becomes a *sajal* and names his father as Ch'ok Wayib Aj Ik' Suutz' K'utim, also a *sajal.* Another K'utim, Aj Chak Suutz' K'utim (perhaps an uncle or brother to young Chan Panak), becomes a *sajal* between the eras of office holding of the father and the son. Clearly, there are family connections here—and also a complex story of the passing of offices from one individual, or perhaps generation, to the next. The last K'utim recorded at El Cayo was Aj Yax Suutz' K'utim, another *sajal*, who oversaw a tomb dedication in A.D. 795, recorded on the Cleveland Panel.

This genealogical information, coupled with the shared last name, supports the idea that courtly positions were not solely a matter of merit but rather depended at least in part on ascribed status and lineage—much like the *k'uhul ajaw*s. Relationships were key in the courtly context, and being a member of a family with history in a particular office was an important factor in becoming a courtly elite. Evidence of family ties helps us understand the structure of the court over time, as well as how social standing was constructed within this institution. While coming from the right family may not always have been a requirement for advancement, the emphasis on kin connections in certain contexts helps to illuminate qualities that contributed to high status for Classic period courtiers.

While textual emphasis on family connections suggests that ascribed status played a part in such positions, the history of the K'utim family also indicates that some types of achieved status were similarly recognized in the construction of elevated courtly identities. In particular, Aj Chak Wayib K'utim—who appears on Altar 4—is

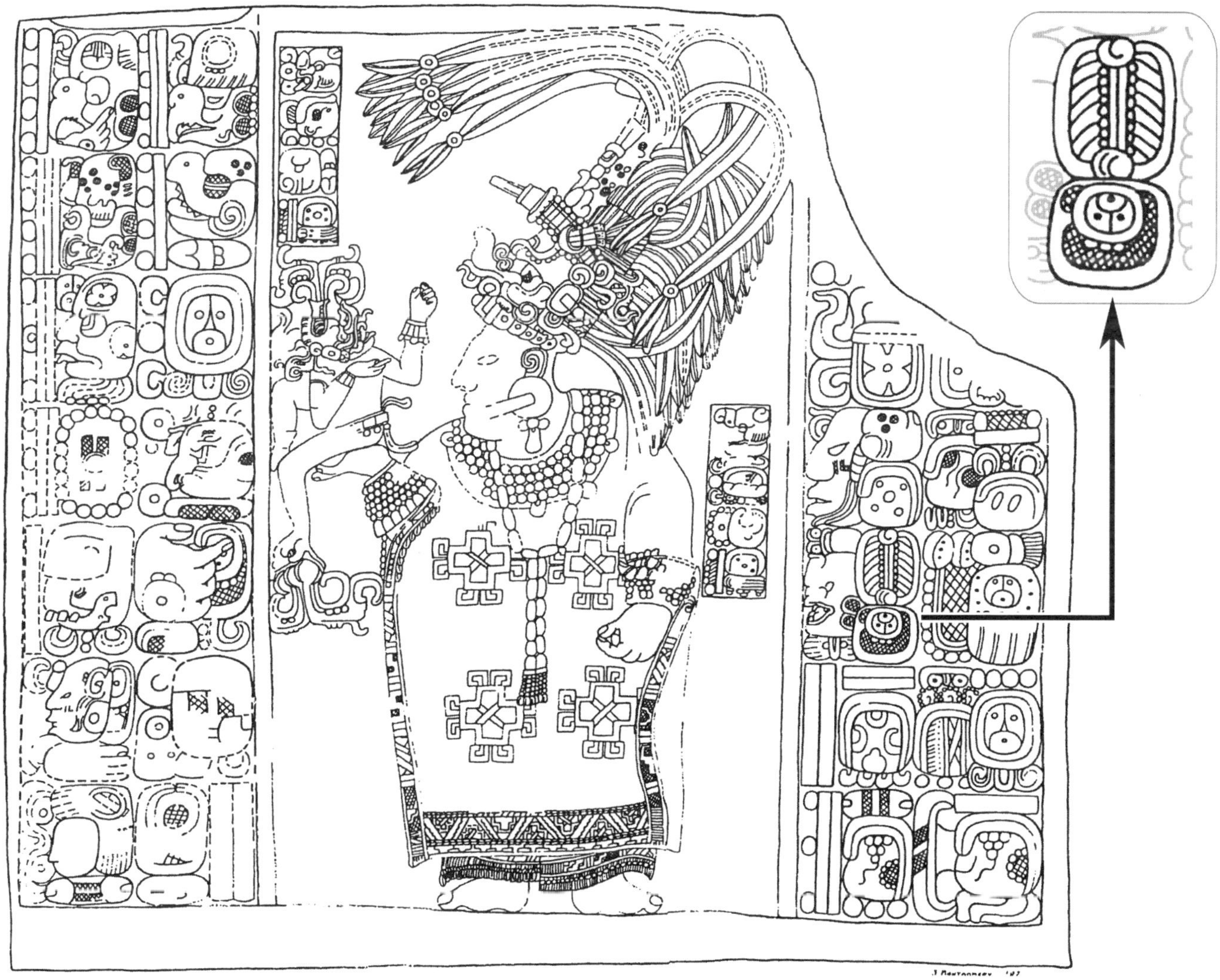

Figure 19. Wall panel, Cleveland Museum of Art. Another El Cayo *sajal*, Aj Yax Suutz' K'utim, is mentioned here. His title is highlighted. Drawing by John Montgomery, © Foundation for the Advancement of Mesoamerican Studies, Inc., www.famsi.org.

called "four *k'atun*" *sajal*, referring to twenty-year *k'atun* cycles (Houston and Inomata 2009:60, 173). Such a description highlights the accomplishment of longevity and the active marking of elders as a group worthy of particular respect.

Before ending our brief visit with the K'utims, let us return for a moment to the complex family story described on Lintel 1, where three related *sajal*s are discussed. These *sajal*s are a father and son and another male relative—perhaps an uncle or older brother of the son. In addition to documenting ambiguous issues of succession, the story of these three *sajal*s in El Cayo is situated within a political framework beyond the confines of this particular site. As mentioned earlier, El Cayo is a satellite site of Piedras Negras, but this monument indicates that the site of Sak Tz'i' also played a part in the local political hierarchy (Anaya Hernandez et al. 2003:179–80). That is, there seems to have been a three-tiered hierarchy operating among these sites. The monument records that a Sak Tz'i' lord oversaw multiple events related to the K'utims: the death and burial of Aj Ik' Suutz' K'utim, the accession of Aj Chak Suutz' K'utim into office, and the dedication of the tomb of Chan Panak Wayib. Despite this apparently extensive involvement in the political life of El Cayo, the monument notes that after the death of Aj Ik' Suutz' K'utim, the young Chan Panak traveled to Piedras Negras. There he visited with Piedras Negras Ruler 5, Yopnal Ahk III (Stuart 2004:3–4). One can imagine that Chan Panak was consulting with him after the death of his father. After this meeting, however, Chan Panak did not take office, despite his visit. (In fact, nine years passed before he did accede to office.) Instead, Aj Chak Suutz' K'utim took office as *sajal*. It seems that Piedras Negras was the ultimate arbiter of the courtly hierarchy at El Cayo, despite Sak Tz'i''s close involvement with ritual occasions there.

Just as the stories of various courtly elites help to show complex rankings and relationships between different individuals within a particular court, this example indicates that the courtly hierarchy would also have structured interactions and machinations between polities in a region—here between El Cayo, Sak Tz'i', and Piedras Negras. *Sajal* roles are also illuminated here. At El Cayo only one *sajal* seems to have held office at a time, likely a result of its status as a satellite site of a larger polity. The *sajal* of El Cayo, then, played a singular leadership role, parallel to the single *k'uhul ajaw* who ruled at Piedras Negras.

Chak Tun of the Piedras Negras/El Cayo Area: Patient in Achieving Office

Chak Tun Ahk Kimi, a *sajal*, hailed from the region of the Usumacinta around Piedras Negras and El Cayo and likely lived at one of those sites, though the extant textual record does not allow for a certain determination. Like the K'utim family, he was also from a family of *sajal*s, one in which three successive officeholders shared the last name of Kimi. As commemorated on the Dumbarton Oaks wall panel (Relief Panel 1) (figure 20) (Coe and Benson 1966:4–15), Chak Tun Ahk Kimi was born in A.D. 649, and in time he became a *sajal*, affiliated with the court of Piedras Negras. Strangely, however, he did not undergo his accession to that office until the ripe old age of forty-eight. Details of his life recorded on the panel indicate that his father, sharing the same surname, was also a *sajal*, and that during Chak Tun's years of waiting to take office he remained engaged with the court of Piedras Negras. He obligingly performed a dance for Piedras

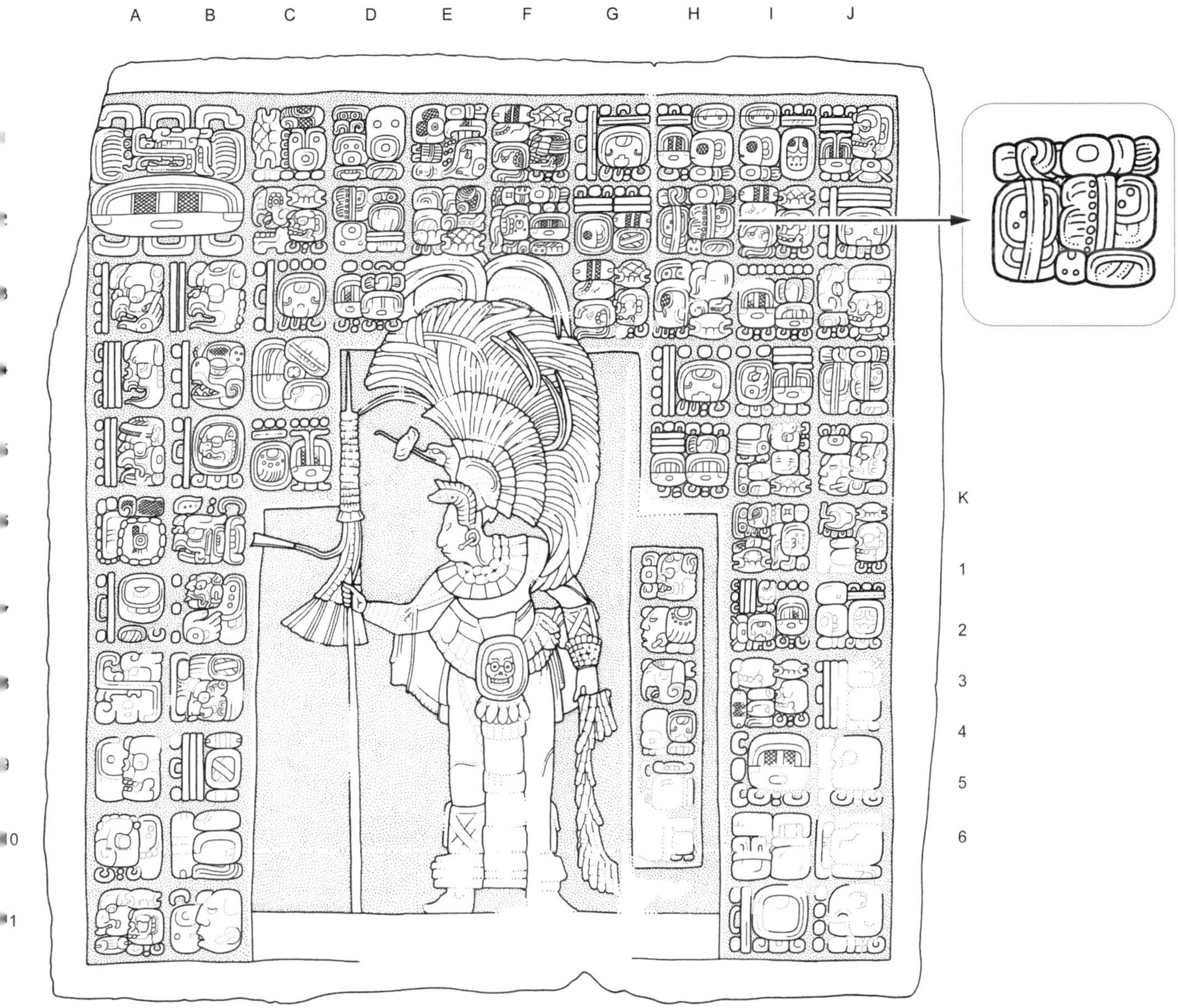

Figure 20. Wall panel, Dumbarton Oaks. This monument records the story of Chak Tun Ahk Kimi, a *sajal* from a family of *sajal*s. Chak Tun's *sajal* title is highlighted. Drawing by Stephen Houston and Alexandre Tokovinine. Courtesy of Dumbarton Oaks, Stephen Houston, and Alexandre Tokovinine.

Negras Ruler 3, Yopnal Ahk II (who reigned from A.D. 687 to 729 [Martin and Grube 2000:142]), on the occasion of that ruler's three-year anniversary of accession. Such loyalty paid off when seven years later Ruler 3 oversaw Chak Tun's inauguration as *sajal*. Chak Tun died, after many years in office, at age eighty-four.

Besides his notable longevity, Chak Tun's story is significant for what it says about patterns of succession, family connections in these roles, and the lack of hard-and-fast rules governing the operation of the formal roles of the court. Reading between the lines of Chak Tun's monument, one might conclude that Chak Tun's father, himself a *sajal*, had to die before the position became open for Chak Tun himself to occupy. (A similar story might be reconstructed for the case of the *sajal* Chan Panak at El Cayo, mentioned earlier, who was also involved in an enigmatic story of succession.) This emphasis on family is seen in other instances and suggests that a key factor in some circumstances was membership in a family that historically occupied such positions. Explicitly recorded family dynasties of courtly elites are exclusively limited to the position of *sajal*, however, indicating another way in which this office is distinctive from the other courtly offices.

That Chak Tun had to wait so long to become a *sajal*—while still appearing in the court in the meantime—is intriguing. This example appears to contradict evidence from several other places, such as Toniná and even Piedras Negras itself, which indicates that multiple individuals could in fact hold a type of position simultaneously. The exclusivity that seems to be at work in Chak Tun's case is not without precedent, however. Perhaps the most striking evidence for the operation of courtly titles as being passed from individual to individual, much as the ruler's position would be, is the K'an Tok Panel from Palenque (figure 21) (Bernal Romero 2002; Marken and Straight 2007:303, 310; Stuart 2003:2). This panel details the history of individuals occupying the office of "banded bird" at Palenque. The "king list" style of text records the names and inauguration dates of each "banded bird" official, as well as the ruler under whom each was seated. Tellingly, the list of supervising rulers does not constitute a complete recap of the known chronology at Palenque, meaning that the cycle of "banded bird" officials proceeded at a different pace from the change in rulers over time. Apparently, some rulers did not have the opportunity to appoint a banded bird official during their reign. This exclusivity of courtly position seems to be the same principle that impacted Chak Tun's late arrival into his office.

As has been mentioned before, *sajal*s at satellite sites have a distinctive type of position from other *sajal*s and, indeed, other courtly elite positions. In ways they may act like regional rulers, or like local leaders standing in for the ruler. In this conceptualization, it makes sense for one individual at a time to have such power. (The Palenque example complicates this, however, since "banded bird" officials at Palenque and elsewhere also experienced such exclusivity of position but were not regional rulers as were some *sajal*s.) Chak Tun's long wait for official recognition, and clear participation with courtly life in the meantime, serve as an important reminder of the presence of untitled individuals playing roles within the court. Chak Tun had access to individuals and activities within this bounded space long before he was awarded official status within it. While individuals in his position are harder to textually identify due to their unofficial status, their impact on this social community must be recalled and recognized for a full understanding of the relationships, interactions, and inequalities that were at the heart of the court.

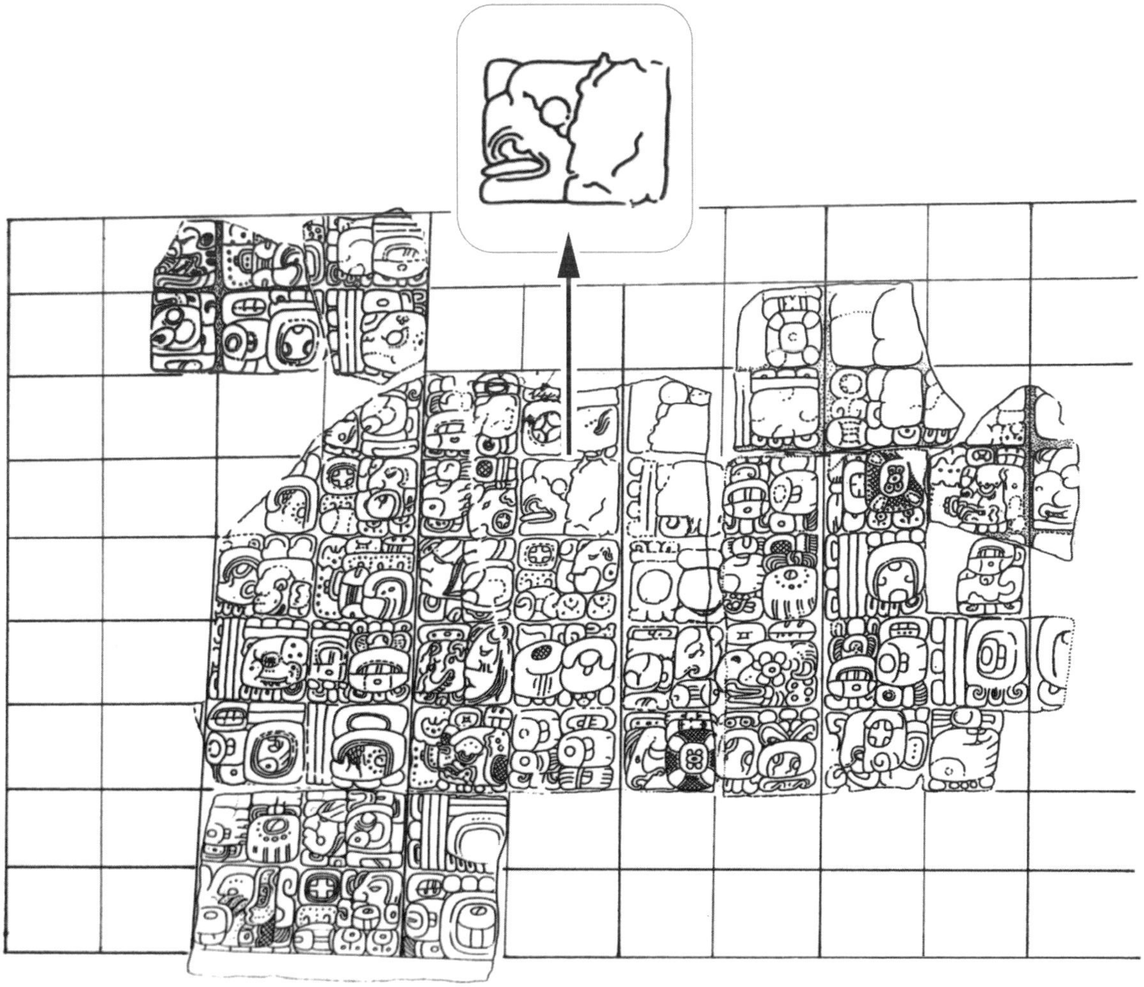

Figure 21. K'an Tok Panel, Palenque. This remarkable panel records the "banded bird" officials who were seated at Palenque and highlights the separate accession cycles for rulers and court officials. One example of the "banded bird" title is highlighted. Drawing by Linda Schele, © David Schele, courtesy of the Foundation for the Advancement of Mesoamerican Studies, Inc., www.famsi.org.

The suite of formalized titles provides strong evidence that many courts across the Classic Maya lowlands shared common characteristics, and the positions within the courts were partially bureaucratized through dependence on some common structural aspects. Nonetheless, there was a notable amount of variation in how positions and courtly institutions worked. In engaging with the details of individual elites' lives, it is important to notice the ways in which processes (such as timing of succession, qualifications for succession, number of officers of a particular type) occurred in a variety of ways within different polities, while still providing the skeleton for similar and shared conceptions of the court.

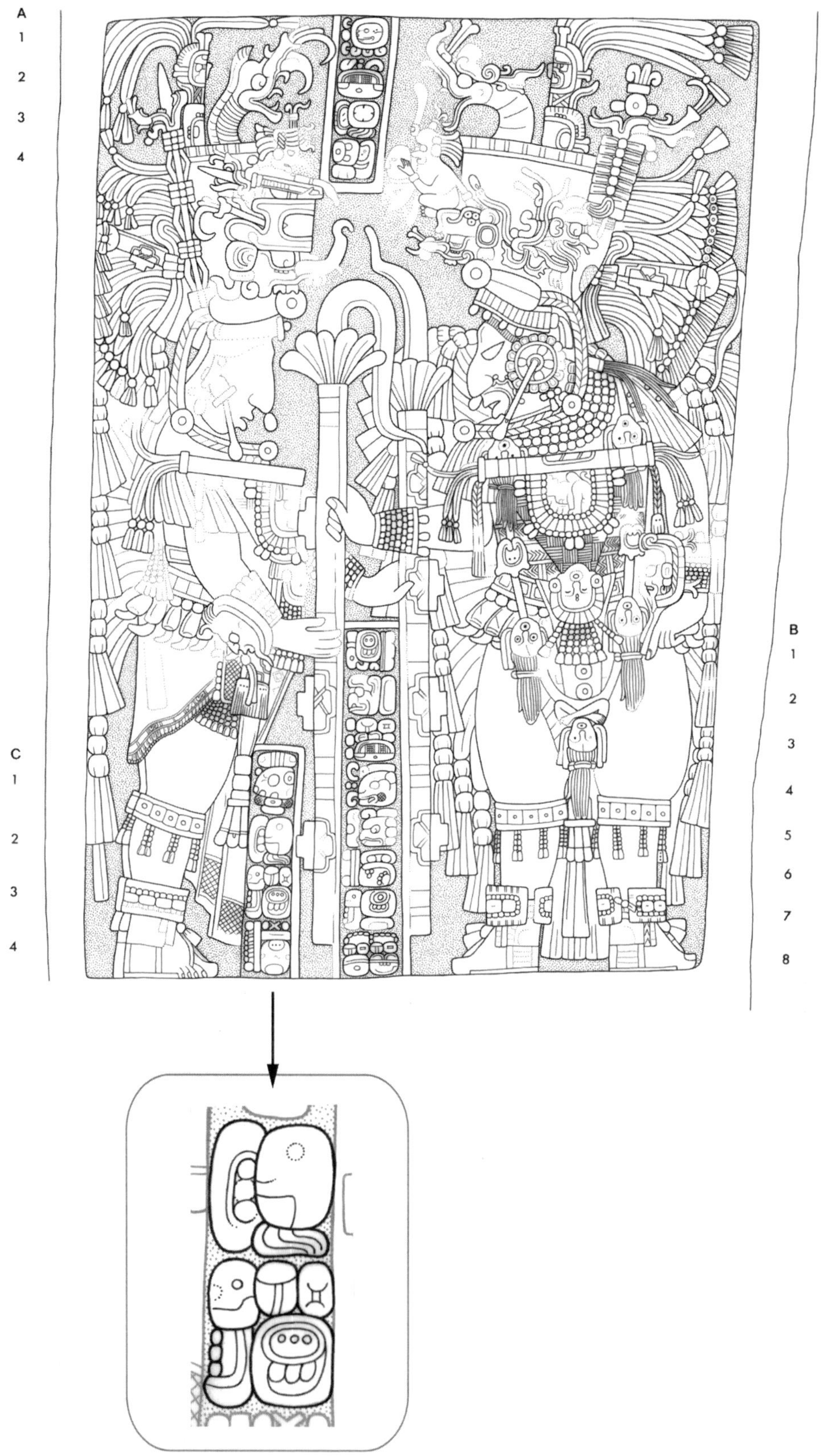
A
1
2
3
4
B
1
2
3
4
5
6
7
8
C
1
2
3
4

Figure 22. *(Opposite)* Lintel 9, Yaxchilán. Chak Jol is named here as a yichaan ajaw, or "uncle of the lord" (highlighted at C2 and C3). This monument may record his elevation to the position of regent for the young Itsamnah Balam III. Drawing by Ian Graham, Courtesy of the Corpus of Maya Hieroglyphic Inscriptions, Peabody Museum of Archaeology and Ethnology, © President and Fellows of Harvard College, 2004.15.6.5.9.

"Great Skull" (Chak Jol) of Yaxchilán: Kin to the Royal Family

Chak Tun, whom we just met, had the privilege of hanging around the court long before he was officially welcomed as a *sajal*. The prominence of the Kimi family, to which he belonged, may have played a part in this. Other instances in which family connections structured an individual's participation in the court take a notably different form. One such case is that of Chak Jol. Chak Jol, the individual commonly known by the nickname "Great Skull," was a well-documented *sajal* at the site of Yaxchilán (Martin and Grube 2000:132, 135; Schele 1991b:78). His affiliation bridged two rulers, Bird Jaguar IV (who reigned from A.D. 752 to 768 [Martin and Grube 2000:128]) and, subsequently, Itsamnah Balam III (in power from A.D. 769 to approximately 800 [Martin and Grube 2000:134]). His connection with these individuals is more profound than other similar relationships between rulers and their titled elites. Specifically, Chak Jol did not just cultivate a close connection with the rulers he served but was actually a blood relative.

On Yaxchilán Lintel 9 (figure 22) and Lintel 58 (figure 23), Chak Jol is named as a *yichaan ajaw*, meaning "uncle of the lord," referring to his relationship with the young heir Itsamnah Balam III (Mathews 1988:285–86; Stuart 1997b:7–8). Itsamnah Balam III was the child of Bird Jaguar IV and "Lady Great Skull," Chak Jol's brother-in-law and sister. When Itsamnah Balam III came to power at the age of sixteen, Chak Jol may have acted as a regent or guardian for the underage ruler. Martin and Grube suggest that Yaxchilán Lintel 9, dating to the end of Bird Jaguar IV's reign, actually records the elevation of Chak Jol to this position (2000:132). The repetition of this title (*yichaan ajaw*, or sometimes just *yichaan*—"uncle") indicates the importance of Chak Jol's relationship with Itsamnah Balam III and puts this kin identification on par with his courtly identifier of *sajal*. In sum, Chak Jol's involvement with the Yaxchilán court is extensive. He holds the position of *sajal* during the reigns of two rulers and further eases the transition between them by playing a close advisory role, based on his kin relationship, to the second of these rulers.

This identification of a direct kin connection between a courtly officer and the royal family suggests that the line between royalty and courtly elites is a permeable one. Titled courtiers may include both specially recognized high elites and members of the royal family who need an alternate outlet besides rulership for expression of power. In fact, the relatively few instances in which titled elites are explicitly identified as members of the royal family almost all seem to represent cases—like that of Chak

A
B
C
D
1
2
3
E
1-4

Figure 23. (*Opposite*) Lintel 58, Yaxchilán. Chak Jol is named as a *yichaan* ("uncle") on this monument (title highlighted at C). Drawing by Ian Graham, Courtesy of the Corpus of Maya Hieroglyphic Inscriptions, Peabody Museum of Archaeology and Ethnology, © President and Fellows of Harvard College, 2004.15.6.6.32.

Jol—in which the individual concerned is of high status but not quite high enough. That is, he or she (and it is, indeed, important to be gender inclusive in discussion of this circumstance) was unable to ever reach the pinnacle of Maya sacred kingship in the role of the ruler and thus sought, or was awarded, an alternate official marker of standing.

Chak Jol's dual roles as royal family member and titled courtier may be better understood by a glimpse at other individuals who occupied similar positions. The majority of the few other individuals known to be part of the royal family, but who also held a courtly office, were women—specifically royal wives named with courtly titles. In fact, with one exception, on Lacanha Panel 1, the only women who are named with courtly titles are members of royal families. They are named in parentage statements, in which the mother of a ruler is named, or as a wife to the ruler. Instances of women named in this way are found at Yaxchilán, Machaquilá, Bonampak, and Pomoná.

For example, "Lady Ik' Skull," a wife of Yaxchilán's Itsamnah Balam II and a member of the royal line of Calakmul, is called *ix ajk'uhuun* on Lintel 53 (figure 24); the *ix* prefix is a feminine agentive marker, indicating that a woman held this title (Houston and Inomata 2009:146; Jackson and Stuart 2001:222). This is a particularly unusual naming, as there are no other *ajk'uhuun*s recorded at all at Yaxchilán. This could support the idea that this was an honorific without the responsibilities of an actual office, since there is not a precedent for that position at Yaxchilán. Lady Great Skull, discussed above as the mother of the young heir Itsamnah Balam III, was named as an *ix sajal* on Lintel 54, for instance (see also Mathews 1988:208–209) (figure 25); her additional elevation was important, given the apparent preoccupation with ensuring the security of her son's right to rule.

What do these examples mean for Chak Jol? The instances in which clearly identified royal family members also held courtly positions largely seem to be ones in which these titles were used strategically by individuals, such as male nonheirs or women, who may have had need or reason to highlight or add to their high status but could not realistically aspire to rulership. These examples do not suggest that all courtly officeholders were actually royal family members, with such positions acting to contain troublesome familial hangers-on. Given the emphasis on articulation of lineage in Maya texts, we would expect to see much more frequent specifications of royal blood, had all such officials been so connected. These apparently idiosyncratic usages of courtly positions do indicate that there was genuine privilege and high respect attached to official court offices, to a degree that they became desirable in some instances even to members of the royal family.

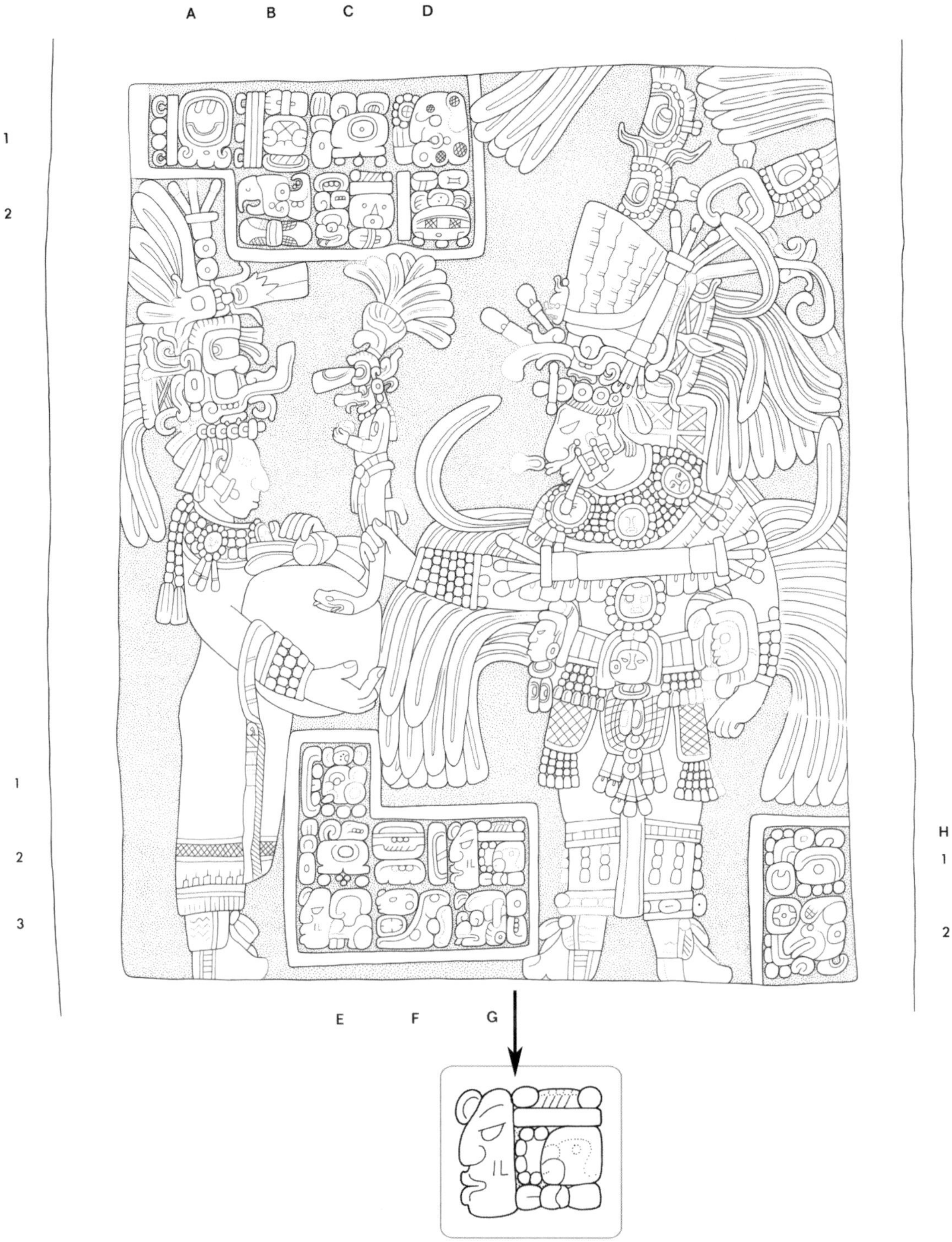

Figure 24. Lintel 53, Yaxchilán. “Lady Ik’ Skull” (*left*), a wife of Yaxchilán’s Itsamnah Balam II, is called *ix ajk’uhuun*, or “female *ajk’uhuun*” (title highlighted at G2). Drawing by Ian Graham, Courtesy of the Corpus of Maya Hieroglyphic Inscriptions, Peabody Museum of Archaeology and Ethnology, © President and Fellows of Harvard College, 2004.15.6.6.27.

Figure 25. Lintel 54, Yaxchilán. "Lady Great Skull" (*left*), the mother of the young heir Itsamnah Balam III, is named as an *ix sajal* (title highlighted at E and F). Drawing by Ian Graham, Courtesy of the Corpus of Maya Hieroglyphic Inscriptions, Peabody Museum of Archaeology and Ethnology, © President and Fellows of Harvard College, 2004.15.6.6.28.

In addition to demonstrating an overlap between the royal family and the titled members of the court, the textual record of Chak Jol's life as a *sajal* sheds light on the nature of elite status. As well as being named as a *sajal* and *yichaan ajaw*, Chak Jol is also referred to with the honorific *aj 7 baak*, or "he of seven captives." This military prowess echoes, to a lesser extent, Bird Jaguar's own impressive reputation as "he of twenty captives" and becomes part of Chak Jol's marking as a courtier of importance.

The emphasis on Chak Jol's achievement as a warrior is important to contemplate as part of exploring functional anchors for the formal roles of the court. Understanding the *sajal* as a war captain is an interpretation that has long existed in the literature (Schele 1991a:10). Despite ambiguous evidence for straightforward functional associations of particular roles with particular titles, examples such as Chak Jol may help to support the idea that the key duties of *sajal*s included—or perhaps even focused on—conquest and military achievement. A survey of all extant examples of courtly elites indicates that honorifics emphasizing captives are exclusively associated with the *sajal* title, suggesting that a war role may have been central to the official identity of the *sajal*. However, such a conclusion must be tempered by the observation that all titled elites, including *sajal*s, are recorded in the hieroglyphic records as participating in a wide variety of events, with a great deal of overlap between activities and titles. While some positions may have had certain areas that were especially important to their duties, the titular system overall was mildly bureaucratized, with positions defined and redefined by the talents of the individuals holding them and by the needs of the court in a particular temporal or spatial context.

Like Mak'an Chanal at Copán, Chak Jol was not alone in shouldering courtly duties for Bird Jaguar IV or for Itsamnah Balam III. Bird Jaguar IV oversaw three *sajal*s at Yaxchilán during his time in office (Schele 1991b:78): Chak Jol, K'in Mo' Ajaw, and K'an Tok Wayib. Chak Jol may represent a chronologically later appointee compared with the other two. The *sajal* Ahkmo' from Site R, whom we met above, and the *sajal* Tilom, from the subsidiary site La Pasadita (Golden 2003, 2010:379–80), were also affiliated with Bird Jaguar IV. Tilom continued his allegiance to the Yaxchilán dynasty during Itsamnah Balam III's reign, and several *sajal*s from the satellite site of Laxtunich joined him. What a welter of *sajal*s (see also Mathews 1988:235–38)! This position was plainly a mainstay of governance in the Yaxchilán region. (Recall, however, that *sajal*s in downtown Yaxchilán held a different sort of position than those operating semi-independently—and singularly—at the outpost sites.) Yaxchilán illustrates the locally determined compositions of Maya royal courts. In courts at other sites, other courtly positions, or combinations of courtly positions, were emphasized.

One final clue to the functioning of courtly elites may be teased out from the story of Chak Jol. One of the *sajal*s with whom Chak Jol shared his position during Bird Jaguar IV's reign was K'an Tok Wayib. K'an Tok Wayib similarly flaunted his military prowess through the repeated appellative "captor of Kokte' Ajaw." Despite Chak Jol's blood relationship to Bird Jaguar IV, K'an Tok Wayib may actually have been the favored *sajal*, sharing three lintel scenes with Bird Jaguar himself, on Lintel 42 (figure 26), Lintel 6 (figure 27), and Lintel 8 (figure 28) (listed here in chronological order), and being named on Lintel 6 as a *baah sajal*, or "head *sajal*." While K'an Tok Wayib was not always specified as *baah sajal* (versus just *sajal*), the use of this relative title

Figure 26. Lintel 42, Yaxchilán. K'an Tok Wayib (*left*), *sajal*, depicted with Bird Jaguar IV (title highlighted at D3). Drawing by Ian Graham, Courtesy of the Corpus of Maya Hieroglyphic Inscriptions, Peabody Museum of Archaeology and Ethnology, © President and Fellows of Harvard College, 2004.15.6.6.13.

Figure 27. Lintel 6, Yaxchilán. K'an Tok Wayib (*right*) again sharing a depiction with Bird Jaguar IV. K'an Tok Wayib is named here as *baah sajal* (highlighted at B7—the *baah* modifier appears in the left-hand section of the highlighted glyph block). Drawing by Ian Graham, Courtesy of the Corpus of Maya Hieroglyphic Inscriptions, Peabody Museum of Archaeology and Ethnology, © President and Fellows of Harvard College, 2004.15.6.5.6.

Figure 28. Lintel 8, Yaxchilán. K'an Tok Wayib (*left*) (title highlighted) portrayed in action, seizing a captive alongside Bird Jaguar IV. Drawing by Ian Graham, Courtesy of the Corpus of Maya Hieroglyphic Inscriptions, Peabody Museum of Archaeology and Ethnology, © President and Fellows of Harvard College, 2004.15.6.5.8.

suggests that his position was hierarchically ranked higher than other simultaneous *sajal*s, such as Chak Jol. Chak Jol's kin connection to the royal family, while a factor in his high status, did not trump other sorts of favoritism from the ruler or other sources of power and status.

Janab Ajaw of Palenque: A Close Connection with Royalty and Gods

Allow me to introduce one final courtier with a brief profile. Janab Ajaw hailed from Palenque, and like Chak Jol he was also a member of the royal family. He was the grandson of the noted Palenque ruler K'inich Janab Pakal I and was the cousin—or possibly even brother—of the ruler Ahkal Mo' Naab III (Stuart 2005b:119). Like Chak Jol, then, Janab Ajaw was a royal male without the ultimate outlet of ruling power. Nonetheless, his political achievements are marked through his courtly position of "banded bird." His short story highlights the importance of court members' proximity to both earthly and cosmological forces.

Janab Ajaw was seated into the position of "banded bird" under the auspices of K'an Joy Chitam II in A.D. 718, as recorded on Palenque's K'an Tok Panel. He is again specified as a "banded bird" official on the south face of the platform from Temple XIX, where he hands the headband of office to the subsequent ruler, Ahkal Mo' Naab III, a momentous occasion on which to assist (Stuart 2005b:117–19). In addition to his close connection to the ruler at the moment of investiture, the broader power of ancestry is also demonstrated in this monument. The accompanying inscription specifies Janab Ajaw as the grandson of K'inich Janab Pakal I. With such an illustrious forbearer, one can imagine that genealogical specificity would be highly valued in the textual record.

The earthly power embodied in this scene has an equally significant cosmological overlay. Stuart has suggested that this scene represents a reenactment of Itsamnah overseeing GI's accession to office (2005:121). This doubling of the power of the court through both celestial and earthly referents to authority will be seen again in other evidence, discussed later in the book. For now, the two meanings of this scene underscore the intertwined nature of courtly power in the Maya context and remind us that courtly officers played a part in both terrestrial and celestial dramas. In the case of this image, Stuart's interpretation is an important reminder of the perceptions and associations that the ancient viewer would have brought to such statements of political power.

As evidenced by the K'an Tok Panel, which records a long sequence of individuals cycling through this position, "banded bird" was a singular office. Perhaps the singularity of this position is what made it appealing to another individual of royal blood. At the site of Seibal located in the Department of Petén, Guatemala, it appears that an actual ruler may have adopted a version of the "banded bird" title, calling himself on Stelae 1 and 6 "holy banded bird" as well as *kalomte'*, a more typical royal appellation and the clue that this individual was likely a ruler. The adoption of one of the courtly titles by an actual *k'uhul ajaw* is highly unusual—unique, in fact. The geographical remove of Seibal from the central area of titular usage, along the Usumacinta drainage, could suggest that this is a more extreme version of regional variation in usage.

For Janab Ajaw, back at Palenque, the office of "banded bird" represented an official position within the court and a recognition of his importance, not only as a descendant of rulers, but as a political and religious authority in his own right.

Interpreting Elite Lives

The life stories detailed above reveal the extent to which Maya history has entered a new era. No longer does the miracle of names and dates read off carved monuments represent the limit of our historical window onto this culture. Instead, our data is now extensive enough that social questions of organization, process, and change become possible to explore. The role of the individual in Classic Maya communities, including persons beyond the figure of the *k'uhul ajaw*, is now a topic able to be examined.

The particular elites discussed in this chapter represent individuals who held important roles in the courts of the Late Classic; each also provides evidence of the ways in which courtly offices operated within the hierarchy of the court. In addition to illustrating circumstances of courtiers within specific courts, these examples make clear that courtly titles were not merely honorifics or random appellations. Rather, they represented actual political positions. While some rules apparently varied from polity to polity, there were shared understandings within particular courts and also within broader political spheres of how accession, succession, and recognition of ranking should occur. Tracking the five courtly titles and recognizing the ways in which they were formalized reveals the shape of Classic-era governmental structures and highlights the nature of governance beyond the figure of the *k'uhul ajaw*.

Despite my argument for formalization and even regularization of courtly offices, the elite profiles in this chapter again and again bump into the issue of variation. Their stories provide unambiguous support for the usage of analogous courtly positions at a variety of sites and also shed light on the systematic, organized ways such positions were implemented. At the same time, however, it is impossible to avoid the inconsistencies that emerge in how such titles operated across different sites. These kinds of differences show that despite the presence of shared formalized elements, courts exhibited a great deal of variety across the Maya world. Such dissimilarities suggest that rather than viewing this variation as random, or as the result of a lack of codification, it might instead be seen as a strategic flexibility. As an active strategy, variation in form would allow the court to adjust to changing circumstances and to incorporate individuals differently as part of the management of power and authority. The ability of elite institutions to provide stability and also to flexibly accommodate change is at the heart of their importance and influence in perpetuating a shared, ongoing understanding of official community identity. A closer look at temporal and spatial variation of the court will be found in chapter 4.

As was argued at the beginning of this chapter, individuals are an important point of departure for understanding ancient Maya politics, in part because the concepts of history, change, and strategic flexibility are dependent upon the actions of individuals. The evidence now available from hieroglyphic texts is powerful in the perspectives that it affords on the ancient lives of certain members of the population, as publicly presented. These courtiers served in a public forum, producing and reproducing a politico-religious narrative that acted as a template for those outside the court. In this way they are key to understanding identity production within Late Classic polities. The brief biographies that emerge from the hieroglyphic texts, as presented in this chapter, are, however, ultimately limited in scope in their ability to offer insight into larger patterns related to courtly institutions. In order to comment upon the usage and distribution of courtly titles as an important part of a formalized court structure, aggregate data must also be looked at to augment and strengthen the observations possible from examining individual agents.

One might usefully imagine the elites discussed in this chapter as attending a cocktail (or pulque) party to which we—citizens of the twenty-first century, investigators of the past—have also been invited. We are charmed to meet these fascinating partygoers—Ahkmo', Kelen Hix, Mak'an Chanal—and, in the way of party conversation, learn a little bit about some of the notable events of their lives, some of the ways they choose to publicly project themselves. At such a party, however, we might feel disappointed that the conversations are so short in length or so superficial in content, leaving us with only a public glimpse of our new acquaintances and little profound insight into their beliefs, identities, or transformations over time. And yet, just as anthropological observation at a modern-day cocktail party might reveal unarticulated aspects of someone's identity or background (their clothing, posture, associates, gesture, accent), so can we read the stories of these Maya courtly elites, not just as texts revealing a story, but as annotated and authored documents (Barrett 1994:37) that illuminate these individuals as cultural experts, knowledgeably navigating their social worlds.

CHAPTER THREE

Membership in the Court

Action and Identity

The present chapter moves on from the cocktail party, leaving behind the pleasantries of one-on-one interaction for a bigger picture. Imagine that we have now left the festivities and gone on Monday morning to visit the make-believe Pan-Maya Office of Regional Affairs, where we have appointments with bureaucrats in the Department of Labor and the Department of Demography. They have recently gathered data from disparate polities across the Maya lowlands on topics related to Maya jobs and work, and on self-identification of status and social affiliation. They have kindly agreed to share the results of their studies with us—especially the parts related to the royal court. The data housed in these offices do not represent on-the-ground situations—after all, what is the meaning of aggregate data on courtly elites, drawn from places that viewed themselves as separate, independent, and likely distinctive? Rather, taking a more inclusive view on records of courtly elites from across the lowlands represents an effort to see beyond the particularistic approach that emerges from engagements with individual stories. The institution of the court utilizes a shared language of political hierarchy in the Late Classic era across different sites that participated in similar cultural traditions, while nonetheless viewing themselves as different and not infrequently oppositional. Ultimately, both the cocktail party chitchat and the hours in the Office of Regional Affairs are necessary to understand the data on Maya royal courts and their members at different levels of resolution.

In the brief portraits of courtly elites in chapter 2, we gained a sense of individual agents. In considering Classic Maya courts, we are not dealing with faceless forces or general entities but rather historical individuals, their choices (free or controlled), and the ramifications thereof. This emphasis on the individual is critical to understanding the active and dynamic construction of the court. However, focusing on individuals has the potential to yield an esoteric and overly particularized view of the past, not to mention quickly succumbing to the limitations of textual evidence. Therefore, while bearing in mind the roles of specific, knowledgeable agents, it also makes sense to consider "courtly elites" as a group for analysis.

Investigating Courtly Elites as a Group

In particular, I am interested in characterizing courtly elites as a group analogous in process and definition to other identity groups, such as those based on ethnicity, gender, or religion. Considering elites as an identity group allows for an understanding of shared aspects of elite identity, acknowledges the dynamic nature of identity formation and expression, and anticipates elite identity being acted out during marked moments of identity production. In order to synthesize what we know about court members, I examine both courtly action and identity in this chapter. In this way I use hieroglyphic data to illuminate courtly work—what did courtiers do all day, as part of their official roles?—as well as courtly identity—how were these people identified and set apart from others?

Membership in the Court

As we investigate hieroglyphic clues about membership in the court and the nature of courtly activity, what is our starting place in terms of identifying the court as a sociopolitical unit? Perhaps surprisingly, this is a difficult question to answer. I have already mentioned that Maya hieroglyphic texts do not record a collective term for "court." Instead, the salience of this institution is identifiable through its centrality in textually documented political discourse, architectural spaces at Classic-era sites, and iconographic representations. Given my emphasis on investigating the terminology and ideas of the Maya themselves, it is disappointing to employ a term imposed from the outside. I toyed with using an invented hybrid term for this institution—"courtly collective," "governing community"—to remind the reader to check his or her assumptions about the meaning of the term "court," but I rejected this option as clumsy and potentially confusing. Instead, my use of the English word "court" throughout the book represents a shorthand that acknowledges the thematic similarities we see between the Late Classic Maya governing structure and what we call "courts" in other times and places. However, I hope the reader will pause occasionally to remember that not all of the modern connotations of this word may be relevant to the Maya court.

As we think about the individuals who composed the court, one of the challenges—and important mandates—for the current chapter is to ascertain how the membership in this political institution was discussed and described by the Maya themselves. The hieroglyphs describing the holders of official, titled positions who surrounded and collaborated with the ruler provide convincing evidence of formalized constituents of this political space; my reliance on accession events as rites of passage provides a common marker, indicating that a meaningful and shared transformation characterized these political offices.

I rely upon the suite of courtly titles as shorthand for talking about the court and its role in Late Classic political life. After all, these officials represent the formalized component of courtly hierarchy and Classic-era governance. Such an extrapolation is potentially problematic, however, in that there were many other people present in the court beyond these titled officials, including other nontitled elites and non-elite individuals with unusual statuses or privileges. Additionally, many sites do not record titled courtly elites.

For those sites that do textually record such positions, the usage of formalized courtly titles is a helpful marker of the adoption of a political institution that includes nonroyal sources of authority and that participates in some shared conventions in the naming of courtly offices. Given the lack of a Classic Maya word for "royal court," the presence of these positions is a synecdochical stand-in but does not mean that their usage in my work as a diacritic precludes other, critical memberships and participations in the court.

At sites where such records of courtly officials are lacking, we are left trying to imagine what types of institutional structures might have been present. While differences between polities across the Maya lowlands may mean that not all rulers felt the need to diversify the governing structure of their city during the Late Classic, hieroglyphic data from various corners of the Maya realm indicate shared usage of these titles and the changes in political hierarchy that they represent. It seems likely that the use of the royal court, and the inclusion of a broader set of individuals in the governing structure, was a wide-ranging adaptation to the changing pressures of the Late Classic—effected in different ways in different places—even when not textually recorded in extant materials. As a next step, we must use evidence recorded by the Maya to illuminate how this group was conceptualized and set apart.

Material and Textual Perspectives

How to talk about Maya social and political organization has proved perplexing over time, particularly when we attempt to do so in ways that mesh with Classic Maya perspectives. The debates about class organization that were discussed in chapter 1 reflect such difficulties. Reliance on material markers to demarcate social, economic, and political differences has been especially problematic (e.g., Palka 1995:388–405), spurring my own use of textual information as a starting place for understanding issues of differentiation in a nuanced way. In particular, use of material markers to identify difference seems to result in broad categories of distinction that are not reflected in the texts as meaningful social units for the Maya (see, as examples, Chase 1992:48, Kurjack 1974, Willey and Leventhal 1979).

Before indicating how I have used textual information as a different approach to this question, let me say a few words about the use of material markers to elucidate Classic Maya hierarchies. Too often in thinking about status differences among the Maya, perceived differences between elites and nonelites are investigated—explicitly or implicitly—in terms of indices of material wealth. Such approaches problematically equate the construction of status difference with a modern sensibility of the dialectic between rich and poor. Assumptions about the relationship between material wealth and status raise questions about non-wealth-based factors impacting status, our incomplete knowledge of what "wealth" (in terms of amount, or substance) meant to the Classic Maya in material terms, and the estrangement of agents from the tools and objects that they manipulated in the past.

Of course, after viewing contents of royal burials, depictions of tribute on ceramic vessels, and tall temple-pyramids, one cannot deny that material investments played an important role for those who could afford it. The Maya were not ascetics, and the costumes, architecture, and ritual paraphernalia that surrounded them acted, at times, as extensions of their own selves (Houston and Stuart 1998:86-92). Indeed, of the privileges and prerogatives that are central to elite identities, access to luxury goods and accumulation of wealth certainly count among them.

Possible paradoxes in the distribution and interpretation of apparently elite material remains, however, suggest the need for caution in reading simplified versions of material-derived status from the archaeological record. Instead of interest in relative "amounts" of high-status materials, the value to the Maya might have been presence/absence, or the ability to meet a certain social requirement (i.e., to practice as an elite). That is not to say that there would not have been competition among high-status individuals or that there is no meaningful contrast between relative displays of wealth and/or authority. Rather, the abstract nature of some sources of Classic Maya status that do not translate easily into the material record obscures the meaning of relative amounts of "stuff." This observation is certainly true when comparing different sites. The variation that is endemic to the Maya lowlands means that material expressions must be contextualized within the spectrum found in the local cultural milieu, and also that the idea of value must be situated not just culturally but at a notably local level.

Similarly, as noted, valuable material objects (e.g., what we classify as luxury items for the Maya) may have carried a great deal of weight. A variety of material signs (including elaborate architecture, sculpture, polychrome pottery, use of jade) without doubt indicated to the observer that an area or its inhabitants were of high status. However, only a few of these material markers (and in small amounts) might have been effective in indicating the privileges or prerogatives of the inhabitants, due to the markers' potency or because they were used in conjunction with perishable objects or nonmaterial markers that similarly signaled the high status of the individual.

Furthermore, the difficulties of matching material expressions to particular, differentiated identity groups is reflected in the fact that many of the material items used by elite individuals were also used by persons both higher and lower on the social scale, by members of royalty and by commoners (e.g., jade jewelry, or on the other end of the spectrum, utilitarian ceramic water jars). Social and cultural processes through which objects end up in a particular locus must then be understood in order to appropriately contextualize these materials.

These observations suggest that construction of value, and by extension articulation of difference, in past contexts involved meanings and assumptions that we still struggle to access. In the case of investigating elite identities, a practice-oriented approach (Bourdieu 1977:78–87) provides one way to excise certain modern and Western assumptions about class and wealth and to build up a concept of what elite identity involved, and how it was constructed in lived contexts. Material remains may best be understood by couching them within contexts of action. Exploring an idea of elite practice as a source for class or status identity opens the door more widely for the integration of nonmaterial data, including epigraphic, iconographic, and ethnohistoric information that may record factors that impacted the successful performance of status-derived identities.

Evidence from hieroglyphic texts—the data source I emphasize in this book—supports the adoption of this type of approach. We can investigate elite action and activity as part of broadening our conception of how elite identities were marked and articulated. The inherent limitations of trying to conduct an elite "ethnography" that would reveal concerted action via fragmentary hieroglyphic sources means that such a perspective will be partial. For this reason, I focus in the present chapter on both elite actions and marked elite identity categories, as expressed and highlighted in Maya texts. Together, these provide a textually derived perspective on what separated courtly individuals from others. Since textual evidence indicates that a courtly/

noncourtly boundary is more relevant than an elite/non-elite one, I focus on indications of these types of difference.

In emphasizing the importance of multiple contributing factors to status or identity, text and image become valuable sources for discovering other factors that contributed to status, including ones that may not be easily detected or correctly interpreted in the archaeological record. In terms of the larger scheme of this book, textual data provide key information for discussing the membership of the royal court and thinking about the characterization of courtly elites in aggregate. While beyond the scope of the present project, these observations will usefully intersect with efforts to rethink or sharpen our interpretation of sociopolitical difference in the material record.

Courtly Work

In attempting to shed light on courtly elites as a group, their actions were identified above as one way to investigate shared responsibilities and shared identity. That is, we can approach the institution of the court and its membership by thinking about the activities that occurred there—the "work" of the court. The nature of Maya hieroglyphic texts means that we do not have transcripts of private sessions, logbooks of appointments, or diaries of courtly officials to illuminate their responsibilities or official commitments. Rather, the roles of courtly members must be read from the more public perspective of the monumental record. Activities, functions, and roles of courtly elites may be gleaned from direct statements in texts and from indirect evidence in visual and textual records. Thinking about courtly work reminds us to animate our images of these past individuals and to contextualize the institution of the court in terms of activities and practices carried out there. I will start with specific discussion of courtly jobs and then transition to a more thematic consideration of the work of the court.

Courtly Job Descriptions

Given what we know about courtly titles—that they represent a change in status, that they do not seem to be random honorifics, and that people identify strongly with them in their official capacities—we might assume that these positions can be correlated with particular sets of duties. After all, if the emergence of a complex court is part of a strategic Late Classic adaptation, it would make sense for its personnel to fill particular roles or responsibilities within the institution.

In imagining Classic-era courtly job descriptions and contemplating the types of work courtly officials undertook, some immediate associations come to mind. In particular, *sajal*s and *ajk'uhuun*s have developed reputations in modern scholarship for certain functional associations. As mentioned in reviewing the decipherment of these titles in chapter 1, *sajal*s have frequently been viewed as war captains or regional governors, while *ajk'uhuun*s have been understood as scribes, or possibly priests, related to holy paper or books. Do written descriptions of elite practice support these ideas?

The anecdotal associations that have been previously suggested for *sajal* and *ajk'uhuun* positions are borne out through the more comprehensive dataset that I consider. When recorded activities and the affiliated offices are tracked throughout the corpus of courtly elite records, *sajal*s are frequently connected to war events. Furthermore, all instances in which an honorific identifies a courtier as a "captor of" someone else, indicating engagement with bellicose activities, feature individuals who are *sajal*s. While this seems like a solid connection, *sajal*s are not exclusively mentioned in connection with war events—rather, *ajk'uhuun*s and *yajaw k'ahk*s are recorded as well. Public documentation of involvement in war was not solely the domain of *sajal*s, despite the fact that they earned recognition in war and capture events.

In terms of testing other associations for the *sajal* position, the role of *sajal*s as regional governors at subsidiary sites is difficult to assess through records of particular actions. Nonetheless, records of *sajal*s who appear to operate as local authorities at satellite sites such as Site R and La Pasadita (both sites outside of Yaxchilán) support the idea that some *sajal* positions involved the exercise of local power, while reporting to a *k'uhul ajaw* at a neighboring primary center (discussed, for instance, in Golden 2010). Our friend Ahkmo' from chapter 2 is one such example.

As for the *ajk'uhuun* title, it is notable for appearing exclusively as the formal title in sculptors' signatures, which identify the scribe or artist who created a monument (Stuart 1989b).[1] This affiliation supports the idea that *ajk'uhuuns*' prestige was derived, at least in part, from the specialized knowledge of writing that they held—echoing the scribal affiliation that has often been attributed to them in modern scholarship. It is important to note that this association is supported here through records of *ajk'uhuuns*' connection to sculpting and writing activities, not through decipherment of the title itself, which has previously been the primary source of support for such an affiliation (e.g., with interpretations such as "he of the holy book"). Regarding such previous interpretations, the *ajk'uhuuns*' status as keeper of the paper, or headbands, is challenged on La Mar Stela 1, where a *sajal* (rather than an *ajk'uhuun*) reaches up to hand the headband of office to the acceding ruler. Again, the proposed functional role of the title has merit, but it is not exclusively mapped onto this position.

In the cases of the two most common titles (*sajal* and *ajk'uhuun*), some of the long-held associations—*sajal*s with combat, *ajk'uhuun*s with artistic production—are confirmed with the data I examine. However, these roles were not exclusive to those positions, nor do they provide sufficiently broad explanations of the other responsibilities that fell under the purview of the individuals in question. (*Sajal*s, for instance, seem to have had a predilection for dancing, in addition to their participation in combat.) It appears that strict specialization or compartmentalization of responsibilities does not easily characterize courtly officials. Functional descriptions of these roles may not be easy to identify and likely were not the primary mode of characterization of the positions in ancient times, either.

In fact, if we move beyond *sajal*s and *ajk'uhuun*s, there is very little evidence of exclusive mapping of functional roles, activities, or events onto particular titles. In examining records of *yajaw k'ahk*'s, *ti'huuns/ti'sakhuuns*, and "banded bird" office-

1. *Anab* also appears in sculptors' signatures; however, this enigmatic title is not one of the official positions I consider in this study, since it does not appear to be associated with a formal accession into office.

holders, a wide and varying set of activities is recorded. While this documentation illuminates the range of work undertaken as part of courtly duties, it does not aid in breaking down the activities of the court into particular job descriptions, pertaining to the constituent offices. This suggests that the primary meaning attached to these positions was not that of a fixed set of duties. Instead, individuals who acceded into courtly office were marked by having achieved a certain status or importance that distinguished them from other members of the population. Nonetheless, notably differential usage of the five titles over space and in terms of relative frequency suggests that they were not merely interchangeable and did not carry identical meanings. As part of the variability and flexibility that made the court such a powerful institution, the meanings of particular offices may have been modified and tailored to local courtly needs or to the skills or talents of the individuals who held them. The shape-shifting nature of the court included the actual delegation of duties within it.

Deriving Courtly Duties

Despite the lack of clear connections between different courtly positions and specific duties, the hieroglyphic texts provide significant information for understanding what work was undertaken within the court and what types of responsibilities were involved. By examining verbs and other descriptions of events found in conjunction with courtly elites in the hieroglyphic texts, one can gain a sense of the roles that were most salient to courtly elite identity as expressed in a public forum. This approach privileges Maya categories of action and event rather than our own assumptions or interpretations regarding what courtly work involved.

Based on these data, elite action may be broken down into several categories, some not at all surprising, some more so. Anyone familiar with Classic Maya culture will anticipate the textual prominence of ritual and celebratory events in the publicly displayed records of elite activity. For court members, these job responsibilities (as recorded in the hieroglyphic data I collected) included participation in a variety of activities, among which were dancing, scattering ceremonies, conjuring, fire-entering and fire-drilling rituals, impersonation, celebration of anniversaries and period endings, and ball playing. Similarly, political events, especially records of capture and of warfare, take center stage.

Based on this data set, the accession into office of courtly elites themselves also forms an impressive segment of the textual record. Records of elite accession demonstrate that these inauguration events were notable milestones (analogous to the kingly transformation that occurred when rulers acceded to office [Houston and Inomata 2009:142–46]); they also indicated the entrance of the elites into a class that would give them the ability or permission to use texts to portray themselves. Sometimes coupled with this textual presence are records of other notable life events for courtly elites—specifically, the dates of their births and deaths.

Activities recorded for elites also include the taking on of artistic or scribal roles, as well as cosmological roles. Artistic work is primarily recorded through elite references in scribal signatures. Impersonation of otherworldly entities is both textually described and iconographically represented.

All of these examples suggest the kinds of responsibilities that would have occupied the attention of those with formal courtly assignments. Other frequently described categories of elite practice may seem somewhat less glamorous, or action oriented, but are equally at the heart of what elite roles were about. One such category is the dedication and ownership of objects (such as ceramic vessels), structures, or specific architectural elements of structures.

In terms of architecture, there is evidence for specific affiliations of titled elites with particular structures, suggesting that they owned, or at least carried out activities in, particular loci at a given site. Records of elite associations with architecture allow for the concrete connection of textually identified courtly officials with the structures or residential compounds where they lived, in a few cases. These instances are found at Copán (Fash 1983; Leventhal 1979; Sanders 1986; Webster 1989b; Willey et al. 1978), Palenque (Rands and Rands 1961; Ruz Lhuillier 1952; Schele 1991a), and Xcalumkín (Becquelin et al. 1994; Becquelin and Michelet 1992; Becquelin et al. 1996; Graham and Von Euw 1992; Pollock 1980). At Copán both Group 9N-8 and Group 9M-18 feature a hieroglyphic bench "owned" by an *ajk'uhuun*. Another example comes from Palenque, where, based on the placement of the Tablet of the Slaves in Building A, Group IV seems to have been inhabited by Chak Suutz' (and possibly other elites, as well). Two structures at the site of Xcalumkín are marked as belonging to two different *sajal*s.

There are also some instances of connections of elites to nonresidential architecture or of more tentative connections of titled elites with architecture. In an example of a courtly elite located at a satellite site, Altar 4—featuring a *sajal*—was excavated in Group E5-1 at El Cayo, though it has been suggested that this was a ceremonial rather than residential complex (Mathews and Aliphat Fernández 1997). Other sites along the Usumacinta such as La Pasadita, La Mar, and El Chicozapote may yield similar textual/architectural connections for titled elites who lived or worked in particular spaces (Charles Golden, personal communication), though these individual connections with specific structures are more difficult to confirm. More anecdotally, at Palenque Stuart notes that at Temple XIX there seems to be a particular elite—Yoktal, a *yajaw k'ahk'*—associated with this space; he may be the caretaker or the ritual practitioner for the structure (2005:123). This suggestion supports the connection of particular courtiers with particular locations, whether for residence or for work.

These types of records suggest that the power or status of titled elites derived in part from, and was represented by, their ownership or affiliation with particular objects or structures. This gives the archaeologist a sense of the physical manifestations of the social landscape of courtly elites and the idea that particular spaces, objects, and even texts (such as those carved on certain architectural elements) were seen as being under the control of elites. Furthermore, part of the publicly articulated identity of courtly officials was based on their relationships with these material items or places; we might frame this type of work as cultivating connections with the material world.

The other category that emerges as a particularly common type of elite role seems quite mundane: the record of courtly elites within textual captions. Such captions are usually brief, smaller texts, which label a depicted person in the image but are not the primary focus of the piece. (We have only to turn back to the last image from chapter 2—Yaxchilán Lintel 8 [figure 28]—to see an example of a caption in the center of that monument.) This is not a type of text that sheds light on elite action in terms of description of activities, but it does yield additional perspective on critical work that courtly elites were expected to carry out. This type of record indicates the importance of an explicitly identified elite presence attending the royal self. This presence was a key aspect of courtly duty, as well as one that merited both visual depiction and textual recording. The role of such attendants as witnesses is conveyed through captions, through image, and also at times through textual description. When described in the glyphs, the verb *yilaji* is used, meaning, "he or she sees it" (Stuart 1987:25). This term reinforces the physical presence of an individual at the scene and the importance of their visual perception of an event (Houston et al. 2006:163–75), just as the names and titles recorded in captions underline the critical nature of particular attendees.

Why might such a seemingly general or passive role be so frequently recorded on monuments? The emphasis on presence as a documented duty of courtiers suggests that not only were these elites physically experiencing and visually witnessing events led by the ruler but that such a role was important to the success of the event being executed. Part of their work was to be an audience. Understandings of Maya conceptions of sight as projective (Houston 2006:140; Houston et al. 2006:166–67), and the role of witnesses as "notarial" (Houston et al. 2006:173) frame such observers as active and critical in ways that might not be obvious to a Western sense of "watching an event" or "attending a ceremony." Acting as a witness is supportive to central work being carried out by the ruler. Examples of court members recorded in captions suggest that courtly officials frequently acted as spectators, witnessing performances by the ruler and by fellow courtiers within the space of the court; the effort that went into identifying them as present indicates that they formed a special, particular type of audience.

Courtly Work as Performance

The visual and receptive responsibilities of courtiers remind us that courtly work often occurred with an audience, large or small. The work of the court can be framed thematically as courtly performances and courtly practices, both formal and informal, abstracting the specific types of activities mentioned above to the social processes that underlay them. Ultimately, this is the crucial work that occurs here. The court is a place where certain practices and selves are performed and subsequently received and replicated. Let us first consider courtly work and identity assertion as formal theater. We have already encountered the court-as-theater equivalence in chapter 1. Courtly theater is discussed here not just as a descriptive model but as a representation of actual activities of the court.

The court as theater represents a critical way in which activities and ideas located within the circumscribed space of the court propagate outward to impact other members of a polity. In addition to conveying particular types of information, this process establishes the relevance of the court as more than a restricted and esoteric island of privilege. Courtly performances, taking the form of rituals or other public events, provide a communicative moment in specific content (e.g., the accession of a ruler) is conveyed, along with cultural ideals, mores, or restrictions (e.g., ideas about elevation, bodily positioning, appropriate access to humans and gods). Public performances of this nature work to clarify cultural identities, enact boundaries, and inspire imitation by the viewer; as such, we can imagine them as important work for court members to undertake.

Figure 29. Stela 1, La Mar. An example of a small courtly audience for actions carried out by the ruler. Courtesy of the Peabody Museum of Archaeology and Ethnology, Harvard University, 2004.29.6461.

Figure 30. A ruler and his mirror in the court, as depicted on a painted ceramic vessel. Here the ruler engages with his own reflection, while an audience of courtiers watches. Rollout Photograph © Justin Kerr, K625.

In imagining audiences, the discussion above positioned courtly elites as the specialized watchers of royal action. But what of larger crowds? The public who attended and watched communal events formed another kind of audience. The key role of witnessing, a defining characteristic of courtly elite roles within the court, occurs on multiple scales. Courtly elites provide visual support and recognition of the ruler; on a larger scale, the attendant audience of individuals drawn from outside the court provides affirmation of the primacy and relevance of the court through their gaze. The spectator plays as critical a role as the performer in defining and upholding courtly action and identity. Such an idea is supported through the conceptualization of the theater as a place of negotiation (Inomata 2006:211), acknowledging the power of the audience as receivers of a message, while also suggesting the possibility of a critical review (Beeman 1993:384), or, more mildly, visual inattention.

In Classic Maya imagery, there is little explicit depiction of larger audiences. Typically, only the immediate audience of courtly members is shown in the company of the ruler in formal moments, such as ritual action, as shown on La Mar Stela 1 (figure 29). Less formal enactments such as the king in front of his mirror—receiving a gaze of another sort—also merit an audience of court members (figure 30). However, others beyond courtiers were present and observant for public events. The presence and attention of captives in images like Piedras Negras Stela 12 (figure 31) provide evidence that other individuals were allowed in proximity to the ruler and paid him visual heed. Spatial settings and the nature of the event would have determined the size of audience that was appropriate and that could have been accommodated.

Architecture provides much of our material sense of courtly performance and how it would have been experienced. Scholars have commented on the suitability of plaza spaces, elevated structures with central doorways, and long stairways for the staging of dramas and the inclusion of the audience (e.g., Houston 1998:360–61;

Figure 31. Stela 12, Piedras Negras. A visual example of an audience made up not of court members but of captives, indicating that visual attention could come from multiple sources. Drawing by David Stuart, Courtesy of the Corpus of Maya Hieroglyphic Inscriptions, Peabody Museum of Archaeology and Ethnology, © President and Fellows of Harvard College, 2004.15.6.19.38.

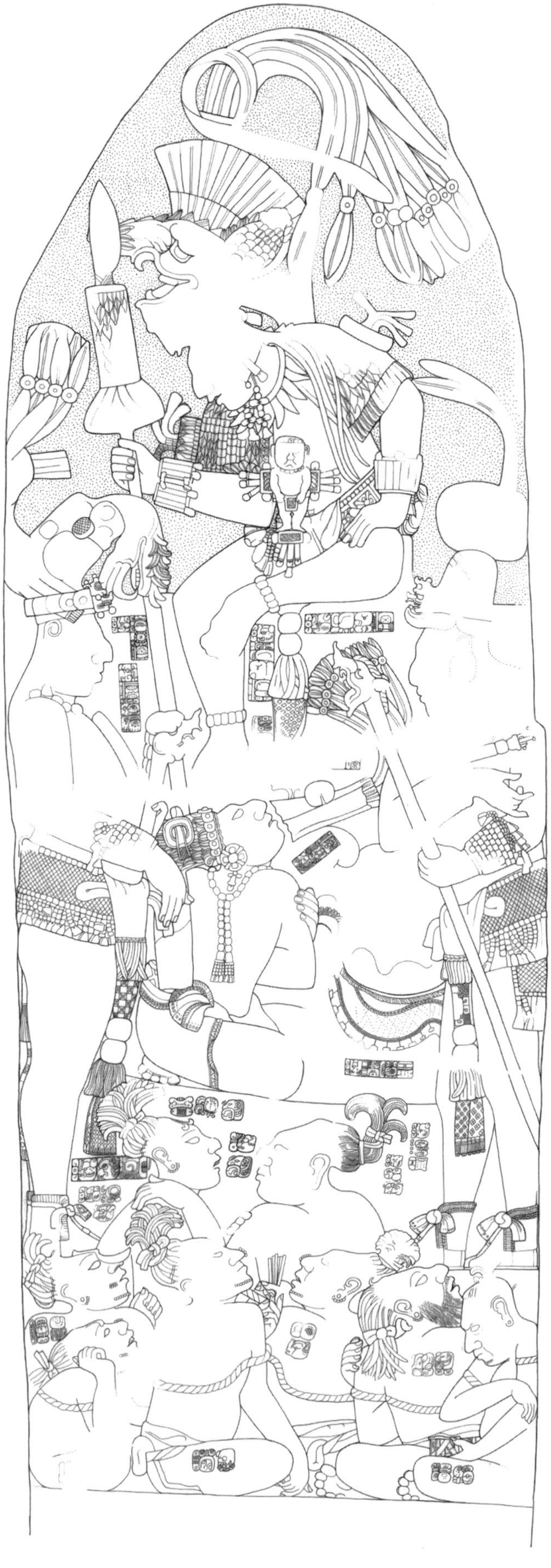

Inomata 2006:198–99; Reents-Budet 2001:202). Such architectural elements would have served as a frame for the unfolding activity that indicated a departure from everyday experience of the site and its structures (Goffman 1974:139). Contrasts between visual availability and the hidden or occluded seem especially important in terms of the reception and the successful enactment of a performance. Use of curtains, multiple doorways, masks, and costumes, as well as attention to lines of sight and even position of the sun (Inomata 2006:198–99, 207; Reents-Budet 2001:196, 199), would have affected the ability to see the performers literally, as themselves, or as other entities that they were impersonating.

In striving to characterize action and identity in the court, moments of performance record—and are—key processes for the public definition of this institution. Strikingly, these performances implicate an audience that often consists of non-court members, who help to verify, define, and make relevant the processes and identities asserted through these scripted events.

Courtly Work as Practice

In addition to intentional, public performances, courtly membership was also enacted through unconscious, everyday performances. We might characterize this as elite practice, or using Bourdieu's language, the habitus (1977:72–73). This may seem like an entirely different thing from the lavish ritual events depicted in Maya iconography. However, both formal and informal performances involve the demonstration of fluency in the cultural grammar of behavior, status, and exclusivity. Despite obvious distinctions, they share central roles in producing locally informed identities and constructing difference between individuals and groups.

Issues of scale, such as the size of the stage, number in the audience, and resources invested, define different degrees or levels of performance. These in turn have different impacts resulting from their enactment. At the most day-to-day level, the habitus represents a personal, local, and continuous identity practice, or performance, constituted of the most simple or unnoticeable acts (Bourdieu 1977:72–73). Individual "practices and works" (Bourdieu 1977:80) serve to mark group dispositions through normalized standards of action. In a performative sense, the habitus represents the internalized, unconscious enaction of identity. It is the opposite of the conception of performance as a spectacle, a disruption of the routine, or a space in which mores or behaviors may be inverted. Furthermore, the habitus may or may not be communicative in terms of being received by an audience.

Nonetheless, everyday practice or action is relevant in understanding courtly members because of the inherently performative and public nature of much of the activity that occurred within that space. Even outside the space of a scheduled and rehearsed event, the court's demarcation of public and private space make seeing, vision, and the gaze (or the blocking of any of these) factors in the courtly experience. Thus, in moments of visibility we might see the carefully articulated behaviors of elites as representing small but legible performances of elite identity through practice.

As we draw to the end of a section on courtly work, we may still be wondering: what *did* Maya courtiers do all day? The specific activities that are recorded in hieroglyphic texts do not, overall, map neatly onto individual titles in ways that suggest a clear-cut or meaningful division of particular duties. While typical elite "work" might encompass a stint at a ruler-directed ceremony, some captive pursuit, and a ritual dance to end the day, these events do not define particular offices in contrast to each other. Nor do they necessarily reveal significant aspects of how these positions were understood, or what set them apart from noncourtly roles involving ritual practice or war, for example.

Rather, elite practice—understood as the actions, forms, and ways of being that signify and reinforce elite identity—might better be conceptualized through what the events detailed in the hieroglyphic texts indicate. For example, titled courtly elites as a group may be seen as marked through qualities of access, prerogative, and proximity, abstract concepts that derive from differential status identities and only indirectly from functional roles. Conceiving of elite identity as enacted connects with the variable and contingent nature of identity groups and acknowledges the distinctively public and performative aspect of life in the court. Multiple conceptions of identity prove useful in attempting to "see" elites in past records. We should attend to messages intended for both internal and external consumption. Despite the fact that access to material wealth without doubt played a part in elite dominance, economic assets might better be contextualized through ideas of elite practice, which focus on more inclusive manifestations of distinctly elite privilege.

Courtly Identity

As seen above, one way to explore the membership of the court is through examination of the types of work carried out there and, more thematically, to think about the actions and practices that characterized its members. Taking this tack has revealed some of the focuses of court energy and some of the responsibilities that its members were charged with carrying out.

Another approach involves focusing on the identities of courtly officials. This perspective examines the things that differentiated courtly officials through descriptions of the qualities and notable markers of such individuals. Analyzing adjectival descriptors to suss out courtly identities provides a descriptive counterpoint to the lively picture that emerges from a consideration of their actions and activities.

Thinking about courtly identity and what it meant to be a member of the court invites a focus on factors that would have distinguished courtly officials. In considering identity in the court, I examine how courtly officials are marked in the textual record with certain qualities. Specifically, adjectival modifiers used to describe titled members of the court provide a useful focus and frequently relate to status factors that elevated elite individuals. For considering this type of construction of difference, civic monuments provide an especially valuable medium. Their intended function was to publicly articulate codified ideals about social norms and behaviors, as related to the privileged individuals who merited mention or depiction on such monuments. Given my interest in avoiding a simple equation of status with measures of wealth, it is interesting to note that material wealth is not directly discussed or recorded in Maya texts; rather, in discussing powerful individuals other personal attributes are emphasized.

Textual Indications of Courtly Differentiation

In examining how the identities of courtly officials are marked, records of court members who are described with a modifier are particularly helpful in understanding how their status or identity was constructed and expressed. In the sections that follow, I examine the types of descriptions that are most commonly found framing courtly elite identities in the hieroglyphic record. These give us clues to the qualities that Classic Maya elites found most relevant in describing their social landscape and differentiation within it.

Respect for Elders: Records of Age

One quality used to mark courtly officials relates to age and the apparent respect accorded to individuals of advanced years. Age descriptors take the form of the modifier *k'atun* plus a number, from one to four in the case of courtly elites. Together, *k'atun* and the number specify an age range and were used to modify titles, to indicate the age of the person holding the title (Houston and Inomata 2009:60, 173; Proskouriakoff 1963:153). This was a common occurrence with royal titles, and *sajal* and *ajk'uhuun* are similarly found with such age-related descriptors. The limitation of age-grade modifiers to the two most common titles may indicate that these positions were the ones most likely to be held for long periods of one's life. The other three titles, which are significantly less commonly used, might have been more specialized and held for briefer periods. There are not sufficient examples to see whether these "X *k'atun*" modifiers of elite titles are added only late in life, or if they progress over time. As is the case with rulers, such age-related titles convey status and importance in relation to elders. Kelen Hix, the Toniná court official, was identified with this type of designation: on Toniná Monument 165, among other designations, he is named as a "two *k'atun*" *ajk'uhuun* at the time of his death.

On the opposite end of the age spectrum, the word *ch'ok* means "young" or "unripe" (Pérez Martínez et al. 1996:58) and in some contexts might be taken to mean "heir." The term *baah ch'ok* (i.e., "head or first *ch'ok*"—more information on *baah* follows below) refers specifically to the heir to the throne and is a position into which someone can be elevated (e.g., K'an Joy Chitam on the Palace Tablet) (Houston and Inomata 2009:144; Martin and Grube 2000:171). For courtly officials, the *ch'ok* modifier is used with the *sajal* title. Although not enough comparative evidence on individual career trajectories is available to prove it, use of this modifier may indicate an initial junior rank, such as that held by Ahkmo' of Site R, named as a *ch'ok sajal* (see figure 15).

Both of these age-related descriptors (*k'atun* designations and *ch'ok* descriptions) indicate that recognition of advanced, or advancing, age seems to have been important. Beyond respect accorded to elders, such marking of age may relate to passage through explicit or implicit stages of experience, in which young/junior/inexperienced and old/senior/experienced are contrasted as categories of positions.

Relative Ranking and Primacy

In addition to marking relative age or experience, attention is paid in the hieroglyphic texts to another type of positioning: the marking of primacy. This marking involves the use of the word *baah*, literally "head," and relates directly to expressions of hierarchy and relative ranking (Houston and Inomata 2009:174–75; Houston and Stuart 1998:73–77; Houston and Stuart 2001:62). This word is used, for example, in the expression *tu baah*, in relationship to the tying of the headband—"on the head." In the hieroglyphs it also denotes a meaning of "first" or "most important."

Of the five titles under consideration here, it is used only with the title *sajal*. Significantly, this is the same distribution as that of the *ch'ok* ("young," "unripe") modifier. This suggests that these may be related designations, located at two ends of the spectrum of advancement, and that for the Maya *ch'ok* may denote a junior or apprentice position rather than focusing on a young age in a calendrical sense.

Baah seems to be used both in contexts related to individual advancement and in settings in which clarification of relative rank may be necessary. Recall that we encountered this term in chapter 2 in discussing the story of K'an Nik Te' of Piedras Negras. He appears earlier (in A.D. 716) as a *sajal* on Piedras Negras Stela 5, along with Yopnal Ahk II (Ruler 3) (figure 11), and then later (in A.D. 749) on Piedras Negras Panel 3, where, in the company of Ruler 4, he is named as a *baah sajal* (figure 12). This temporal succession could provide evidence for achievement of this title over time. However, on Panel 3 there are other *sajal*s pictured as well. Thus, the naming of K'an Nik Te' as *baah sajal* ("head *sajal*") might be a necessary clarification, to identify him as the most important (or senior or elite) *sajal* when in the context of other *sajal*s. The present evidence does not allow for conclusive support of one of these ideas over the other.

The Role of Personal Achievement

Qualities or characteristics associated with the *baah* modifier, and possibly the *k'atun* modifier, may be connected with experience acquired over time. These descriptors do not provide an enumeration of particular achievements, however. Modern readers (and perhaps ancient ones, too) must accept the described status elevation without knowing what achievements or other factors contributed to it.

Another category of modifier, in contrast, does make explicit the role of involvement in certain activities in promoting one's courtly career: emphasis on experience or achievement in warfare. Here I refer to the trope of recording the number of prisoners that an individual has captured. This achievement is expressed in the formula *aj* [number] *baak*, or "he of [number] captives" (Stuart 1985a). At times, in the case of an especially important captive, a courtly official will be named as "the captor of [name]," even in contexts outside of the capture event. An example of this phenomenon is the *sajal* K'an Tok Wayib of Yaxchilán, who was the captor of Kokte' Ajaw (pictured in figure 28). The use of an achieved status marker, reflecting combat prowess, is restricted to the *sajal* title, providing evidence for the interpretation of *sajal*s as connected to war and being leaders in battle.

Other types of personal achievement are not specifically highlighted in the texts, though one might argue that some of the actions or work identified earlier in this chapter may be included in the public record because they brought recognition to the actors. The categories of work represented—including participation in political, ritual, and war events—provide general outlines of the areas in which recognition might be granted.

Gender Consciousness

The final type of titular modifier to consider in explicit records of courtly differentiation is gender markers. The infrequent feminine versions of official courtly titles, indicated through the use of the prefix *ix* (Houston and Inomata 2009:146; Jackson and Stuart 2001:222), were mentioned in chapter 2. (Examples of the *ix* hieroglyph can be seen in figures 24 and 25.) As explored there, these examples seem mainly to represent instances of overlap with royal family members, potentially as an outlet or honorific for royal women (though, I argue, not simply taking their husbands' titles [Josserand 2002:121]). The grammatical marking of gender in these titles, and the predominance of men as holders of the positions, indicates that gender consciousness played an important role in determining eligibility and position. Two women from Yaxchilán, also discussed in chapter 2, illustrate such marking of gender in courtly titles. Lady Ik' Skull is publically designated as an *ix ajk'uhuun*, while Lady Great Skull carries the title *ix sajal*. In assembling the constellation of traits that form a distinctive elite identity, gender thus plays a role in terms of determination of membership in public courtly cadres.

Data from the hieroglyphic texts indicate some of the recorded factors that would have contributed to the determination of social standing and membership in an elite group. These factors represent a mix of ascribed and achieved qualities and provide further indices to investigate in conceptualizing difference, in addition to material or economic measures of wealth or privilege. The factors discussed here impart a sense of the qualities that social-climbing denizens of the Classic Maya world might have kept tabs on and give an idea of how these qualities were asserted and recorded. These factors have limitations as well. They signify only those characteristics that were overtly and plainly articulated in the texts. It seems likely that a constellation of other traits, achievements, and connections (including the family connections that came up in chapter 2) also played a role in determining the makeup of sociopolitical hierarchies at Maya sites. Additionally, it is difficult to ascertain which identity traits are specific to court members and which are larger categories that would have been used to recognize differential status among Maya people more generally. While the documentation here only allows for specific commentary on qualities considered remarkable for titled members of the court, it is likely that this evidence is applicable to a broader reexamination of our understanding of status in ancient Maya contexts.

Identity Boundaries

Much of the discussion above is concerned with what elite identity "looks like" within the space of the court, suggesting that identity—and our latter-day detection of those traits—is dependent upon markers of content. Another way to look at courtly identity is to consider its boundaries and edges—something I reflect on in this section. Ultimately, both of these perspectives are illuminating in understanding courtly identity and in homing in on categories that were meaningful to the Maya themselves.

Jones, drawing upon Barth's work (1969), makes a compelling argument for particularly strong marking of identity in archaeological contexts occurring at places of contestation—that is, at border areas (1997:128–29). These are loci where the performance of identity is especially salient because it is in direct contrast to, or even in conflict with, a different entity. The elaborate courtly performances of ritual, framed here as theater, serve this function: flashy demonstrations of difference at the moment in which the most intensive contact with non-court members occurs. Given that courtly performances serve to unify at the same time that they emphasize difference, this apparent "border defense" might be relatively one-sided in the case of the court. That is, commoners or extra-court members are not—as far as we know—simultaneously making efforts to mark their estrangement or difference from the court. Instead, they may be striving to imitate certain aspects of courtly presentation, ritual observance, and organization through scaled-down versions of hierarchical enactment, cosmological framing, and religious action at the level of their own households. Thus, when class or status (or other identities in which one group is framed as more desirable or advantageous than another) is part of the identity equation, such marking of borders occurs in a different way than in the examples of ethnic identification on which Jones focuses.

Hieroglyphic data provide other ways to examine elite identity boundaries. Recall that the five formal courtly titles involve an accession event parallel to that experienced by the ruler on the occasion of his taking the throne, indicating a lower boundary for the courtly elite identity group. This important transition distinguishes courtiers in formal offices as having endured a socially and politically meaningful change of state. The accompanying status change is subsequently marked through the titles and offices used to record and describe these courtiers' public identities. Such a change in state serves as a reinforced boundary, separating courtiers from others who have not experienced this official recognition of status identity. Thus, textually, a clear boundary emerges on the lower edge of courtly identity through the use and record of accession ceremonies for individuals as officially recognized members of the court. In contrast, the upper boundary of the group of courtly officials is not clearly marked and indicates a lack of emphasized distinction, as well as some actual overlaps, between courtly and royal identities.

Even though courtly elites could hold more than one position over their lifetime, multiple offices do not seem to have entailed multiple accession events. The elevation in identity that occurred through the rite of passage of accession, once accomplished, did not need to be repeated for other positions that the individual might hold during his life. This brings to mind the Maya Colonial-era reliance on a group of *principales*, town nobles who acted as a pool for official positions. At any given time, there were many more *principales* than offices; different *principales* moved in and out of office over time, not continually holding positions, and generally represented a state of eligibility in which they met status and identity requirements for access to elite privileges (Restall 1997:69–71). Similarly, Classic period accession events may have represented social/political movement into a state of eligibility or potentiality, framed by the entrance into one's first office. These "eligibles" would have been granted membership in the court, with its attendant privileges and prerogatives. Thus, the transformation of identity that occurred through entrance into this group represented a marked boundary.

Elites who have acceded into a courtly office are not the only ones who attended events within the royal court, however. How does one explain the variety of untitled or not formally titled individuals who appear in depictions of the court, apparently enjoying similar proximity to the ruler and access to the space and privileges of the court? Looking at depictions of the court painted on ceramic vessels provides evidence that the court encompassed a variety of "palace people," not all of whom were graced with formalized offices (Houston and Stuart 2001:68). Some of these individuals seemingly did not fit into traditional categories of elites. Captives and servants, for example, occupy the same physical space as the ruler, but not the same social space. These categories of court attendees (to the extent to which presence by coercion or obligation can be termed as such), together with more exotic categories of non-elite court presences such as dwarves or eunuchs, threw into relief the identity and features of the elites proper by providing an artificially constructed boundary within the space of the court (Houston and Stuart 2001:61; Inomata 2001a:40). In a similar vein, juxtapositions of howling captives with staid rulers highlight idealized elite bodily and emotional control (Houston 2001:210); the contrast of states makes such lack of affect especially striking.

In addition to contrasts of differing identities within the courtly space, the court acts as a physical and metaphorical container (Giddens 1984:262; Moore 1996:15–17) for a wide and varied collection of high-status individuals. Some of the individuals who are not named with offices may be in the limbo of the pool of *principales*. Additionally, the presence of positions of distinction outside of the formalized offices is suggested by the use of opaque terms such as *anab* (Houston and Stuart 2001:72), or general terms like *ajaw* ("lord") (Houston and Inomata 2009:131–35, Houston and Stuart 2001:59–61), which seem to function as honorifics but may not boast the same change of state associated with more formalized titles. The accession boundary separates titled elites from others who were nonetheless likely important people of resources, including individuals who appear to have attended court, but without a title. Thus I do not argue that this is the edge of an elite class group but rather a category, marked by the Maya, of culturally significant "movers and shakers." The identity of untitled individuals at the court requires further study. Based on available hieroglyphic evidence, however, the most clearly marked boundary of membership is represented through accession into office.

In contrast to the lower boundary of titled elites, delimited through the rite of passage of accession, the upper boundary is apparently permeable, with known examples of overlaps with members of the royal family (for instance, Chak Jol of Yaxchilán, one of our elite acquaintances from chapter 2). Significantly, these examples indicate that royalty were not exercising strict boundary maintenance with regard to courtly positions and that in certain circumstances it was indeed appropriate for royals to advertise their connection with these offices and their attendant privileges and rights. Royal personages, especially the ruler himself, are generally noticeably differentiated from other elites in image, text, and the material record, and Maya emphasis on lineage (e.g., written records of parentage statements) means that such familial membership would have been closely attended to. However, royals were less invested in representing the exclusivity of royal and nonroyal roles—that is, non-ruler roles—in the context of the court.

The overall lack of genealogical advertising of royal family connections in the texts makes me confident that courtly elites did not merely represent a spillover of royal family extras looking for an outlet. But this fuzzy boundary does raise questions. Ideas about boundary maintenance of identity groups (Barth 1969:15–16) suggest that one might expect clearer assertions of association or identification to be enacted in opposition to another group or identity. In fact, this makes sense in understanding the court. Official courtiers are offset from the rest of the population who do not perform similar roles embodying exemplary identity and status. While these courtiers are not royalty in most cases, their group aims are complementary to those of the royal family, and the groups are thus seen as aligned. Thus, the oppositional quality that highlights group boundaries does not exist at the upper edge of the courtly elite group. The contrast between the treatment of upper and lower boundaries of courtly officials indicates which division was of particular salience to the Classic Maya themselves. With these observations, we can begin to see the shape of the political hierarchy and can comment on the nature of courtly membership.

Recall that we began this chapter with the image of the Pan-Maya Office of Regional Affairs (and its Departments of Labor and Demography), an invented institution that nonetheless reminds us of the types of information about courtly members, membership, and identity that emerge when we consider data in aggregate. The approach in this chapter has been to take a more inclusive look at the people who constituted the court through consideration of textually articulated action and identity. Together these angles illuminate court members as marked or distinguished by both ways of acting and ways of being. The result is an increased awareness of the nuanced factors used to describe courtly elites and the recognition of content and boundaries that were relevant to the ancient Maya in articulating and enacting a courtly elite identity.

One of my intentions for this chapter was to steer us away from overly simple understandings of what it means to be an elite and explore how court membership was experienced by those who held it. If we recall the individualistic and sometimes idiosyncratic life stories of particular individuals from chapter 2, however, we quickly realize that we must also be careful not to use the characteristics and practices discussed here to yield a static and singular picture of elite identity. Rather, dynamism is a quality noticed in individual elite life stories, as well as in the composite portrait of the Late Classic court across the Maya lowlands. I would argue, in fact, that change and variation are crucial parts of the Late Classic courtly experience. We must now consider how such an adaptively useful anchor of central authority and long-term cultural continuity like the court could simultaneously have been so marked by an almost mercurial variability and local interpretation.

CHAPTER FOUR

Courtly Variation and Change

Hieroglyphic and iconographic data make clear that the Classic Maya royal court was an active and productive institution. As a political unit it was composed of individuals who structured and restructured not only the institution of the court itself but also the social, political, and religious messages that radiated outward from this culturally idealized space. As we have seen, the performances of roles and cultural mores that took place in the court enacted shared ideas that were visible and influential beyond the confines of the physical space of the court. Thus, courtly practices reinforced the meaning and the power of the court through the solidifying process of repeated actions. The repetition of court-originated action such as ritual duties, celebratory occasions, and even modes of interaction would have occurred outside of the court as well, with the activities that were performed on the courtly stage subsequently reenacted by extra-courtly individuals within their own residential spaces.

Discussing the enactment and reenactment of cultural forms must not lead to the conclusion, however, that these courtly processes involved perfect repetition or that they precluded change. Indeed, analogous criticism has been leveled at Bourdieu for his elision of transformative processes in his discussion of the habitus (see King 2000 for an overview), which emphasizes "durable," "regular," and "structured" ways of being that are repeated by both individuals and groups (1977:72). Instead, we must look to scholars like Giddens to understand how making/remaking through temporally situated individual action is intimately tied with both change and variation (1979:198–33, 1984:227–80). Particularly useful to us here is Giddens's focus on temporal contexts, cultural process, and knowledgeable individuals or agents (1979:217; 1984:281–82)—all elements that play a part in situating the Classic Maya court as a dynamic and strategic institution.

This chapter explores how the composition of the court varied and changed over time, as part of situating the institution within a dynamic framework of Late Classic politics and strategic adaptation. Thinking about change in the court brings it to life, serving as a reminder that it was a vibrant social space. Indeed, some of its power and authority derived from its ability to manage that dynamism in a way that incorporated change while also promoting continuity. In order to understand the shifts that occur in the Late Classic court, it is also necessary to look carefully at how change occurs and how the Maya themselves conceptualized it. Ultimately, this chapter considers change, variation, and even continuity, as we investigate the nature of courtly shifts, how individuals in the past would have been implicated in these processes, and how changes and variations in the court represented strategic adaptations.

Courtly Offices over Time

Temporal Distribution of Titles

In considering variation and change related to courtly offices and the structure of the court, we see that one of the clearest trends is temporal in nature. A well-recognized pattern in the appearance of titles like *sajal* and *ajk'uhuun* is their apparent "boom" in usage in the Late Classic. These titles are recorded in notably increased numbers during this period (Houston 1993:127–34). Tracking their usage chronologically makes the pattern apparent and also suggests some possible interpretations of the development of the positions and how they were used.

Within my database of courtly titles, 122 entries are associated with readable dates, representing data points that can be used to reconstruct a chronology. An examination of these dates supports previous observations that an increasingly large elite group was featured in texts during the Late Classic (Houston 1993:130–31; Houston and Stuart 2001:73–74; Stuart 1985b:24). However, additional observations may be made that illuminate not only the final trajectory of these offices but also their initial emergence. Looking at the range of time over which these titles were in use, as textually recorded, indicates that the employment of such offices was not only a late effort to combat shifting or failing political institutions. Rather, the emergence and usage of formalized courtly positions might better be seen as a long-term strategic political adaptation to changing circumstances.

A simple bar graph by date shows that titular usage peaked around A.D. 725 (see chart 1) and that almost all of the dated records of these titles fall squarely within the Late Classic. Separating this distribution by courtly title indicates similar curves within each of the positions (charts 2.1 and 2.2), providing information on the adoption and implementation of the various formalized offices. Given the discrepancy between the extents of numerical usage of different titles, one might expect that less common titles like *ti'huun/ti'sakhuun, yajaw k'ahk'*, and "banded bird" would make later appearances, given the apparent specialized and less-developed nature of their roles, in contrast to the positions of *sajal* and *ajk'uhuun*. Such a hypothesis is not supported, however, as the usage of all of the titles spans approximately the same period, overlapping both at the beginning and end of the period of use.

Interpreting Changes in the Court over Time

What do these temporal distributions mean? Despite the Late Classic prominence of *sajal*s, *ajk'uhuun*s, and their compatriots, the range of dates associated with titled elite individuals is actually much wider, covering 446 years from A.D. 435 to A.D. 881. We must pay attention to when such textual documentation was set down, however. The earliest contemporaneous record of a courtly title (i.e., in contrast to a retrospective one, or one that was recorded at a later date) was in A.D. 613, at Toniná, a date that does fall within the Late Classic. Records of these titles that occur prior to the Late Classic are almost entirely retrospective ones, raising questions about the nature, and even

Chart 1. Distribution of all courtly elite titles over time (in years A.D.)

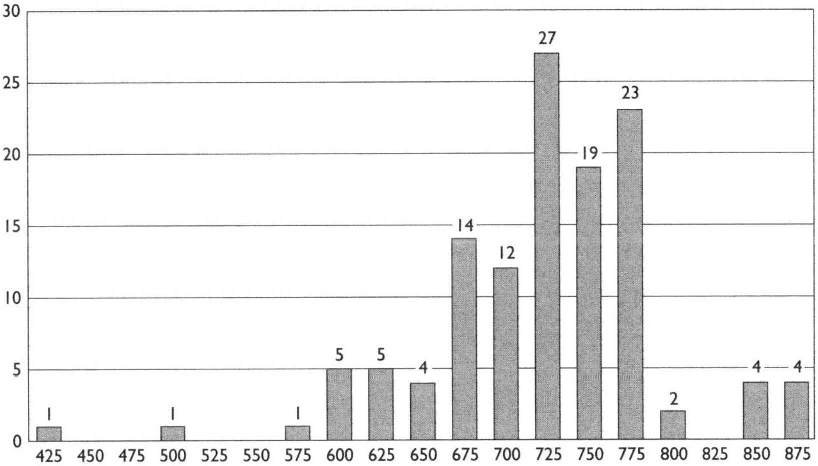

The year refers to the recorded date associated with the titled individual, not the date that the monument was carved. Note the peak in usage during the Late Classic period (A.D. 600–900).

accuracy, of these records. The K'an Tok Panel from Palenque, discussed in chapter 2, is an example of this type of retrospective record, in which courtly officers and their associated dates were documented years later. (It is possible—though not verifiable—that such data [names and dates] may have been recorded contemporaneously in texts that no longer survive.) Retrospective dates could belie efforts to create a particular historical trajectory after the fact, a strategy that would raise doubt about the reliability of retrospective records. While they may represent different historical truths than do contemporaneous records, a wholesale creation of *post-factum* retrospective records seems unlikely, particularly given their occurrence across multiple sites. It is my interpretation that they represent genuine time depth in usage of these titles, even if the titles were not recorded or emphasized in the same way in these earlier periods.

Interpreting this pattern as a change in recording styles supports the idea that the offices were present over a long period of time but were used and emphasized differently in the Late Classic. Not only was there an increased interest in filling and highlighting such positions in the Late Classic, but there were renewed efforts to refer to earlier-era officeholders, who at the time received less textual "air time." (Recall that a monument like Piedras Negras Panel 3, for example, provides evidence for the memory of courtly officers from earlier eras, who were not textually documented until later.)

It is likely that the notable change in the number of titles used in hieroglyphic texts during the Late Classic period is the product of intertwined processes (Houston and Stuart 2001:73). Such processes include a shift in recording practice in which elites merit, or demand, a more central role in word and image. Simultaneously, these records may also reflect an actual shift in political structures of power sharing, in which the ruler extended his power base by including increasing numbers of elites in the functioning of the court and governance of the polity. Certainly these positions appear to have increased in importance over time.

Chart 2.1. Distribution of *sajal* titles over time (in years A.D.)

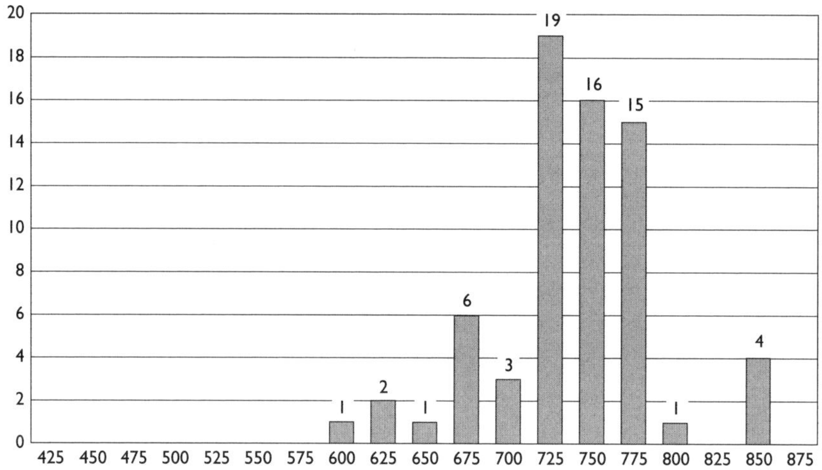

Chart 2.2. Distribution of *ajk'uhuun* titles over time (in years A.D.)

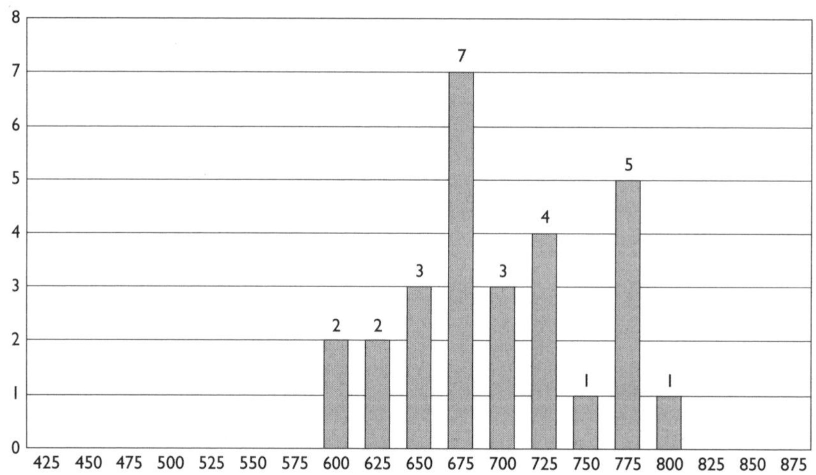

In both of these charts, the year refers to the recorded date associated with the titled individual, not the date that the monument was carved. Note that even when separated by title, the temporal distribution remains largely the same. Since *sajal* and *ajk'uhuun* are the two most common titles, they yield the most data for comparing chronological distributions. However, the other titles display similar curves. The one exception is "banded bird," which, because so many of the dated examples of this title come from the retrospective K'an Tok Panel at Palenque, shows a more even distribution across the Classic period.

Can we further illuminate the temporal patterns of usage of these titles by looking at each position separately? Rather than an evolutionary process in which different positions developed over time, these formal positions emerged and were used over analogous time periods. In the Late Classic the chronological distributions of all of the titles show that a full-fledged cast of titled elite players existed from the beginning of their appearance in the monumental record. Records of accessions into these positions, a marking of formalization, almost uniformly occur quite early. This indicates that the system of courtly offices was already fully formed from their earliest textual appearances. First records of accessions for each of the titles occurred as follows (as found in the database I compiled): "banded bird"—A.D. 435 at Palenque; *ti'sakhuun*—A.D. 608 at Palenque; *yajaw k'ahk'*—A.D. 610 at Palenque; *ajk'uhuun*—A.D. 613 at Toniná. The one exception—surprisingly—is *sajal*, for which a recorded seating does not occur until A.D. 697, in the El Cayo area. While perhaps a vagary of the preserved hieroglyphic record, this may also serve as evidence that the position of *sajal* operated in a different way from the others, especially since this record, on the Dumbarton Oaks panel, represents a *sajal* at a satellite site. Additionally, it is hard not to note Palenque's prominence in the enumeration above of first records of the seating of these positions. Palenque's distinctive record will be further considered below.

According to the evidence, the apparent expansion of the formal membership of the court was not a late effort in response to pressures of the increasingly unstable Late Classic period. The observations above indicate that importance of the court as a political institution was a long-term adaptation. The shared temporal boundaries of these titles' textual records also indicate a degree of intentionality in the highlighting of the institution. Whether the positions had been previously present and only now deserved special emphasis (the interpretation I would favor), or whether they represent an institution created *de novo* as a conscious adaptation, there seems to be an element of strategy in this shift away from textual and iconographic emphasis on the ruler as the sole axis of power and source of authority.

The temporal data on members of the court plainly illustrate some type of change over time—whether a shift in actual governmental positions or a shift in the recording practice that highlighted them, or likely a combination of these two processes. One type of dynamism characterizing the court, therefore, can be understood as occurring over time. Looking at records of courtly elites in another way reveals that significant differences in the usage or emphasis of courtly positions also occurred across the geographic space of the Maya lowlands.

Courtly Offices across Space

Spatial Distribution of Titles

We know that the same suite of courtly titles appears at sites throughout the Maya world—this is not a phenomenon limited to a specific site. However, reliance on courtly offices as part of the governing apparatus of a polity is documented in distinctly different ways across the Maya lowlands. Others have recognized previously that occurrences of the *sajal* title tend to cluster in the region of the Usumacinta River (Stuart 1985b:23–24). This observation turns out to be true for all of the courtly elite offices.

The largest concentration of formal elite titles occurs along the Usumacinta River, including sites directly on the river, as well as in the larger Usumacinta drainage (map 2). This clustering suggests the operation of a sphere of political interaction, and perhaps competition, centered on the Usumacinta. Usage of the titles, and the offices that they represent, is not limited to this region, however. The northwest section of the Yucatán peninsula also features a tradition of title usage. Additionally, a few examples are found from Tabasco, and from the southeastern periphery of the Maya world, in the Copán area. Despite the fact that the central Petén is frequently seen as a core area of Maya politics, only a few examples of titles are recorded at sites such as Tikal, Naranjo, and Najtunich. In short, the appearance of titled members of the court varies significantly from place to place. Their strong presence in the texts and monuments of the Usumacinta region is not similarly echoed in all areas of the Maya world.

This spatial distribution of records of court members is not the same for all offices, however. If individual titles are plotted geographically, using the data I compiled, an interesting divergence emerges between *sajal*s and *ajk'uhuun*s (maps 3 and 4). These two are the most useful for identifying patterns, since they occur in the largest numbers. Like the overall distribution of courtly titles, references to *sajal*s cluster tightly along the Usumacinta, with a few exceptions appearing in other areas. In contrast, *ajk'uhuun*s are found spread much more widely across the landscape. This disjunction is intriguing because it indicates that titles were not merely interchangeable honorifics but rather they displayed elements of differentiated uses, meanings, or possibly roles for the ancient Maya.

The distribution of courtly offices also offers a view on the nature of governance in different areas of the Maya lowlands. Plotting the spatial distribution of courtly titles provides information on what a court looked like in different places. Only one site, Palenque, exhibits a complete suite of all five formal offices. Toniná comes in a close second, missing only "banded bird." Most polities did not have (or record) courts that contained a complete contingent of formalized positions, indicating that a full complement of titles was not necessary for a functional court. Additionally, this suggests that courts in different areas utilized varying types of governing structures, as represented by differences in the specific offices of the court. This profound regionalism is thus seen in the types of localized adaptations used to successfully accommodate particular circumstances. In the case of the Classic court, such circumstances might mean needing to include powerful locals within the court, having the resources available in the court to support courtiers, and having stable elite officials available to help with challenging ruler transition.

Spatial Variation in Courtly Offices: Two Ends of the Spectrum

In considering variation as a notable quality of courtly composition, employing the lens of spatial distribution points both to sites with remarkably rich records of courtly officers and, at the other end of the spectrum, sites that retain no such record at all. I consider both here, including temporal data that may point to a place of origin for the emergence of these distinctive positions.

When temporal and spatial records are examined in concert, we see that use of courtly titles did not emerge evenly across the spatial landscape of the Maya lowlands. This provides another nice illustration of the phenomenon of sociopolitical

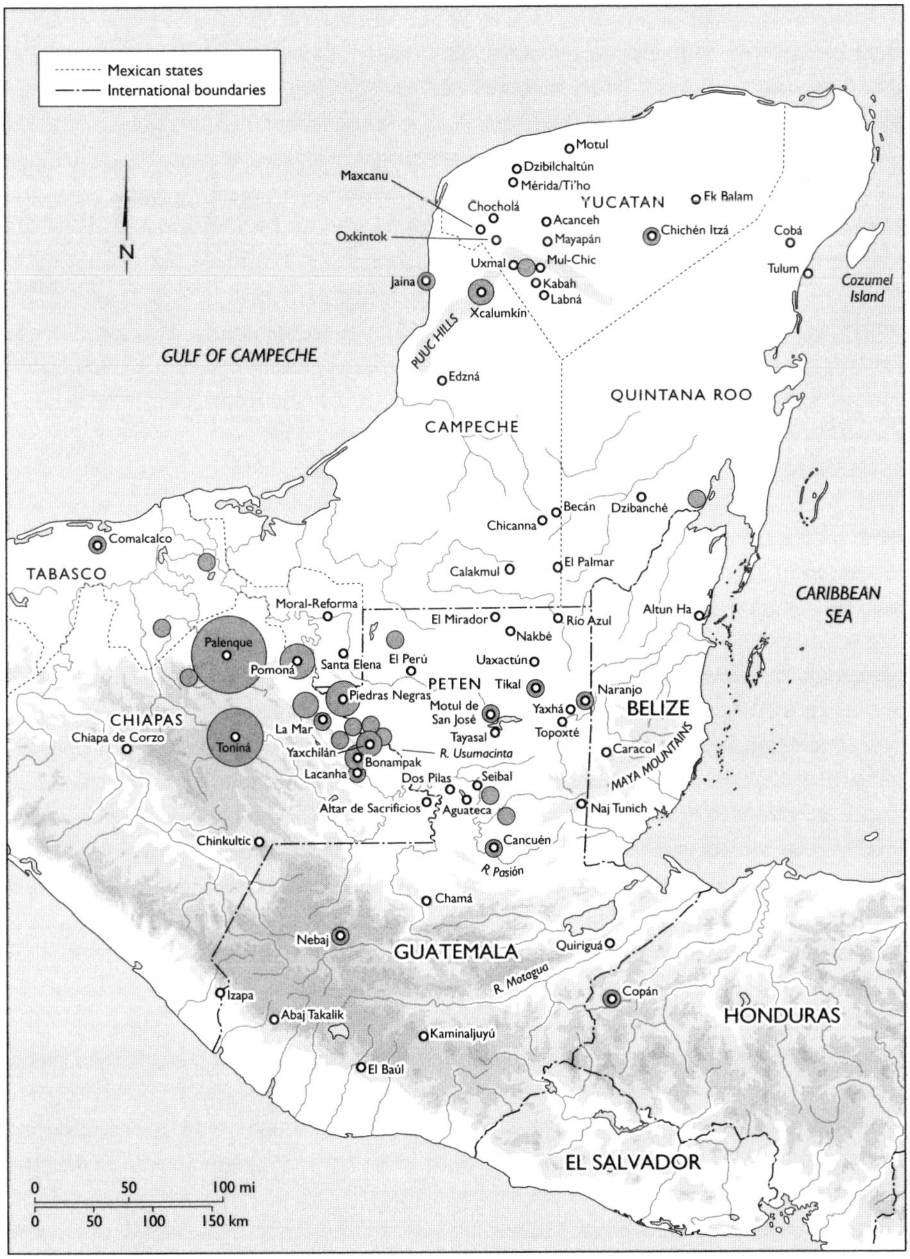

Map 2. Map of the geographical distribution of all elite titles, indicated by the placement of shaded circles; the relative size of the circles indicates the relative number of titles recorded. Note the high concentration of title usage in the Usumacinta corridor. Map adapted from Miller and Martin 2004: figure 3. Copyright © 2013 by the University of Oklahoma Press.

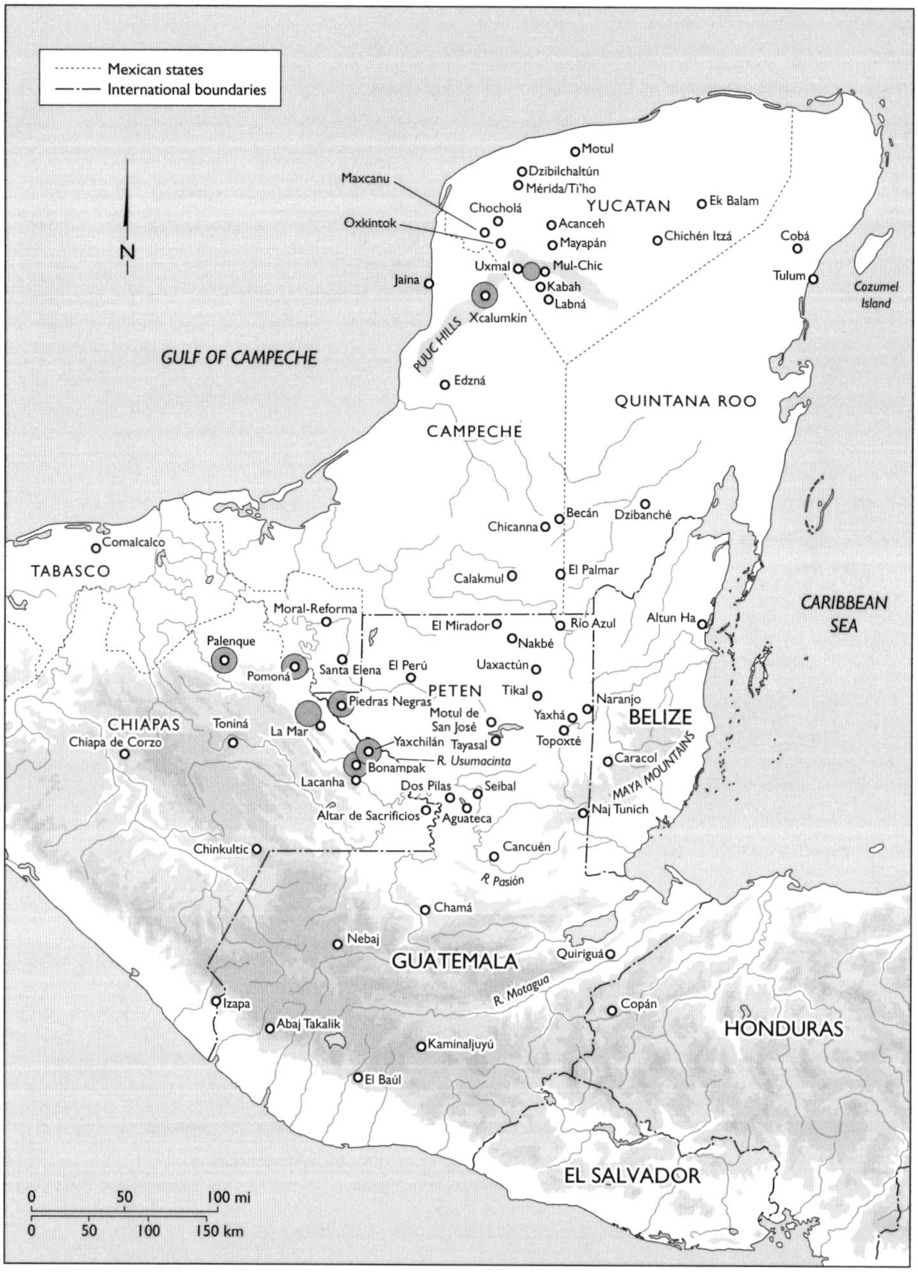

Map 3. Map of the distribution of *sajal* titles, indicated by the placement of shaded circles; the relative size of the circles indicates the relative number of titles recorded. Again, note the high concentration of titles found in the Usumacinta corridor. Map adapted from Miller and Martin 2004: figure 3. Copyright © 2013 by the University of Oklahoma Press.

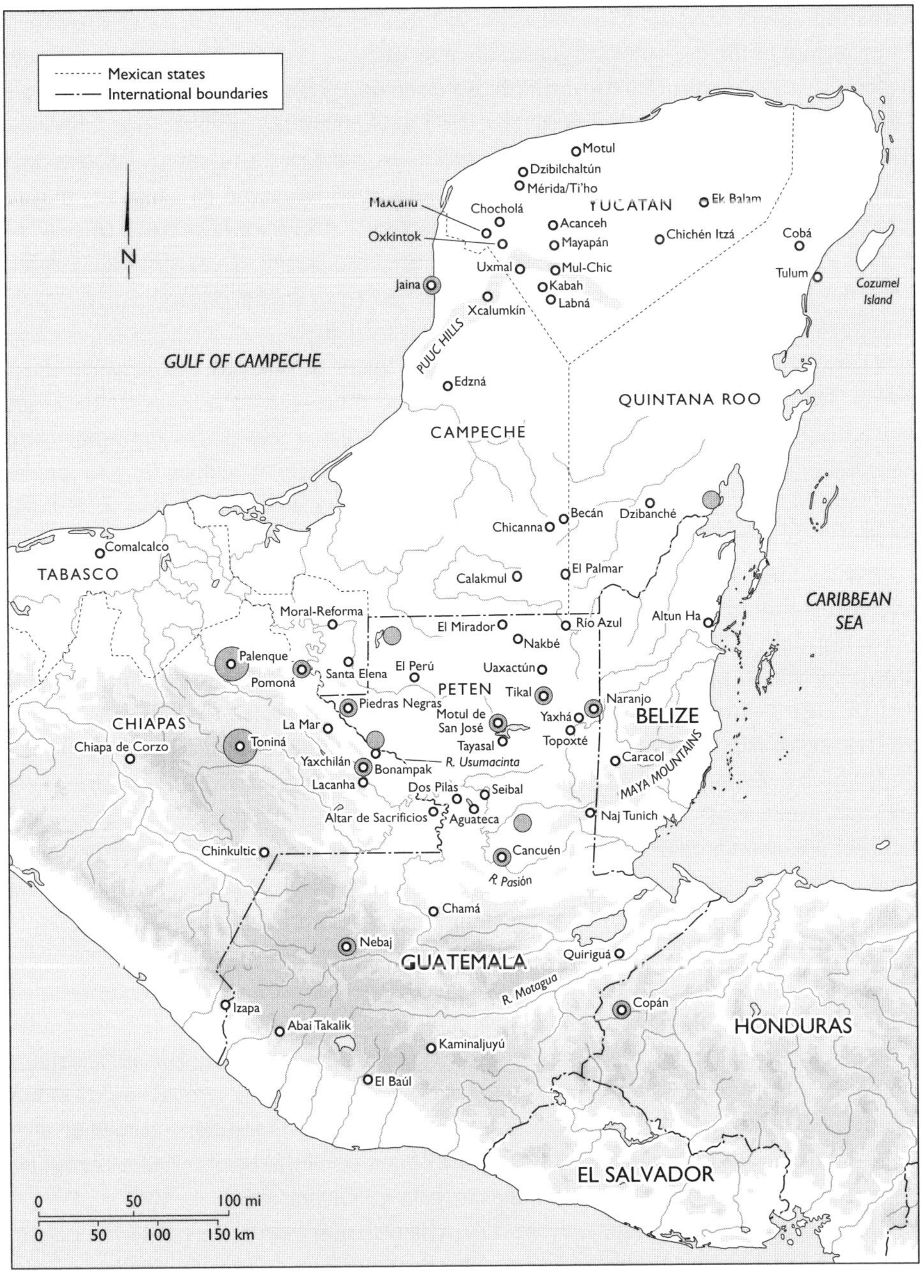

Map 4. Map of the distribution of *ajk'uhuun* titles, indicated by the placement of shaded circles; the relative size of the circles indicates the relative number of titles recorded. Map adapted from Miller and Martin 2004: figure 3. Copyright © 2013 by the University of Oklahoma Press.

variation across the Late Classic world. In thinking about the genesis of the court, approached in terms of chronological change, one site takes particular prominence: Palenque. (Miller and Martin similarly note the importance of Palenque as a center "demonstrat[ing] the ideals of courtly life" [2004:200–201], though their observations focus primarily on architectural and artistic data and on the royal dynasty, rather than on the presence of titled courtly officials.) Palenque, the only site to display the entire suite of five courtly titles, is located in the area where these titles were used most extensively, in a zone surrounding the Usumacinta River drainage. Recall, too, that Palenque is dominant in terms of the first records of accessions: three of the five positions were first recorded as acceding at this site.

Palenque's apparently intensive use of courtly positions has particularly deep roots. The presence of the K'an Tok Panel (also discussed in chapter 2) provides intriguing evidence for a long tradition of elite titular usage at this exemplary site (see figure 21). As we have seen, this carved stone panel documents a long sequence of "banded bird" titles, recorded over 332 years during much of the Classic period. In each recorded event, the accession of a new "banded bird" official was overseen or watched over by the Palenque king or queen in power at the time. However, the patterns on this panel make it plain that individuals being seated as "banded birds" were not doing so in sync with the accessions of rulers; that is, "banded bird" officials came into power on a schedule that differed from the accessions of Palenque rulers. Furthermore, not every ruler oversaw the seating of an elite into the position of "banded bird." Likely, the officeholder would have held the position until death, reflected by the twenty- to thirty-year spans of office indicated on the panel. This unique monument suggests not only a long history at Palenque of official courtly officers but also some degree of independence of elites from their rulers, since each *k'uhul ajaw* could not have created his court from scratch. It also suggests that courts were resilient institutions, with political continuity operating below the hierarchical level of the actual ruler.

Nearly all of the records of courtly officials on this monument are not contemporaneous, providing evidence for the legitimacy of retrospective records. In the tradition of king lists such as the one seen on Altar Q at Copán (where the site's sixteen rulers are pictured and named in sequence around the edge of a carved square stone altar) (Stuart 1992:170–71), the K'an Tok Panel illustrates a long-term record of successive holders of the banded bird position. While these refer back to earlier eras, the specificity of the records does not suggest wholesale invention.

The idea that a courtly hierarchy and courtly positions were integral to the political scene at Palenque is also supported by the additional complexities in courtly ranking found at this site. Palenque is the only site with evidence for the ruler/courtier hierarchy becoming even more nuanced through the nesting of positions, in which certain titled courtly elites explicitly control other titled elites below them. This is seen in the example of Aj Sik'ab in chapter 2, for instance. Palenque's primacy in the emergence and usage of courtly offices also seems to have led to its further development, as seen in these nested hierarchies. Such an overt articulation of hierarchy is not seen at other Classic sites but might have eventually radiated outward from Palenque.

Certainly Palenque is known for having an unusually rich and extensive textual record (Miller and Martin 2004:201; Schele 1991b:80; Stuart 2007:207). This local style may be the source, at least in part, of its apparent primacy in usage of the courtly structure. Observations about Palenque's distinctive record related to courtly positions suggest that the Late Classic usage of these positions as part of the court structure might have originated at Palenque, to be imitated and adopted to varying degrees across the Maya lowlands. Just as material goods, such as Chablekal Fine Gray ceramics, were known to have been mimicked and imported from Palenque to other sites (Kovacevich et al. 2005:42), so might their system of governance have been replicated at sites in both their immediate vicinity and farther afield.

The example of Palenque, where courtly officials are recorded in abundance, can be contrasted with other polities in the Maya lowlands that lack such records entirely. Tracing records of courtiers across the Maya lowlands reveals the fact that many areas have no textual record of these official positions whatsoever. What can one make of these striking lacunae? As has been seen in different emphases on certain positions at different sites, so may there have been variation in which sites engaged with the formalized elite hierarchy of the court. Some rulers may have avoided granting elites particular positions within their government, for instance. Rather than suggesting that governing structures in these areas completely lacked a formal internal organization or political hierarchy, however, it is also possible that the gaps point to distinct regional differences in recording practices. Just as different styles, emphasis on particular media, scribal hands, and other visual cues help identify images and representations from different parts of the Maya world, such differences in recording styles would also be reflected in what topics are emphasized in preserved texts. In areas with a scanty record of courtly positions, these individuals might have been less frequently highlighted in text, or they may have been recorded on media that were less likely to survive until the present.

To summarize, clear distinction exists between the Usumacinta region and other parts of the Maya world, in terms of the relative textual emphasis on formalized positions within the court. Nonetheless, differences in recording practices—and, in a larger sense, regional identities or styles—likely mean that this distinction is not as black and white as it might initially appear. That is, the map showing the distribution of preserved records of court members (see map 2) should not be read literally as a map of the extent of usage of courtly governing structures. Courtly positions of some type were almost certainly in play in other areas of the Maya world but are not accessible to us due to vagaries of preservation or the trends in recording just suggested. At the same time, we must recall the heterogeneous nature of the sociopolitical landscape of this era, which was marked by the existence of distinctive, independent polities. Coupled with the differential use of titles in locations that do have extensive hieroglyphic records, we are left with a reminder of the importance of investigating and recognizing local organization of power structures. Given the evidence of variation, modern interpreters of ancient Maya polities should not be surprised to find polities that governed themselves in a wide variety of forms.

Thinking Theoretically about Late Classic Change and Variation

The observations discussed above about the distribution of titles on temporal and spatial axes provide clear evidence of the dynamism of courtly positions and the institution of the court. This dynamism can be characterized both by change over time and by spatial variation in usage. Tracking these textual records provides a broad view of courtly shifts, setting the stage for considering the implications of a dynamic Late Classic court and the possibility that it was employed as a strategic adaptation to a shifting cultural landscape. In order to contextualize and understand these processes, a brief theoretical discussion is warranted. The reflections that follow shed light on both how we might conceptualize change and variation for past cultures and how they actually occurred. I begin by thinking expansively, before discussing the specific case of the Maya.

Conceptualizing Processes of Change and Variation

In considering what is meant by change and what processes of change look like, one might think of the imagery of movement. Using this visualization, one can imagine change as represented by a variety of types of movements—vectors (moving from point A to point B with explicit direction), circles (cyclical patterns of repetition), clouds (generalized, undirected movement in an area), as well as others. Theoretically speaking, this idea of movement—and in particular repeated movement—is integral to conceptions of change. Recall that Giddens's work (1979:198) makes the important leap of situating ideas of ongoing practice *in time* and characterizing them as recurring processes; picture: cycles of repeated movement. Significantly, this temporal context introduces the possibility of change through intentional and unintentional misfires, that is, imperfect reproductions of existing structures (Giddens 1979:219–22); picture: tracings that are inexact, the subtle shift of tracing paper during the redrawing. This imperfection—or, if intended, improvisation—is an important concept for uniting theoretical ideas about how the social world is created and re-created through the actions of agents, with real-world evidence of individuals living and operating in this world (see, e.g., Bricker 1981:162).

To continue with the analogy of movement, shifts or imperfect reproductions differ from the original version. Depending on their directionality, or lack thereof, one might characterize different types of movements as change versus variability. What is the significance of this distinction? As archaeologists, and inhabitants of the present, one of our challenges is how to interpret aberrations in the record of the past. How we interpret unexpected evidence, or evidence that deviates from previously established patterns or expectations, may depend on our understanding of the *type* of misreproduction at play. We must interpret different types of misreproduction, even though they all stem from the same process of imperfect replication.

Variability and change, then, are related concepts (Fischer 2001:163). Making a distinction between them may ultimately be more important to us, as we attempt to grapple with fragmentary and contradictory evidence from the past, than it would have been to the denizens of the past. Recognizing the processes that operate behind these concepts helps to place the origins of agriculture and the erratic and unusual remodeling of a temple structure in the same cognitive category, as agent-inspired moments of shifting reproduction and as adjustment to changing circumstances affecting past peoples. While there are different implications for these processes, they are both ultimately representative of inexact reproductions yielding structures that diverge from the original. Considering the concepts of variability and change helps us to imagine the processes that led to the usage, and textual documentation, of courtly offices in various places in the Maya world during the Late Classic period.

In visualizing the movements characterizing change and variation, one might imagine change as suggesting movement from one structural configuration to another. In contrast, variation is pictured as a lack of codification or regularity in the form that a structure takes and does not necessarily indicate a trend. With variation, the trope of directional movement that is frequently associated with a discussion of change is largely absent. Instead, variation can be understood as representing the flexible elements of structures, which allows them (or rather the individuals in charge of reproducing them) to respond effectively to a variety of situations. Indeed, the habitus may be seen as an improvisatory strategy (Bourdieu 1977:78), representing a range of possible culturally logical responses (Fischer 2001:15–19).

Suggesting that variations are representative of flexibility does not suggest, however, that they are without meaning to those who enact them. In fact, even apparently trivial variations may be an important strategy in defining the boundaries of a group (Geertz 1980:51) and asserting, therefore, identity through group practice. Thus, variation can still represent strategic use—although it may also result, of course, from less conscious or intentional processes of arbitrariness (Bourdieu 1977:164) or irregularity (Geertz 1980:26) in reproduction. Such possibilities represent less rich contexts for interpretation and indicate the importance of attempting to distinguish between meaningful variation and variation resulting from human error.

Enacting Change and Variation

In addition to thinking about what the processes of change and variation look like, it is also necessary to consider how these processes were actually put into play by individuals in the past and how we interpret them from fragmentary evidence. Thinking carefully about this allows for an appreciation of what data on Classic-era political structures represent, in terms of the ancient processes that we are attempting to reconstruct.

Enactment of change or variation presupposes several entities or qualities: a dynamic system (or the possibility thereof) (with inspiration from Bricker 1981:180–81, Fischer 2001:16, and Marcus 1993:121), knowledgeable agents or actors (Giddens 1984:281–82), and cultural logics that help to determine what a consistent and legible cultural system looks like (Fischer 2001:15–19). The enactment of change by agents, whether intentional or unintentional, involves directionality (as discussed above) and constraints on their actions as determined by the logical operation of the milieu in which they are operating.

Different types of change may be posited as responses to a variety of contextual pressures or situations (e.g., environment, demographics, resources, conquest, etc.). However, the enactment of structural replication is carried out by people who are likely aware of the relationship—potentially imperfect—between their action and its context and the cultural constraints and logics against which their action is measured. Thus, an individual may not plan ahead or intend to make an error (e.g., a cooking pot that is not the same shape as other cooking pots in their village). Nonetheless, their recognition of their action (making a pot of X shape) and how it relates to culturally prescribed actions (making a pot of Y shape) means that even if the pot resulted from carelessness rather than an intentional act of ceramic rebellion, it is still an informed act. This is due to the ability of the actor to contextualize it, thrusting individual action into relief against group or cultural logic. Indeed, an important aspect of the project undertaken here is understanding political changes of the Late Classic in reference to records of individuals.

In the preceding paragraph I used the words "error" and "imperfect" not to criticize a less-than-optimal choice but rather to highlight the fact that change results from "misfires" (to use Austin's term for speech acts that do not produce the expected or desired result [1962:16]). These are situations in which restructured structures diverge from the original through revisions enacted in practice. The words "imperfect" or "misfire" do not, in this context, have pejorative implications but rather highlight how the action of practice is not a cycling of endless repetition. Instead it involves rereadings, revisions, reenactments, and reinterpretations that in fact do *not* perfectly echo the original and that yield subtle or not-so-subtle differences through the process of real world engagements (Bricker 1981:180–81). In the case of a textual society, like the Maya, some of this cycling (e.g., the appearance of a *sajal* at Xcalumkín, where such a position had not previously been recorded) is caught vividly in written evidence, as has been demonstrated by changes and variations evident in use of courtly elite titles.

Perhaps most interesting in dissecting ideas of change and intentionality is to analyze chains of structuration and restructuration (or decision making). What does our errant potmaker do after she or he makes the ill-formed pot? Break it? Hide it? Ignore it? Decide it is her or his signature style and assert it as distinctive of her or his house group? Each of these subsequent actions would highlight, in different ways, how individual action is experienced and how these small moments are part of a larger sweep of change or scurry of variation. Alternatively, might this potter *not* recognize that the pot is a little different from others in the village or from others she or he has made previously? It is certainly possible. In the case of fields in which the actors are experts, such as craft specialists, we might reasonably presume that they are quite sensitive to variations in process or product. However, we may at times be dealing indirectly with agents who were not experts in a certain material, structural, or social field. Additionally, our own, modern analytical lenses may focus on elements that were not salient to individuals in the past. In these cases, which I suggest will not present as the most robust instances of change in material or other evidence, change or variation may still be occurring but cannot be meaningfully read as intentional or knowledgeable.

In terms of the textual data on courtly elites under consideration in the present work, I argue that choices both small and large guided the changes and variations in political organization and hierarchical structure that are observable in these records. (Does a *k'uhul ajaw* create and allow an official political position in his court because he is trying a new strategy for controlling wayward local nobility? Because he is in ill health and needs a deputy to occasionally attend ritual ceremonies on his behalf? Because he has two younger brothers who are always underfoot?) These choices were made by individuals and groups of individuals with complex understandings of precedent and possibility. That is, while not all of the examples related to courtly elites that are reviewed in this book exhibit calculated intention in terms of culture change, nor are they random sorts of shifts. By looking more closely at the evidence, we can hope to pull apart some of the meanings and strategies influencing these individuals in the past. The present, admittedly abstract, considerations are necessary to clarify how I am conceiving of processes of change and variation and how these happened in the domain of actual people. The result is a perspective on Maya history, and particularly the processes of the Late Classic period, that breaks down general characterizations or sweeping shifts and plumbs the rich data sources to reveal nuances that are newly available in this golden era of textual investigations.

Before thinking more concretely about what enactment of change meant for the Late Classic members of the court, one more—possibly surprising—topic must be broached: that of continuity. In the face of an involved engagement with changes, one must also consider continuity as a process with a profoundly related kind of movement. Continuity is a topic that comes up frequently in considering the Maya—Classic, Colonial, and modern. Our assumptions and beliefs about continuity underlie many accepted hypotheses about Classic Maya lives and serve as the basis for using aspects of Colonial and modern Maya culture as comparative material for illuminating Classic Maya contexts. These are assumptions that bear close examination, and some would suggest that past work has relied overly much on an inappropriate comfort with the similarities between modern and ancient Maya lives.

It is critical to understand ideas of continuity within the models of movement to which I again return. That is, continuity in cultural practice should not be seen as indicative of stasis but rather of individual choice and action that maintain carefully guarded cultural reproduction, closely mimicking original forms. Palka considers this topic with regard to the modern Lacandon Maya, a group often considered as uniquely untouched, and proves that apparently unchanging situations may be complicated by considering hetereogeneity of experience, examining issues of resistance and control, and exploring the ways that new situations are fit into existing structures (2005:1–8). Apparent continuity in a typical schema of movement might be represented by a smooth, flowing line. In actuality, it involves repeated cyclical restructuring movements, of the type already discussed, beneath the apparently smooth surface. Thus, situations of continuity involve the same processes of knowledgeable restructuring as seen in situations of clear and radical change. Indeed, I argue that the institution of the court represents both a change and a continuity.

Both shifts and continuity operate within certain guidelines or constraints that serve to make behaviors and choices culturally logical, and culturally logical action stems from shared frameworks that constrain what kinds of behaviors may occur (Fischer 2001:15–19). In many cases these cultural logics allow for the coexistence of change, including responses to radically new circumstances, *and* the simultaneous maintenance of experiences of continuity, by allowing for widely variable behaviors that nonetheless conform to larger cultural models (Fischer 2001:15).

Change and Variation within the Late Classic Court

In applying these ideas about the unfolding of change and variation to Late Classic courts, we can distinguish trends that seem to extend over the period of the Late Classic (what we might term as change, as well as a range of versions that represent specific responses to local circumstances—i.e., variation). Both of these phenomena are represented in examining hieroglyphic data on courtly officials. In the case of data on Maya elites and courts, recognizing both of these processes helps to identify two important things: (1) institutional changes in the Late Classic resulted in the development of new power structures (i.e., a different kind of court); and (2) the Late Classic court took on a variety of acceptable forms in different contexts. These observations allow us to detect critical and unwavering aspects of the court, as well as the ways in which the court was functionally flexible in accommodating a range of circumstances.

The longer-term developments of the Late Classic period represent structural changes—potentially intentional. Viewed diachronically, the reproductions of courtly structures move directionally to include greater numbers of elites and in more formalized positions, a shift that is visible through graphs that chart the notable increase in usage of formalized titles during the Late Classic era (e.g., see chart 1). At the same time, the distinctive variation of how royal courts were both experienced and recorded across the Maya lowlands during the Late Classic indicates that there was not only one acceptable, recognizable, or "logical" version of the court. The representation of a formalized and formally structured court was highly variable across the Maya lowlands, with a noticeable degree of variation apparent in the adoption and usage of different titles. This reflects different ideas of what exactly constitutes a functionally effective Late Classic court as a mechanism for dealing with particular societal challenges of that period, even while using similar building blocks.

Accessing Related Maya Perspectives: Maya Ideas about Time

Using modern theoretical ideas to talk about change and variation aids us in awareness of our own assumptions and perspectives related to these topics. In order to comprehend the political changes that characterized the Late Classic Maya court, we also must consider how such shifts would have been experienced from an ancient Maya point of view—the Maya theoretical perspective, if you will. Ideas about time are especially helpful for revealing something of the cultural model that would have couched conceptions of change and variation.

In plumbing the hieroglyphic texts for information on Maya perspectives on change, commentary on the nature and meaning of time is particularly useful. In particular, it helps to illuminate the framework within which Classic-period people experienced societal reproduction. It is already a well-accepted idea that time, as measured through multiple calendars of different shapes, is a potent force in daily, generational, and intergenerational experiences of Maya life (see Rice 2008 for an excellent overview of the significance of time to the Maya). Nonetheless, understanding the importance of keeping track of and recording time, and the ways in which time is personified and marked, allows us to situate ideas about change within the temporal landscape of Maya lived experience.

For the Maya culture of the Classic period, ample evidence in the hieroglyphic record supports the idea of temporal reckoning as a critical element in framing and contextualizing events, both in individual lives and in polity-related happenings. At a basic level, our understanding of hieroglyphic texts indicates a specific calendric framework for narratives. Texts often referred to an anchoring date within the linear timeline of the Long Count (recording time elapsed since a mythical creation date) and/or a potentially ambiguous connection to the cyclical form of the Calendar Round, a system of reckoning that repeated every fifty-two years. (Coe and Van Stone [2001:37–48], Houston [1989:48–50], Marcus [1976:39–41], and Rice [2008:282–84] provide useful syntheses of the workings of the calendars described here, for readers seeking additional details.) The lack of fixity of the repeating, cyclical Calendar Round date is, in many ways, hypothetical. Those viewing a monument would likely have easily understood the placement of the text in the current temporal context or cycle. Even today, comparative and contextual analyses usually yield an educated assessment of the correct cyclical affiliation. Nonetheless, the nature of the Calendar Round as a cyclical calendar makes explicit a certain shape of time and evokes other temporal possibilities, each separated by fifty-two years, to which such a sign potentially refers. Additionally, distance numbers, marking the time elapsed between sections of a narrative, form a relative temporal framework within texts and serve to link components of a story into a temporally paced narrative.

What is the significance of these temporal structures? They reflect a concern in public or official narratives with temporal positioning of multiple types (linear, cyclical, relative), which provides a distinctive social contextualization. Ong discusses the transformative process of being temporally or calendrically aware as choosing a culturally relevant "point of reference" for placing oneself (1982:96–97). However, given the cyclical nature of time, this contextualization is not tied to a singular temporal space. Understanding the associations of these temporal frameworks provides the necessary foundation for seeing how change over time was experienced.

The connection of multiple temporal spaces is also evident in other aspects of the Maya calendar. Meanings attached to different calendar days, for example, are more multivocal and weighted than simple associations (Tedlock 1982:107). Barbara Tedlock's discussion of modern calendrical and divination rituals indicates that day names are not simply associated with a nominal or verbal counterpart. Instead, more complex mnemonics, phrases, and associated prognostications might have been apparent in any given day name to the Maya observer (Tedlock 1982:107). Events would have been contextualized by these calendrical meanings, providing an additional layer of significance surrounding the temporal space in which action and change occurred.

Examples of how the temporal dimension proved important in structuring social and political lives appear in both Classic and modern Maya evidence. Passage of time, framed as an individual's age, has been identified in chapter 3 as a marker within the ranks of courtly elites, with modifiers such as "two *k'atun*" indicating temporal prowess and age achieved. This achievement of longevity indicates not only the respect reserved for those who were of older ages but also a personal consciousness of passage through time. The use of day names of birth for personal names, a practice noted in multiple Mesoamerican cultures (Marcus 1976:39–40), similarly marries individual life experiences to a larger movement of time. As positioned within the cyclical Calendar Round, this naming practice relates individuals to events and people that came before and those that would come after. This idea also intersects with the importance and presence of ancestors for both Classic and modern Maya. Taken even further, Stuart has argued for a complex interweaving of temporal concepts and celebrations thereof with the assertion of regal authority through the medium of carved stelae (1996:156–57), indicating the interrelationship between time and political structures. Other temporal clues in the hieroglyphic texts that indicate a focus on the passage of time include the significance of anniversaries, which, like age, indicate an awareness and experience of events in light of units of time. Similarly, the emphasis on period endings shows the power or desirability of certain dates, frequently in connection with certain actions.

These observations reveal how actions would have been understood and experienced within the temporally specific environment in which they occurred. A temporal framework for action provides the context for variations or changes that unfold and that gain meaning within a culturally specific sense of time. These examples illuminate the sensitivity of the Maya to detailed records of time, reflect an awareness of their temporal situation and the passage of time, and indicate a set of important meanings attached to these contexts. Meaning would have been constructed through actively cultivated references to the past, representing a temporal space that continued to be relevant within the frame of the present. Neither continuity nor transformation, as exclusive concepts, adequately represents Maya history or experience. Effective analyses must examine how Maya populations themselves controlled, managed, and resisted impacts on their cultural systems. In understanding the changes occurring during the Late Classic period, these insights into the experience of change contextualize the simultaneous experiences of shift and continuity that seem to have been a hallmark of Maya elite strategy. Changes in the political institutions of the Late Classic, including the expansion of the membership of the court, would have been comprehended against the background of these ideas about the structure and nature of temporal experience.

Implications for Interpreting Dynamism within the Late Classic Court

Relating data on change and variation within the court to ideas about how change and variation occurred or were understood results in a synthesis that aids our understanding of the political changes that characterized the Late Classic court and its members. In particular, the discussions above yield several concepts that inform an interpretation of the Late Classic royal court as a dynamic space. These concepts are the role of the past in the present, the relationship between cyclicality and change, and the presence of continuity as a process even within dynamic, changeable systems. With these ideas in mind, we can consider their implications for interpreting the Late Classic political landscape and, in particular, the observable changes and variations of royal courts and their officers.

The Role of the Past in the Present: Ideas of Accumulation

An understanding of the interrelationship between the past and the present within Maya culture provides important context for the courtly experience of change. Tedlock has suggested that the idea of temporal imbrication or overlap characterizes shifts of time or movement between periods of time for the Maya (1982:203). Specifically, her research indicates that rather than experiencing an unequivocal movement between or through temporal units, Maya experience of time involves graded shifts and includes gray areas in which both units of time are considered present or relevant (Tedlock 1982:203). This means that movement in a temporal sense is not reflected by the Western concept of the clock striking midnight or the calendar flipping over at the end of the month. Instead, the potentially liminal periods of transition between time units provide another way of accessing Maya perceptions of time and movement through it.

This idea of imbrication conjures an important aspect of Maya conception of time and change: the role, and presence, of the past in the present. The overlaps that Tedlock identifies are examples of the ways in which it can be difficult to leave behind the past in Maya contexts. Examples in which a rupture with the past occurs (e.g., Copán dynasty founder Yax K'uk' Mo' 's building of the Copán acropolis in a shifted space from the previous focus of occupation [Fash 2005:79–87] or the lack of textual reference—barring Piedras Negras Panel 3's enigmatic allusion—to the interregnum period at Yaxchilán [Houston and Stuart 2001:71]) are moments in which blatant disregard for the past is self-consciously enacted as a strategy of breaking from a problematic history. With the exception of these situations in which rulers or others apparently ignore ancestry and history in order to assert inorganic or unexpected change, present time among the Maya is inexorably structured by the past.

This is not an unexpected observation. References to ancestors, dynasty founders, and historical/mythical events, and even past personal accomplishments, permeate Maya texts. In the material record, structures may contain architectural or iconographic references to earlier constructions, objects from earlier eras may be curated, and sacred sites may be dedicated to ancestors. The location of burials at the heart of structures further highlights the idea of the past, and individuals from the past, continuing to play an active, ongoing role in the present.

This connection between past and present meanings is part of a conceptualization that associates time with the idea of accumulation (Tedlock 1982:202). That is, rather than just a cyclical rotation apparent in repetitive calendars, we might also usefully think of processes of addition, of piling up, of adding on or augmenting. This idea of accretion is important in thinking about change because it indicates that new or different actions, events, or identities may be added on to, rather than just replacing, an earlier or accepted way of doing or being. This is especially relevant to an understanding of change because the trope of addition, rather than replacement, can powerfully characterize cultural shifts, adjustments, and adaptations.

Such ideas are also relevant in terms of other structures that are expressed within temporal and chronological frameworks—such as the political organization of the court. In the realm of political hierarchy, Tedlock mentions that municipal positions among the modern Quiché are not discarded after a term is over but rather are added on to over the course of a lifetime (1982:202). Intriguingly, there is evidence—as has been insinuated in previous chapters—that Classic courtly offices operated in the same way. As in the case of Aj Chaanah, a compatriot of Kelen Hix at Toniná discussed in chapter 2, investiture into office seems to have represented a critical change in state. Aj Chaanah held both the positions of *ajk'uhuun* and *yajaw k'ahk'*, yet only underwent one recorded accession event (probably as *ajk'uhuun*—Toniná Monument 3). The initial change in status associated with accession heralds entrance into a certain segment of society. Thereafter, titles—sometimes culminating in a full list at the time of death—are accumulated. Such an accumulation of roles is also an accumulation of action over time.

Hieroglyphic texts treating courtly elites and political hierarchy also emphasize

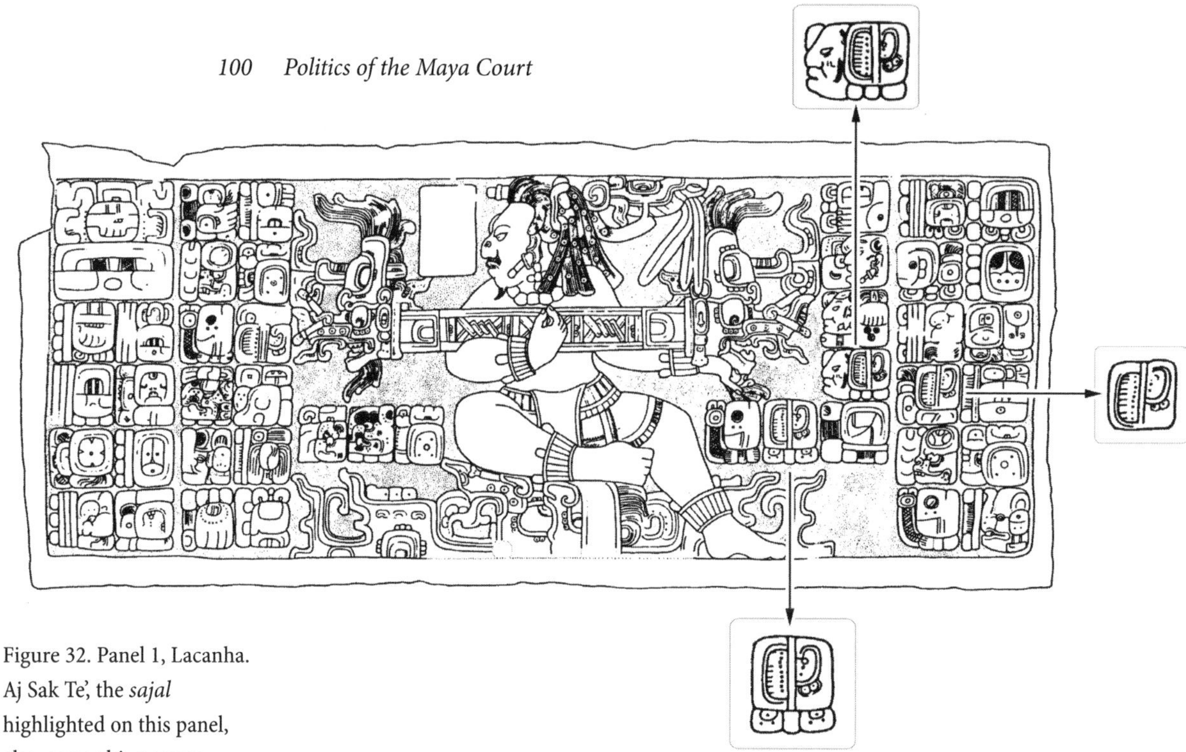

Figure 32. Panel 1, Lacanha. Aj Sak Te', the *sajal* highlighted on this panel, also names his parents, who held the same courtly position. The three *sajal* titles—father, mother, and son—are highlighted. Drawing by David Stuart. Courtesy of David Stuart and Dumbarton Oaks.

ancestors and lineage, highlighting a theme in Maya culture of the ongoing role of ancestors in the lives of their descendants. Textual records are rife with references to those who came before, using such references to provide support for claims of identity and authority for present-day individuals, and in this way indicating how precedent and legitimacy are accumulated. While emphasis on lineage is often discussed in terms of ruling dynasties, courtly elites are no exception in terms of these references to the past.

Panel 1 at Lacanha (figure 32), for example, features the seating into *sajal*-ship of a fellow named Aj Sak Te', who cites his parentage, both mother and father. On this panel, Aj Sak Te' is named as a *sajal*, and also with the less formal honorifics of *anab* and *ch'ajom* (censor). Interestingly, his parents share similar titles, with his father bearing all three and his mother named as an *ix sajal*. (This is a rare instance in which an apparently nonroyal woman carries a courtly title.) This suggests that in some cases (especially for *sajal*s, as it turns out), family connections played a significant role in gaining office. For Aj Sak Te', the citation of his parents provides an important contextualization in the present, both in terms of officers who preceded him and in terms of his particular genealogical connections. This type of reference relates past and present temporal frameworks, indicating connections between individuals and eras and using the past as a foil to contextualize meaning in the present.

These same processes of active reference to the past and use of the past in the present in reference to courtly elites are reflected in a different manifestation on the K'an Tok Panel at Palenque (figure 21). The early mistaken interpretation of this monument as a king list indicates the parallelism between the representation of a "dynasty" typically associated with the ruler and the apparent "dynasty" of titled nobility named in the panel. Significantly for the discussion here of the past in the present, this record of a chain of courtly individuals not only indicates continuity but also suggests the idea of the accumulative weight of the past. A monument such as the K'an Tok Panel emphasizes documentation of history and precedent. Monuments like Altar Q at

Copán, commissioned by Yax Pasaj, the sixteenth ruler, and depicting the sequence of previous rulers at that site (Stuart 1992:170–71), demonstrate this idea graphically as well as textually, by showing on the four sides of the altar the symmetry and completeness that the presentation of self in the company or context of ancestors provides.

In terms of an understanding of change, references to the past—whether textually or materially recorded, and whether true or invented—provide a backdrop of meaning onto which present-day events and practices are superimposed and added. Bricker frames this dual presence of precedent and innovation in terms of blurred distinctions in Maya tradition between myth and history (1981:3–9), an observation that critically reminds us of the relative nature of such categories and the dynamic nature of history and myth in Maya traditions (1981:181). In the Maya worldview, changes are not departures but rather additions, or reconfigurations, and the ability to refer to the past provides necessary justification that these processes represent additional layers, not new structures.

A Close Relationship between Cyclicality and Change

In order to situate what we perceive as important organizational changes of the political landscape of the Late Classic period, we must understand how, for the Maya, change and cyclicality are related concepts. Thinking about accumulation also provides a more nuanced way to think about cyclicality and the effects of conceiving of temporal structures as repeating or circling back. In particular, the idea of accumulation provides a way to conceive of cyclicality as repetition that can also involve change. One can usefully refer here to the modern Tz'utujil concept of *jaloj k'exoj* (Carlsen 1997:50–57), a conception of time that hinges on interlocking concepts of cyclicality (and that also has Classic-era resonances [Carlsen 1997:57–67; Taube 1994:669–75]). The idea of *jaloj k'exoj* combines ideas of change between generations (e.g., replacement of grandparents by grandchildren [Carlsen 1997:54–55; Mondloch 1980]), reflected in the word *k'ex*, and change over the course of a single life cycle (i.e., individual growth and maturation), embodied in the word *jal* (Carlsen 1997:50). These two types of change may be conceptualized as cyclical processes located one within the other, operating simultaneously in order to yield changes at different levels of resolution. Like the idea of accumulation, this concept provides an explanation for how replication does not necessarily yield stasis. Rather, the model imagines incremental change through imperfect or displaced replication that occurs at a variety of scales and for a variety of reasons (intentional or unintentional).

Significantly, the people of Santiago Atitlán couch the concept of *jaloj k'exoj* in agricultural terms (Carlsen 1997:50, 54–57). This contextualization indicates the extent to which natural cycles and agricultural rhythms pervade rural Maya life in the present and would have been similarly important in Classic times. Such ways of life provide a template for understanding a variety of cultural processes. Within this trope, intergenerational change is framed as successive crops of maize plants, with each year's crop replacing the previous, embodied in the seed; individual change is understood as the sprouting and growing of a particular plant.

Such ideas about cyclicality and replacement as a mode of change appear in the Classic period textual record of courts through naming practices, in which personal names are repeated and reconfigured through the generations. Recall the K'utim and Kimi families, both family lines of *sajal*s from the polities of El Cayo and possibly Piedras Negras. In these examples, personal names are repeated through multiple generations of officeholders. This indicates not only that family connections played a role in courtly positions but also that repetitive naming processes indicated a sense of similarity, and even replacement, from generation to generation. Other agricultural connections within the royal court will be discussed as part of a consideration of courtly metaphors in chapter 5. The relationship between cyclicality and change represents a critical point in contextualizing perceived political shifts and strategies of the Late Classic period within central tenets of the Maya worldview.

Long-Term Continuities: Complementary Evidence from Later Sources

Just as I argued in the previous section that change and cyclicality need to be understood as related in order to properly contextualize the Maya royal court, so must we see continuity as a related and important process in describing dynamic cultural institutions. While continuity may seem at odds with the change and variation highlighted in this chapter, identifying variation in courtly configurations conversely suggests key, continuous concepts that underlie the idea and function of courtly structures. Evidence from another era of Maya culture reminds us of continuities that characterize the court over time. Specifically, some aspects of political structure exhibit a basic, shared form over time and were replicated more precisely than others. Looking at much later records of elite political structures from the contact period and postconquest era reveals components of the court system and elite political hierarchy that were especially resilient. These continuities represent profound parts of a system that endured over long periods of time and through significant change in historical context. With these data, one recognizes that the concepts of accumulation and cyclicality discussed above can also yield long-term continuities.

Colonial-era dictionaries and wordlists, recorded by Spanish priests as part of their efforts to learn indigenous languages and hasten the conversion process, bring to light much about the kinds of elite political and organizational structures extant at that time. I have previously examined (Jackson 2005:328–416, 2011) data drawn from four regions in order to shed light on political continuities across multiple eras of Maya culture. The regions and linguistics groups considered were: Yucatán (Yucatec) (Acuña 1993; Ciudad Real and Arzápalo Marín 1995; Pérez and Michelon 1976), highland Chiapas (Tzeltal, Tzotzil) (Ara and Humberto Ruz 1986; Laughlin and Haviland 1988), the Tabasco area (Chontal, Choltí) (Morán and Gates 1935; Scholes and Roys 1968; Smailus 1975), and highland Guatemala (Cakchiquel) (Coto and Acuña 1983; Edmonson 1965; Sáenz de Santa María 1940; Vico and Gates 1913).

Examinations across a wide variety of Colonial contexts reveal that despite considerable linguistic and organizational diversity, a few characteristics are shared across the board among these later-era cultural groups *and* also appear in Late Classic elite contexts (Jackson 2005:411–13, 2011:719–22). Such robust characteristics visible in Colonial-era sources include the presence of one central ruler; the reliance on a council, cabildo, or court, representing shared governance; and the presence of a public political space—court or council house—that houses and embodies community political processes. Tables 1, 2, and 3 show that these characteristics are present in dictionary sources from all four of the linguistic regions examined, demonstrating their ongoing relevance in the political discourse of that historic moment (Jackson 2011:692–93, 696, 707). These fundamental political elements are notably consistent over time between the Classic and Colonial periods. Identifying the importance of a ruler, a group of *principales*, and the building they met in may seem like a less than profound observation. However, the principles of power sharing and negotiation among an elevated group and this group's location within a physical space in the community are critical, if broad, characterizations of both Late Classic characteristics and contact-era political configurations. These components provide a basic political structure for the Late Classic period that is as important for the strategic use of the court as a tool of political continuity as the flexibility and variability that overlaid it.

Notably, the variations that I have argued characterize different versions of Late Classic period courts are similarly visible among the different geographic regions represented by the sources mentioned above. One notable example is that of the Quiché system, which depended on a system of quadripartite rule that combined familial and political hierarchies (Carmack 1981:170) and stands out as a distinctive organizational system. Regional differences such as this one support the idea that specific configurations of courts and positions were contextually driven and varied regionally, even given the presence of the basic shared structures and components identified above.

Change, variation, and continuity are seen in both Classic and Colonial evidence in relation to elite political structures. These observations indicate that imperfect replications allow for adjustments of structures to varying contexts and also yield directional shifts of structures over time. Ongoing replications that show some exactitude of reproduction (that is, continuity) also play a part in the enduring power and stability of political institutions, especially when present in combination with change or variation in other parts.

Table 1. Data from Colonial dictionary sources, indicating the ongoing usage of terms for one central ruler, in multiple regions of the Maya world

Mayan term	*Language*	*Translation*	*Notes*
ahau	Yucatec	rey (king) (Pérez and Michelon 1976:2); rey o emperador, monarca, príncipe o gran señor (king or emperor, monarch, principal or great lord) (Ciudad Real and Arzápalo Marín 1995:7)	
batab	Yucatec	casique que gobierna el pueblo (cacique who governs the community) (Acuña 1993:161)	Interchangeable with "cacique," "gobernador" (Restall 1997:63)
halach uinic	Yucatec	gouernador, nombre de dignidad (governor, dignified name) (Acuña 1993:370)	May be an honorific for a powerful batab (Restall 1997:64) Literally, "true man"
ahau	Chontal, Choltí	rey, señor (king, lord) (Smailus 1975:127); señor (lord) (Morán and Gates 1935:58)	
yum	Chontal, Choltí	señor, also dueño, padre, amo (lord, father, master) (Smailus 1975:179); amo, dueño, señor (Morán and Gates 1935:3)	
aghabetic	Tzeltal	noble, principal (noble, principal) (Ara and Humberto Ruz 1986:241)	
'ojov	Tzotzil	king, lord, master of slaves, prelate (Laughlin and Haviland 1988:151)	"Note that '*'ojov'* is universal for any individual of authority. They even call the alcaldes of their town, the prefects, and the provincial fathers '*'ojov'* in respect. When it is necessary to explain the difference between the king and the others, one must add to king '*sba[1] 'ojov, muk' 'ojov, batz'i 'ojov'*" (Laughlin and Haviland 1988:151). *Ba* is "best," "first," "first in everything," "the first" (Laughlin and Haviland 1988:161); *muk'* is "big," "fat," "greater" (Laughlin and Haviland 1951:263); *batz'i* is "fine," "pure," "very" (Laughlin and Haviland 1988:162)
yumil	Tzeltal	señor (lord) (Ara and Humberto Ruz 1986:314)	
ahav	Cakchiquel	lord (Edmonson 1965:6)	Edmonson notes that this is "a title commonly used in reference to any titled official" (1965:6)
ahau or *ajau*	Cakchiquel	señor, rey, caçique o prinçipal q[ue] gouierna (*ahau*) (lord, king, cacique, or principal who governs) (Coto and Acuña 1983:440, 478, 518); señor, dueño, jefe, cacique (*ajau*) (lord, boss, cacique) (Sáenz de Santa María 1940:34)	

(Table 1, cont.)

Mayan term	*Language*	*Translation*	*Notes*
ah pop	Cakchiquel	king (Edmonson 1965:5); el señor del petate (lord of the mat) (Vico and Gates 1913:319); el s[eño]r dél petate (Coto and Acuña 1983:423)	
camal ruxiquin	Cakchiquel	*ahau*, tiene buen oido (has a good ear) (Vico and Gates 1913:70)	
tepév	Cakchiquel	king, sovereign (Edmonson 1965:121)	Also means "fire" (Edmonson 1965:121)

Source: Jackson 2011:692–93.

1. Should be *ba* rather than *sba*—possible error in Laughlin and Haviland.

Table 2. Data from Colonial dictionary sources, indicating reliance on a council, cabildo, or court, representing shared governance

Mayan term	*Language*	*Translation*	*Notes*
nicteil na	Yucatec	casa de cabildo (building for the cabildo) (Pérez and Michelon 1976:531)	Literally, "flower house"
popol na	Yucatec	casa de cabildo (building for the cabildo) (Pérez and Michelon 1976:531)	Literally, "mat house." Both this and the example above reference long-time symbols of governance
yotoch cah	Yucatec	cabil[do] y lugar donde se juntan a tratar negocios (cabildo and place where they get together to do business) (Acuña 1993:160)	Literally, "the house of the *cah* (or village)"
popol otot	Choltí	cabildo (Morán and Gates 1935:13)	*Popol*—"comunidad" (community); *otot*—"casa" (house) (Morán and Gates 1935:13)
jcha'kel	Tzotzil	council (Laughlin and Haviland 1998:195)	References the root *ch'ak*, which has a wide variety of meanings related to governance and legal cases (Laughlin and Haviland 1988:194)
popol	Cakchiquel	counsel (Edmonson 1965:91)	References a similar root to those seen in Yucatec and Choltí. *Pop*—besides meaning "mat"—can also mean "assemble, meet, group, form a crowd" (Edmonson 1965:91), a reference to the social nature of community rule

Source: Jackson 2011:696.

Table 3. Data from Colonial dictionary sources, indicating the ongoing presence of a public political space—court or council house—that houses and embodies community political processes

Mayan term	*Language*	*Translation*	*Notes*
'ajvalel na or *'ajvayeb na*	Tzotzil	palace (Laughlin and Haviland 1998:152)	Literally, "the house of a master" (Laughlin and Haviland 1988:151)
na 'ojov	Tzotzil	house of the lord (Laughlin and Haviland 1988:265)	
na tekpan	Tzotzil	royal palace (Laughlin and Haviland 1988:265)	Echoing the Nahuatl term and suggesting the impact of interactions with groups from Central Mexico
aghaybna	Tzeltal	palacio (palace) (Ara and Humberto Ruz 1986:241)	Literally, "the house of the lord"
teqpan	Cakchiquel	palacio, casa principal (palace or principal house) (Sáenz de Santa María 1940:360)	Analogous to the Tzotzil example above
nicteil na	Yucatec	casa de cabildo (building for the cabildo) (Pérez and Michelon 1976:531)	Literally, "flower house"
popol na	Yucatec	casa de cabildo (building for the cabildo) (Pérez and Michelon 1976:531)	Literally, "mat house"
yotoch cah	Yucatec	cabil[do] y lugar donde se juntan a tratar negocios (cabildo and place where they get together to do business) (Acuña 1993:160)	Literally, "*cah* house"; etymologically, focused on the broader community
popol otot	Choltí	cabildo (Morán and Gates 1935:13)	Literally, "community house." "Comunidad" is translated as *popol* in this source (Morán and Gates:13)

NOTE: Notice the contrast between the first and second sections (representing emphasis on royal palaces and residences, versus council or community houses).

Source: Jackson 2011:707.

The Late Classic Court as a Strategic Adaptation

Both changes and variations involved in the institution of the court have been discussed in this chapter, as textual data points, as theoretical concepts, and as applied to the interpretation of the Maya royal court. A clear temporal trend for the Late Classic court is represented by a radical increase in records of formal elite positions, and spatial variation unambiguously indicates that the idea of a "court" may have looked very different (or, at the least, been documented with distinctly different emphases) in different places. Explanations that are often given for the apparent boom in courtly elites are sometimes passive (e.g., demographic necessity [McAnany 1993:73-74]) and sometimes active (e.g., kingly efforts to incorporate trenchant nobles [Fash 1988:168; Fash and Stuart 1991:168-75]). Adopting the approach to change and variation espoused here, the Late Classic political shifts seen in the court can be viewed as strategic actions implemented by individuals and groups of individuals, actively responding to local contexts. Let us delve a little deeper into this idea of strategic adaptation and examine how identifiable political changes nonetheless clearly intersect with underlying, continuous cultural concepts.

Sifting through textual data gives us an inkling of the logics that drove Classic Maya behavior, and thus the ways in which change was enacted in culturally meaningful ways. Some of the most familiar tropes of Maya studies emerge when we consider concepts that appear to inform the expansion of the court. These concepts include the conflation or intertwining of religious and political authority, replication of societal structures at multiple levels, agricultural and organic models of a variety of aspects of society, and profound ideas of cyclicality. These concepts, as "cultural logics" (with reference to Fischer 2001:15–19), might be expected to appear in a variety of guises and forms in different realms of Classic Maya life. These are underlying ideas that constrain the processes of change in particular directions. The emergence of courtly elites in terms of numbers, in force of representation in text and writing, and in power or influence becomes legible or comprehensible through the ways these changes obeyed a variety of established cultural dicta apparent in Maya culture. These concepts frame the royal court as both logical and adaptive.

The Nature of Authority

First, the nature of these elite positions echoes the long-term nature of authority in the Maya world, namely the integration of political and religious power. Early evidence in Maya culture (e.g., the San Bartolo murals [Saturno et al. 2006:1282]) suggests that from the first emergence of the office of *ajaw* ("lord"), political leadership involved ritual practice. Political authority was based in part on the prerogative of access to gods and otherworldly spaces and experiences. The very title *k'uhul ajaw* ("holy lord"), used by Classic-era rulers, reflects this political and religious unity. The intertwining of these roles continued throughout the Classic era and likely beyond.

The formalized courtly elite titles seem to follow this pattern of status gained from a combination of political and religious sources. In examining texts and images for evidence of courtly identity, very real and pragmatic activities related to governance and political operation, like the taking of captives (especially for *sajals*), figured large in the depiction of the accomplishments of courtly elite individuals. Similarly, these courtly folk may have been in charge of satellite sites, as in the case of some *sajals*. Courtiers helped to control the flow of information and specialized knowledge, as in the case of scribal or craft knowledge (Stuart 1989b), such as at Aguateca (Inomata 2001b). They also organized their own hierarchies of elites below them (as in the example of Aj Sik'ab at Palenque).

At the same time, like the ruler, courtly elites are marked by access and responsibility to the spiritual world in a way that complemented their terrestrial responsibilities. Courtly elites are frequently depicted as assistants or witnesses at ritual events carried out by the ruler (e.g., Chak Tun and K'an Nik Te' of Piedras Negras and others discussed in chapter 2). In some situations they seem to have had their own personal relationship with otherworldly entities, such as Kelen Hix's connection to the paddler gods at Toniná. Some courtly roles are even cast as a cosmological doubling of the world-bearing *pauahtun*s (with examples seen at, e.g., Pomoná and Laxtunich, a topic further explored in chapter 5). In this way, these newly foregrounded courtly positions nonetheless conform to expectations of the nature of authority.

Structural Replication

In addition to continuing an ongoing trope of political/religious conflation of authority, these courtly elite roles also—in a related way—involve the replication of social and political structures at multiple levels. This kind of replication has been noted previously (e.g., Vogt 1969:571–81) in terms of households, social structures, and settlement patterns. In the case of the court, it involved a nesting of roles, in which courtly elite positions imitated the ruler at a lower level in the authoritative hierarchy, as in the parallel sources of power just discussed. The echoing of processes of investiture similarly suggests an imitative aspect or parallel between these various types of roles. Too, the grammatical and metaphorical "possession" of courtly elites by rulers (indicated by possessed forms of titles—for example, *yajk'uhuun* or "his *ajk'uhuun*") is at times imitated through the claiming of lesser elites by more exalted elites (as in the case of Aj Sik'ab from Palenque, discussed in chapter 2). At a more theoretical level, recall the consideration of models for the court in chapter 1, in which the nested concept of the house society was identified as potentially useful for understanding Maya organization (Joyce and Gillespie 2000; Lévi-Strauss 1984). At an institutional level, the court could then be seen metaphorically (if not theoretically [Houston and McAnany 2003; Watanabe 2004]) as an exalted household space, writ large.

All of these instances indicate imitation or replication happening between different levels of organization. The logic of the structure of the court and its membership seems to be underwritten by its placement, at both individual and institutional levels, within repeated frameworks. New or different configurations are strategically folded into a nested and replicated structure that couches them as integral and sensical.

Agricultural Connections

In examining courtly structural replication, the bringing together of different levels not only juxtaposes cosmological and political realms but unites political realms with less exalted quotidian spheres. In particular, we might think of the agricultural cycle, a structuring experience for many Maya people, the vast majority of whom were involved in food production. Elites and political authority are linked to these fundamental processes through the use of words that echo organic and plant cycles. These ideas will be explored in greater detail in chapter 5; I provide a few brief examples for now. One such example is the naming of young people (possibly including heirs) as *ch'ok*, or a green or unripe person, a descriptor that came up in chapter 3 and that we have seen applied to individuals like Ahkmo' from Site R. We also see iconographic and textual representations of elites (both rulers and their courtiers) as trees, sprouts, and plants. A prime example of this is the iconography on the sides of Pakal's Sarcophagus at Palenque, an example to which I will return. Additionally, governmental processes of change and oversight are described through agricultural vocabulary of tending and growing.

Here a cognitive model that is inarguably explicitly available to the entirety of the population, and which harkens back to the mythological importance of organic substances such as maize, frames the upper echelons of the reigning hierarchy in an accessible and integral way.

Location within Larger Cycles

Connected to these agricultural ideas is the final "logic" proposed above: an experience of time and history as cyclical. Of course, an agricultural trope leads to the experience of time in this way (e.g., as signified by the modern Tz'utujil concept of *jaloj k'exoj*, describing the organic cycling of short- and long-term change [Carlsen 1997:50]). The Maya Calendar Round similarly provides an obvious impetus for understanding the movement of time as repeating. These types of cyclical change are represented in the court in several ways. They are documented through reference to past rulers, as seen on Altar Q at Copán, with its visual documentation of the history of Copán rulership, providing a wonderful symbolization of this concept. The repetition of formalized offices occupied by different individuals through time, as exemplified by the K'an Tok Panel, is similarly powerful. Additionally, the commemoration of anniversaries by rulers with the assistance of elites, such as the celebrations shown on Piedras Negras Panel 3, illustrates this concept.

All of these instances, and the underlying ideas, suggest that not only was change viewed as organic (and thus natural or unthreatening) but also shifts such as the changes in the structure of the Late Classic political system would have been contextualized in larger historical loops, in which the present was transitory and the past could or would be revisited.

The Adaptive Mechanism of the Court

As a strategy for adjusting existent political systems to the changing historical contexts of the Late Classic era, increasing the elevation of and reliance on titled courtly elites was an extremely adaptive solution. Governing structures continued to emphasize continuity and connection with the past by operating within profound cultural systems and models. Simultaneously, Maya rulers were able to change the distribution of power from an Early Classic emphasis on a single axis mundi of *k'uhul ajaw*-ship to a cosmic model of central power (still denoted by the ruler himself) and integrated supports. This new-old model, by activating the cultural concepts discussed above, incorporated elites seemingly effortlessly into the ruling system as critical parts of the political system. The apparently flexible form that courts took in different places allowed for the successful adaptation of this mechanism to local circumstances.

Having seen the ways in which courtly changes make sense within larger conceptual spheres, we can better understand these changes as resulting from logical behaviors that were neither random nor desperate but rather reflected actions that operated successfully within the bounds of cultural constraints, while accommodating new pressures faced by the rulers. Late Classic rulers chose to modify the political order in particular ways in order to maintain their authority, while also responding to historical circumstance. Their "imperfect" replication of previous structures was profoundly adaptive, at least temporarily, allowing them to use change to express continuity for themselves and those beneath them in Maya society.

This chapter has examined change and variation in order to understand what was going on in the Late Classic period in the realms of political hierarchy and organization and, subsequently, how these processes of change were actually enacted. The ideas and data discussed in the chapter are especially important in understanding movement (whether change, variation, or continuity) as a culturally legible strategy that grew out of long-term Maya traditions, even while it represented an observable change in hierarchical organization and governance. These data and ideas provide a context and framework for understanding the political landscape of the Late Classic period. The chapter has also made clear that the processes at work in this era were culturally meaningful and contextually specific. The cultural meanings of the Maya royal court are further explored in the next chapter, where I examine metaphorical framings that illuminate the significance of this institution in Maya terms.

CHAPTER FIVE

Metaphors, from the Quotidian to the Sublime

In this chapter I turn to culturally informed ways of understanding elite hierarchies and the Classic Maya royal court. Accessing internal perspectives on these topics involves thinking about kinds of change or transformation different from those discussed in the preceding chapter. Here I consider the transformation of real-world political structures into metaphorical ways of representing and thinking about these institutions, a change that involves both a flexible movement between two realms of communication and understanding and the use of metaphor to talk about political organization. I refer here not to metaphor invoked by modern scholars but rather metaphors that were used by the Maya themselves and that reveal important aspects of their conception and understanding of political systems and differentiation.

Two metaphors are used in Maya sources to couch the work of the court and the identity of its members: an agricultural one, in which the court is connected with the work of farming and organic growth, and a cosmological one, in which the court is compared with exalted, other-worldly spaces and organizations. I translate these metaphors into two suggested equivalences that frame the Classic royal court: rule and agriculture, and status and godliness. These associations will be explored in the pages that follow; for now, let me put two images in front of your eyes in order to plant the seeds of these metaphors. Figure 33 shows an elite individual—an ancestor of Palenque's ruler, Pakal, as a sprouting, fruiting shoot, emerging from the surface of the earth. Figure 34 shows a courtier from Laxtunich holding up the Celestial Monster, an embodiment of the cosmos, which also supports the ruler who sits upon it. We will return to both of these examples and to the equivalences that they represent.

This chapter focuses on metaphors that are significant for understanding Maya political hierarchy. Courtly metaphors provide a window onto perceptions of the meaning and power of the court in Classic Maya times. To what extent can a close examination of metaphor reveal the intended meanings that were assigned to the court? Do these metaphors reveal anything about strategic management of Late Classic political change? While a number of the concordances that I discuss have previously been identified by other scholars (e.g., the association of elite individuals with natural or plantlike models [see, e.g., Houston and Cummins 2004:367] or the divine mandate for earthly courts [including Houston 1998:352–56; Miller and Martin 2004:51–65]), they have not been discussed in a unified way, or using a theoretical and explanatory framework of metaphor, in order to illuminate the royal court. In order to contextualize the metaphors that were used to talk about the Maya

Figure 33. Close-up of east side of Pakal's Sarcophagus, Palenque. An image of one of Pakal's ancestors, sprouting from the surface of the earth as a plant, representing the first of the courtly metaphors I discuss. Drawing by Merle Greene Robertson. Copyright Merle Greene Robertson, 1976.

Figure 34. Close-up of Lintel 4, Laxtunich. A courtly elite individual simultaneously appearing as a cosmological support, representing the second of the courtly metaphors I discuss. Photograph courtesy of www.mayavase.com.

royal court, I begin by considering some brief theoretical commentary on metaphor; I also discuss metaphor use in Mesoamerica. With these foundational pieces in mind, the particular metaphors that couch the court can be more transparently understood as part of Maya strategies that use metaphor to frame certain practices and institutions.

Metaphor as Powerful, Constructive, and Systematic

Before turning to metaphor in Mesoamerica and the specific metaphors that framed the court, I want to briefly suggest a few ideas about metaphor that indicate how it moves beyond a literary device and how it helps us understand cultural institutions like the Classic Maya royal court. We will see that metaphors accomplish constructive work and form systems of meaning that reveal culturally constructed ways of thinking.

Metaphor is a term familiar from junior high school English classes, where one learns that this figure of speech involves comparison between two unlike things in order to highlight certain similarities. Metaphor, as discussed in this chapter, takes on additional significance beyond a purely literary device; nonetheless, the elements of metaphor as a figure of speech remain useful in thinking about how it operates. Fundamentally, a metaphor juxtaposes two entities or ideas in order to emphasize (and sometimes hide) particular aspects (Lakoff and Johnson 1980:10–13). The shared characteristics that build a connecting bridge between the parts of a metaphor are subsequently extrapolated in order to explicitly or implicitly suggest other similarities between the two parts—an extrapolation that activates the creative powers of metaphor. This chapter moves beyond directly stated metaphors to consider the ways in which cultural metaphors may be systematically represented through verbal expression and imagery. As a starting point in looking at both textually and visually recorded metaphors, we may deploy a basic working definition of metaphor as a culturally defined comparison between disparate entities that serves to draw attention to particular real or desired commonalities held by the two.

Metaphor must be understood as more than an expression or a turn of phrase (Lakoff and Johnson 1980:5). Why are metaphors powerful? What work do they accomplish that makes them a key part of the larger quest to understand a culture? Metaphors do more than reveal something about a particular time and place. Metaphors actually accomplish things. Austin has argued that language does not merely describe events as they happen. In his view, language can actually make things happen—such as in performative phrases like those connected with naming, betting, and marrying ("I hereby pronounce you man and wife!") (1962:5). This perspective recognizes that language can be active, accomplishing actions and effecting change through words themselves. In the Maya metaphors discussed in this chapter, implicit and explicit comparisons are not used as literary adornments or simple descriptive operators. Instead they create and subsequently reinforce certain realities and relationships—such as the systems of difference that underlay the court—based on repeated use of certain metaphorical systems. Lakoff and Johnson argue that, rather than being esoteric or flowery, "metaphor is pervasive in everyday life, not just in language but in thought and action" (1980:3). If metaphors are omnipresent in how people act and interface with their social and physical surroundings, then accessing such metaphors represents an important route for entering an emic perspective of a given culture.

In addition to functioning as isolated comparative devices, metaphors can operate systematically, forming a consistent structure of discourse and revealing important beliefs or perspectives. Metaphorical concepts that describe or address entire ideas, processes, or collections of objects serve to communicate statements beyond the immediate comparison constructed. In a classic example, the North American expression "time is money" is a metaphor in its unification of two disparate entities in order to highlight or create similarities between them (discussed, e.g., in Lakoff and Johnson [1980:7–9]). This metaphor is indicative of a larger conceptual system in North American culture, in which time—and work and productivity—are understood in economic and monetary terms. We see both time and money on similar meters—numerically saved up, spent, or wasted; such ideas demonstrate very real ways in which our culture then operates, such as the saving up of vacation days. While such conceptual metaphors may be reduced to a single statement ("time is money"), the offshoots of this root metaphor can be seen in many other expressions, actions, and ways of thinking. In this way, the two entities that are drawn together through metaphor are not single things or ideas but rather domains that allow for a complex set of illuminations to occur through the implementation of the metaphor. In thinking about evidence for metaphors from the Classic Maya world, I focus on two conceptual metaphors—one that references agriculture and the other, cosmological entities and spaces—that define the royal court and, by extension, ancient understandings of hierarchy and sociopolitical difference.

Metaphors in Mesoamerica

Transpositions and Transitive Thinking

Let us first consider the presence, in the Maya worldview, of what might be termed transitive thinking. Maya thought in past and present contexts frequently invites movement between diverse realms or meanings. Multiple examples of substitutions or transformations are present in the Maya worldview, and these operate in ways analogous to metaphorical pairings.

Those familiar with the Maya recognize the pervasiveness of metaphorical connections, highlighting interrelationships between different levels of experience in the Maya world. Examination of the landscape, for example, reveals intriguing equivalences between geographic features (e.g., mountains, caves, springs) and religious spaces, as part of a Mesoamerican conception of the sacred landscape (Carrasco 1990:51–52). In a particularly notable example, the connections drawn between mountains and temples are not only attested to verbally (in ethnographic contexts) and visually, but also include overlaps in glyphic descriptions through the use of the term *witz*, or "mountain," to reference temple structures (Stuart 1997a:263).

In another realm of transformation or transposition, rulers appear to have had particularly powerful bodies that harbored profound connections with other entities. Stuart has discussed correspondences between rulers and stone monuments, suggesting that carved standing stelae may have acted as stand-ins for the ruler taking part in ritual action (1996:160). This type of substitution plays on apparent visual similarities between carved representations of ruling individuals and their actual bodies and accesses culturally specific understandings of the meaning of representation and the nature of the self (Houston and Stuart 1998:90–92; Stuart

1996:158–65). Rulers and gods were also at times able to share the same identity or corporeal manifestation through the practice of deity impersonation (Houston 2006:145–49; Houston and Stuart 1996:297–98), representing a moment in which different entities from separable realms were brought together with dramatic effect. Rulers (and others) also embodied multiple essences and exemplified substitution of different entities through coessences or *way*s (animal alter egos) (Houston and Stuart 1989:6–7). Belief in animal others highlights a profound connection between human beings and particular animals, as well as the possibility of personal transformation (Monaghan 1998:142–43). The use of masks in Mesoamerican contexts similarly relates to the possibility of enacting equivalences between different things (e.g., Markman and Markman 1989: xix–xx).

Another example of a powerful correspondence in Maya thought is illustrated by the symbolic importance of maize. Maize was important as both a subsistence resource and a religious one. As referenced in the sacred Maya book *Popol Vuh*, human flesh and maize are a shared substance, with humans being created by the gods from corn dough (Christenson 2010:580–83; Taube 1993:53–54). The "lifecycle of maize," and agricultural practice generally, forms a basis for much of Maya religious belief and mythology (Carrasco 2010:601, 602), uniting two separate realms of practice (agricultural work and religious observance) in a paired framework. Within these joined worldviews of agricultural and religious action, the Maize God figures particularly prominently. The figure of the Maize God directly evokes an ear of corn in his representation (Taube 1985:171–73). In turn, depictions of rulers indicate correspondences between their own physical attributes and those of the Maize God (e.g., as seen in depictions of Pakal at Palenque), referencing the conception of the Maize God as an ideal to which they would aspire (Miller and Samayoa 1998:57). The centrality and value of both maize and the Maize God in Maya contexts leads to additional associations between other precious materials and corn. Miller and Samayoa argue for similarity between quetzal feathers and maize silk (1998:65) and for jade beads as metaphorical maize kernels (1998:58). Practice in agricultural and religious realms also echoed each other: sacrifice events, such as those depicted in the Bonampak murals may represent the "husking" of captives' bodies (Miller and Samayoa 1998:65).

As can be seen through these examples, the precious substance of maize provides a substrate for a variety of other meanings in both daily and exalted realms and is a material of particularly rich, multivocalic interpretation in Maya contexts. It is a base for metaphors or comparisons of a variety of types and in this way becomes a touchstone for the construction of diverse meanings. As will be seen below in discussing Classic-era court-specific metaphors, maize and agriculture figure prominently in framing governance as well. In a larger sense, the use of maize to construct meaning in various realms further underlines the presence and power of metaphorical and transpositional thinking in Maya contexts.

The examples discussed above indicate that there are predispositions in Maya belief and practice to understand different realms of the world as overlapping and having meaningful connections. Indeed, Marcos argues—in thinking about bodies and religious metaphor—that "Mesoamerican thought is framed by metaphors" (2006:64). While not all of the examples mentioned here are expressed as metaphors per se, they indicate sensitivity to the possibility of transposition and to the meanings that may result from the connection of ostensibly separate or different entities. The more overt metaphors used for the court are not just descriptive devices but rather part of a larger set of understandings of transformation or transitivity present within the Maya worldview.

Metaphors in Action in Mesoamerica

In addition to identifying a pattern of metaphor usage in Mesoamerica, we must also consider what cultural work metaphors carry out. Two examples of metaphors in comparative Mesoamerican contexts illustrate the power of what metaphors do: they help to instruct, and they structure action. Metaphors are particularly useful for exploring structures of institutions—like the court—because of their didactic role and relationship to "normative discourses" (Marcos 2006:67, 70), referencing cultural perspectives and practices that we can derive from them. The examples I explore in this section are not from the Classic era, but they do provide evidence for how metaphors have operated and been used in Mesoamerican contexts in more recent time periods.

An early Colonial example of metaphor recorded in Mesoamerica provides evidence for the idea of metaphors as instructional and used to reinforce societal mores, in this case among the Aztec. A manuscript written by the Spanish priest Fray Andrés de Olmos demonstrates the codified nature of metaphors and how they were used to communicate and teach fundamental concordances in the world (Maxwell and Hanson 1992). *Arte para Aprender la Lengua Mexicana*, dating to 1547, represents Olmos's efforts to record linguistic and ethnographic evidence of the people and cultures he encountered. Olmos recorded them "as examples of elegant language use" and illustrations of ancient or typical ways of speaking (Maxwell and Hanson 1992:19). Their "metaphorical nature" involves the multiple layers of literal and implied meaning that they encode. Some of these even relate to governance. For example, one Metaphor of Olmos's, titled "Authority as Bearer," reads: "Carrying cloth, carrying frame/he spreads the cloth, he straightens it./He is wise, he is centered./He carries the load, he bears the burden./Deftly he cradles it/as the back he bears, as shoulders he/supports great burdens./He sows, he rules, he governs" (Maxwell and Hanson 1992:170). The metaphorical references (burdens, agriculture) are familiar to us from Maya contexts as well (indeed, analogous usage of figurative language can be found in Maya texts such as *Popol Vuh* [Tedlock 1996] and *The Annals of the Cakchiquels* [Recinos et al. 1953]). The flowery, evocative language provides a taste of what the performed forms of Classic period texts might have been like.

Maxwell and Hanson argue that, over time, some correspondences between components of metaphors, including these, would have progressed to a point where a productive comparison between unlike objects would no longer have been comprehended, yielding a connection in which one thing stands directly for another; they term such instances "fossilized" or "frozen" metaphors (1992:23). Given the paucity of literary sources from Classic contexts, one wonders if the only metaphors emerging in modern analysis are those that would qualify for the frozen status, due to their ancient ubiquity. Frozen metaphors are also those which were likely referred to in the past with frequency, in formal or informal didactic contexts. Certainly, the ones accessible to us must represent only a small selection of a rich symbolic framework employed in the Classic era.

While the Maya instances discussed below are not codified into an instructional text, as the Olmos examples are, they may still be scrutinized for repeated references that suggest fundamental ways of understanding. The Olmos manuscript reminds us of the oral nature of some metaphorical expressions, the ways that metaphor would have tied into a long pan-Mesoamerican tradition of speech making and poetic expression (Houston and Stuart 2001:59; Stuart 1995:190–91), as well as the role of such expressions in teaching appropriate "manners of speaking"—and of thinking, or being in the world.

In considering what metaphors are able to accomplish, ethnographic examples from Yucatán illustrate the ways in which metaphors are imbricated with, and inspire, action. Hanks's linguistic and anthropological work with modern Maya groups in Yucatán provides a source for understanding the processes by which linguistic and cognitive connections are made and are dynamically enacted through lived practices (1990, 1999). His discussions of ritual practice, in particular, reveal that such charged moments involve the crossing and drawing together of disparate spaces and times (a common description of ritually active space [e.g., Turner 1969]). This is a dramatized version of what metaphor accomplishes.

For example, Hanks discusses the parallels between agricultural work and ritual activity. In describing the carefully prescribed boundary marking activities involved with the placement of a new milpa, or cornfield, he observes that the actions undertaken by a farmer establishing a plot for his crops "are homologous with ritual practices" (1990:356). There are telling similarities between marking off and preparing land for crops and ritually demarcating spaces inhabited by particular spirits or intended for particular religious activities.

This close association between different spatial or functional spheres in Maya thinking is also apparent in a temporal sense. Hanks records a conversation he had with Don Seéb, a modern-day Yucatec Maya shaman, while they were walking together at the archaeological site of Labna: "We were visiting the site together, when he [Don Seéb] told me that he often came here and walked the ground. The difference was that when he came, it was still densely populated with Maya nobles and there was a great bustling marketplace in the center. The Labna that I knew well was an archaeological monument, partly in ruin and surely not inhabited by anyone other than the INAH guard and his family. Walking side-by-side, we were nonetheless inhabiting different temporal frameworks" (1990:230).

Don Seéb's ability to access experiences of the Classic period world was, in part, a result of his powerful position as a shaman; his talent in transposing his thinking (or self) would not be accessible to all Maya peoples, past or present. However, like the example of milpa placement mentioned above, it illustrates the familiarity of juxtaposed and even overlaid layers of perception in Maya thought. These correspondences operate similarly to the juxtaposition that is inherent in metaphorical constructions. Both serve to highlight and strengthen ties between disparate entities.

Hanks discusses ritual practice as characterized by the inhabitation of different temporal schemes (1999:230): it represents a "borderzone between the local emerging present and the global memorial past [that] can be crossed in both directions" (1999:236). He observes that the experience of such moments indicates a permeability between distinctive spheres (1999:237), the bridging of which involves processes of relating and transforming—both of the present reality into another space/time and of a distinct space/time into the present (1999:237, 238–39, 241). The result is a "dynamic field" associated with ritual practices, "in which the infinitely many potential differences between things are recast into meaningful opposition" (Hanks 1999:246). The transpositional modes of thinking and experience that I have suggested permeate Maya and Mesoamerican thought also impact action in the real world. That is, these lived "metaphors" frequently relate to experiences and occurrences.

Hanks's ethnographic observations have a larger implication for understanding metaphor in Mesoamerican contexts and for our project of exploring courtly metaphors. They illustrate that aspects of everyday experience could be penetrated by influences or entities from other places and times. That is, identity or self was not fixed in space or time in the ways that a twenty-first-century North American might imagine. Extending the textual sense of metaphor to this field of action, connections or similarities drawn between human individuals and entities inhabiting another time/space effected transformations based on this affinity; this "metaphor" is enacted in ritual or otherwise marked moments. Hanks's discussion of ritual transpositions reminds us of the lived and experiential aspects of metaphor. Courtly metaphors would not have been pretty descriptive devices but rather embodied ways of thinking that impacted how actions and decisions unfolded.

Ethnohistoric evidence, such as that of Olmos, as well as ethnographic evidence, such as that discussed by Hanks, provides support for the idea that metaphor (even when not named with that term), as a process of culturally informed concordance, operated as a powerful force. It impacted communication and understanding in patterned ways in Mesoamerican cultures of the past and the present. Such metaphorical connections are written literally in texts but are also recorded through religious action and linguistic practice.

These examples may not all qualify as formal "metaphors," but they do convey the senses of transitivity that have colored Maya individuals' interaction with, and understanding of, the world. The metaphors that frame the royal court discussed below are much more explicit—I address clear evidence of culturally specific relationships, not just general interpretations of connection—and are reflected in glyphic, iconographic, and historical linguistic records. These remains of Late Classic metaphors may seem static or skeletal. I ask you to imagine the beautiful and influential language of Olmos's informants and the transformational experiences of Hanks's collaborators performing intertwined ritual and agricultural practices. These comparative examples provide possibilities for envisioning how earlier metaphors would have had a life of their own and been important parts of the lives and ideas of Classic Maya individuals.

Classic Maya Metaphors in the Court

What can metaphors reveal about the meanings and significance of the Late Classic Maya court? Can they help us to comprehend how this institution would have been understood by people of that era? My goal in investigating courtly metaphors is to find evidence of the conceptual systems that were operating at the time and that framed the institution of the court. Comparative material from Colonial and modern contexts should be taken not as proof—we know that metaphors may shift organically or intentionally and may be locally situated—but rather as potential support for particularly deeply rooted ways of thinking. In light of the project of this book, I focus on unearthing metaphors that were related to ideas about elites and governance and how inequality and rule were conceptualized and articulated. Two recurring and ultimately interrelated tropes highlighted—in the most simply articulated form—equivalences between rule and agriculture, and status and godliness.

Agricultural Connections

The quotidian aspect of the first framing casts the work of the court as agricultural. Organic and plantlike connections in the court surface in several ways, some of which indicate connections between people of the court and plants; others describe the political trappings and undertakings of the court in light of plants and harvesting. In a culture in which maize agriculture has long provided the basis of subsistence, and in which maize itself is a sacred substance connected to the mythical process of creation, such a metaphor would have resonated at a fundamental level with all members. In his consideration of records of maize in linguistic as well as iconographic evidence in Mesoamerica, Stross reminds us of fundamental connections between maize and the human body in Mesoamerica (2006:581); Sandstrom makes similar points based on ethnographic work in a modern Nahua village in Mexico (1991:216). (Interestingly, profound connections between elite authority and agricultural practice are also noted among the Inca of South America, where ruling individuals even took part in ceremonial plowing and planting [Bauer 1996:327, 328, 330]. Like the Maya, the Inca saw their ruling elites as defined by connections to both divinity and agriculture [Bauer 1996:333].) The line between corn and living people is a permeable one, making this an ideal site for an evocative and powerful metaphor.

The connection between people and plants originates early in life, with the use of the word *ch'ok* to refer to young people (Houston and Stuart 2001:67). As has come up earlier, *ch'ok* literally means a green or unripe thing (in a modern Ch'orti' dictionary it is defined as *tierno*—"tender" or "fresh" [Pérez Martínez et al. 1996:58]). This equation casts the body not just as related to the organic world of growth but specifically as a plant itself. There may be particular connections between the term *ch'ok* and heirs or young lords, as indicated by the use of the apparent ranked appellation, *baah ch'ok* ("head youth"), or by naming royal sons *ch'ok ajaw* ("young lord") as is seen on Piedras Negras Panel 3 (Houston and Inomata 2009:144). Examples of *ch'ok* recorded in combination with official titles include *ch'ok sajal*s at Laxtunich (Lintel 2), Site R (Lintel 1), and Sak Tz'i' (Randel Stela), and the use of *chak ch'ok* (or "very young") with the *sajal* title at Xcalumkín (Column 3) and Xcombec (carved pier). Individuals who are new to a position, or destined for a future position, are green or unripe before they "grow into" it.

The correspondence between bodies and growing, sprouting plants is made visually unequivocal in imagery on the sides of Pakal's Sarcophagus at Palenque. Here ancestors of Pakal, including former rulers, are depicted as sprouting from the surface of the earth (figure 35). They display attributes of plants (leaves and fruits), which some scholars have associated with particular species (Greene Robertson 1983:65–73; Miller and Martin 2004:207; Schele and Miller 1986:284–85). Schele and Mathews refer to this remarkable assemblage of sprouting elites as "an orchard

Figure 35. East side of Pakal's Sarcophagus, Palenque. Pakal's ancestors are portrayed as leafy and fruited plants, sprouting from the surface of the earth. Drawing by Merle Greene Robertson. Copyright Merle Greene Robertson, 1976.

of ancestors" and emphasize the connection of generational rebirth or resurrection with plants (1998:122–23). Pakal's body within the sarcophagus would have been positioned in the central place, in death as in life, embodying a world tree among a larger, sprouting wood (Schele and Mathews 1998:125).

The imagery on Pakal's Sarcophagus connects with themes related to the court and governance through the framing of political power and authority in organic terms. McAnany points out the intentional association between the valued, multigenerational resource of fruiting orchards and Pakal's ancestors, who represent resources of power and authority (1995:75–76). The powerful moment of Pakal's resurrection that is depicted on the face of the sarcophagus lid is also connected to the seasonal rebirth invoked by depictions of sprouting plants. The organic aspects of his symbolic resurrection as the Maize God (Aldana 2007:122; Martin 2006:162) are reinforced through both his own representation and those of his ancestors. The naturalized cycles of rebirth and replacement depicted in this imagery (Stuart and Stuart 2008:180) are similarly used to frame processes of elite governance, as will be seen below.

While the individuals shown on the sides of the sarcophagus are members of the royal family and not explicit representations of titled members of the court, they are depicted here as providing organic support to Pakal's central claim of power in an analogous way to courtiers. Martin reminds us that as sprouting plants, these surrounding figures draw strength from the decomposing body within the sarcophagus (2006:162), another layer of the theme of replacement and regeneration that characterizes the iconography of Pakal's burial and demonstrates the dendritic nature of hierarchical authority. The significance of the sprouting ancestors' presence here is as evergreen witnesses to Pakal's moment of rebirth, as embodiments of valued resources, and as offshoots of the central stem of Pakal.[1] These are similar roles to

1. The interconnection and interchangeability between older and younger generations, as described by the concept of *k'ex* (Carlsen 1997:51; Mondloch 1980:9), suggests that a strict distinction in role between ancestor and descendant may not always be appropriate.

those played by courtly members and may serve as a template for the desired positioning and responsibilities of nonancestral supports. The royal ancestors shown on the sides of the sarcophagus represent idealized versions of the plant/body; court members play parallel roles in their plantlike framings.

Later sources support the idea of elite bodies, more generally, having organic or vegetal aspects. In Colonial dictionaries, elite bodies are described as plantlike; the Yucatec example of *u chun thanob*, meaning "principales o primeros del pueblo" (i.e., "principal or first people of the village") (Pérez and Michelon 1976:708), which may be literally translated as "principal words," recalls speechlike associations with other Mesoamerican leadership terms, such as *ajaw* and *tlatoani* (Houston and Stuart 2001:59; Stuart 1995:190–91). However, this term may be understood more abstractly as "root of power" (*chun*—"foot or root of a tree" [Ciudad Real and Arzápalo Marín 1995:251]; *than*—"force or power" [Ciudad Real and Arzápalo Marín 1995:734]). In this instance, the body/plant connection is extended beyond royal bodies and is used in a political sphere, indicating that this is not solely a reference to ancestors but rather a mode for describing roles and interconnections between ranked individuals. The image of elites as roots or parts of trees conjures up a metaphor commented upon by López Austin: the pan-Mesoamerican "archetype of the plant cycle" (1997:10–11), which positions the ruler as a world tree among four directionally situated, smaller trees that "represented natural models for ancillary lords at court" (Houston and Cummins 2004:367).

Olmos's text, discussed above, includes references to governance framed in an agricultural model. These echo the metaphors seen in Classic Maya contexts, providing evidence for the fossilization process of the metaphor through the replication of a conceptual model across multiple cultural contexts. The examples that Olmos collected include several instances in which rulers are described as sprouting or rooting (Metaphor XLI—Succession) (Maxwell and Hanson 1992:183). Authority "fosters the growth, the greening" (Metaphor IV—Authority as Model) (Maxwell and Hanson 1992:170), and the leader "sows," "rules," and "governs" (Metaphor III—Authority as Bearer) (Maxwell and Hanson 1992:170), suggesting an organic model for understanding leadership and responsibility in that later era.

In considering the salience of an agricultural metaphor for the Classic Maya court, the parallels are animated beyond a simple association of human and vegetal bodies. This metaphor also references larger processes—including political processes—that reflect those of the natural world. *Jaloj k'exoj* (also mentioned in chapter 4) provides a point of access for examining organic or agricultural framings for courtly work. The framing of life processes—for elites and nonelites alike—as part of cyclical patterns that replicate agricultural cycles is cogently discussed for modern Maya settings by Carlsen (1997), who notes that *jaloj k'exoj* represents two intertwined types of changes. Individual change is referred to by *jal*—change within a particular, individual life, represented by the husk of a plant (Carlsen 1997:50). Generational change is *k'ex*, represented by crop cycles or life cycles and connected to ideas of ancestry and replacement by offspring, seeds, and sprouts (Carlsen 1997:50). These terms are used to discuss pragmatic, quotidian matters, such as naming practices, but they also represent a key structuring mechanism of Atiteco traditional religion (Carlsen 1997:51). The concept of *jaloj k'exoj* provides a way of understanding change at both human and cultural levels as related to the seasonal, organic, and growth-related processes so familiar to Maya individuals in both the present and the past. These types of change are documented in early Colonial sources and likely provide hints of conceptualizations from the Classic era as well.

Glimpses of earlier incarnations of *jaloj k'exoj* are documented linguistically in ethnohistoric materials dating to the decades after initial contact between the Spanish and Maya populations (Jackson 2011:713–17). Evidence for the presence of organically oriented thought in connection with ruling elites emerges through the use of terms for types of political change that cast elite players in plantlike roles. In particular, words linguistically related to *jal* and *k'ex* are used to describe the transfer of authority from one officeholder to another (table 4). The use of terms related to both *jal* and *k'ex* emphasizes different types of change: the personal evolution of a maturing individual into an officeholder or principal, as well as the replicative process (echoing that which occurs in generations of a family) by which new officials replace old ones. While these terms are not explicitly recorded in the text that runs around the edge of Pakal's Sarcophagus, for instance, the imagery there highlights the Classic-era conception of the close connection between transfer of authority and organic processes of change.

These Colonial examples indicate that ideas of organic change that are readily identifiable in present-day ethnographic contexts were also present in post-contact situations. Furthermore, these post-contact instances related specifically to elite community members. Colonial examples indicate that the same connections to the botanical world implied by the Atiteco metaphor very likely informed discourse on change in the Colonial era as well. It is significantly more challenging to locate a direct connection to *jaloj k'exoj* in Classic-period evidence; one possible example is naming patterns that appear to follow the rules of *k'ex* have been cited in support of the longevity of this framework (e.g., Houston and Inomata 2009:211). Nonetheless, indirect references to the same concepts of organic change and substitution seem to be employed.

As we consider the agricultural metaphor used to frame the Classic-period royal court, we have already seen evidence to support the bodies-as-plants trope. In surveying instances in which elites are discussed or portrayed in connection with plants, it emerges that courtly elites may also take the role of planters, serving to protect and care for the community, portrayed as a metaphorical milpa. These are observations that Houston and Cummins have made in relation to the ruler himself (2004:367) but that in reality apply to authority that extends beyond the parameters of royal prerogative.

Not only in Colonial- but also in Classic-era texts, models of government officials as farmers emerge through descriptions of political work as related to agricultural tasks. In Tzotzil such a conflation is seen in terms such as "winnowing," used, for example, to describe the task of selecting a new person for office: *jt'ujom* ("elector"), coming from the root of *t'uj* ("winnow") (Laughlin and Haviland 1988:324). Furthermore, Houston and Cummins have commented on the use of the term *u-chab'-jiiy* (or spelled *u-kab'-jiiy*) in both Classic and Colonial periods (2004:368; Houston and Inomata 2009:145; Stuart 2005a:283–84). This term seems to indicate an overseeing role in Classic hieroglyphic monuments; in Colonial Tzotzil *chab* is translated as "to govern." Both such terms mean, in root form, to "cultivate" or "plow" (Houston and Cummins 2004:368; Laughlin and Haviland 1988:184). Usage of this glyph

Table 4. Examples of Colonial records of *k'ex* and *jal* that refer specifically to governmental or political contexts, and the transfer of office

Mayan term	*Language*	*Translation*	*Notes*
hel	Yucatec	sucesor en cualquier oficio o cargo, o lo que sucede o se pone en lugar de lo que se gastó, quitó o faltó; paga, trueque, retorno, recompensa y retribución de otra cosa (successor in an office or cargo/burden, or that which succeeds or which is put in place of something that is spent, taken off, or lacking; payment, exchange, return, recompense and retribution of another thing) (Ciudad Real and Arzápalo Marín 1995:305)	
*u **hel**in hun pay* or *uatal u **hel**in*	Yucatec	suceder en ofiçio (succeed or follow in office) (Acuña 1993:600)	
*u **hel**in hunpay u **kex**ul*	Yucatec	suceder in oficio (succeed or follow in office) (Peréz and Michelon 1976:741)	
*va'an **k'ex**ol*	Tzotzil	entrust one's office or rank to another (Laughlin and Haviland 1988:325)	
***k'ex** ba*	Tzotzil	change office (one entering, one leaving) (Laughlin and Haviland 1988:231)	Literally, "to change head"
***k'ex**ol*	Tzotzil	deputy (of warden or governor), substitute, vicar (Laughlin and Haviland 1988:232)	Ideas about substitution
***k'ex**ol rey*	Tzotzil	viceroy (Laughlin and Haviland 1988:232)	Ideas about substitution
***k'ex**ol sancto padre*	Tzotzil	papal legate (Laughlin and Haviland 1988:232)	Ideas about substitution
hal	Cakchiquel	suçederse vnos a otros en offiçios, ocupaçiones, etc., que se van mudando (succeed one to the other in office, occupation, etc., that are moving) (Coto and Acuña 1983:534)	The entry notes: *hal* es la mudança o suçession así (*hal* is change or succession in this manner)
***hal**atah*	Cakchiquel	be succeeded in office (Edmonson 1965:37)	

Note: *k'ex* and *jal* terms are in bold type for clarity.

Source: Jackson 2011:716.

is seen, for example, on the K'an Tok Panel (Palenque), where each "banded bird" accession event is described as being overseen by a ruler, using the term *u-chab'-jiiy*. These observations cohere nicely with a variety of politically related titles from Colonial Tzotzil, each of which also contains the *chab* root (Jackson 2011:718-719). The titles in table 5 reference both literal and metaphorical types of guarding.

All of these examples of "overseeing" or "guarding" may be understood as both agricultural in tone (as a farmer oversees his crops) and as fundamental to leadership roles at a variety of levels. In this way the suggestion of an agricultural metaphor becomes more complex, extending from a proposed equivalence between bodies and plants to leadership roles that involve the cultivation of such plants. How do these different perspectives on people/organic connections come together to reveal something about court members?

As seen through these discussions, references to agricultural and plant-related activity crop up in unexpected places and are found in Classic, Colonial, and modern contexts. The examples discussed in this section weave through these different time

Table 5. Examples of terms in Tzotzil related to *chab* involving both literal and metaphorical guarding

Tzotzil term	*Translation*	*Notes*
*j**chab**ivanej*	custodian, guard, guardian (Laughlin and Haviland 1988:185)	
*j**chab**iomal*	custodian, governor, guard, government (Laughlin and Haviland 1988:185)	
*j**chab**iomal-padre*	prelate (Laughlin and Haviland 1988:185)	
*j**chab**i ch'u*	priest (Laughlin and Haviland 1988:185)	Literally, "guard of (the) god" (Laughlin and Haviland 1988:184, 200)
*j**chab**i tak'in*	treasurer (Laughlin and Haviland 1988:185)	Literally, "guardian of metal or money" (Laughlin and Haviland 1988:184, 307)
*j**chab**i k'anal tak'in*	treasurer (Laughlin and Haviland 1988:185)	Literally, "guardian of yellow metal" (Laughlin and Haviland 1988:184, 233, 307, 308)
*j**chab**i-na*	house watchman or religious secretary (Laughlin and Haviland 1988:185)	Literally, "guardian of the house" (Laughlin and Haviland 1988:184, 265)
*j**chab**i muktal k'op*	secretary (Laughlin and Haviland 1988:185)	Literally, "guardian of the secret or hidden word" (Laughlin and Haviland 1988:184, 234, 262)

NOTE: *chab* is in bold type for clarity.

Source: Jackson 2011:718.

periods. Some of the correspondences remain tentative linkages, but they are nonetheless suggestive of shared ideas over time. Agricultural tropes are ones that would be familiar to many Maya people and that are used to discuss realms of existence removed—at least in our modern perspective—from that of subsistence farming and natural cycles. The extension of this metaphor beyond the literal space of the agricultural world suggests relationships that are useful to the modern observer in understanding structuring ideas of Maya culture. In particular, a somewhat surprising comparison is the use of a quotidian agricultural metaphor to describe individuals and processes within the exalted spaces of elite governance and the court. Within these courtly spaces, the language of organic entities and processes frames powerful individuals as plants and as planters, a strategic, multilayered association that—like many other aspects of the court—both unites and divides the people and space of the court from those outside of it.

Houston and Cummins cite the importance of this concordance as an "elite appropriation of common activity as a strategy for buttressing royal authority" (2004:367), with reference to Maurice Bloch (1987). I venture that the importance of these associations is actually much more lofty. They represent the structuring importance of agricultural activity at all levels of society. This occurs not only through the referencing of activity familiar to commoners in a subversion of expectation, but also through the sharing of a commonly understood language of "work," "duty," and "guardianship" in order to cast increasingly complex hierarchies and governmental organizations within a traditional light. In this way, processes of culture change involve invocation of cultural logics in order to highlight continuity even in the midst of shifts (Fischer 2001:15-19)—here, from much earlier traditional and egalitarian communities to the baroque differentiations of status of the Late Classic period. The fact that elites are evoked both as planters and as plants marks their roles as masters of their own metaphorical cornfields (or communities) at the same time that they play organic (and thus vulnerable) roles in a god-governed world. These dual roles exhibit elite skill at maneuvering between positions of power and of submission as they mediate between earthly and cosmic realms.

Cosmological Connections

The cosmic realm is the second framework that describes the Maya court in conceptual terms. As has been suggested by Miller and Martin (2004:51–65), the divine realm may, in fact, have provided a model or mandate for courtly roles and proceedings within the terrestrial realm. Miller and Martin discuss broader connections between myth and Classic politics or practice; they suggest a compelling idea of a "royal ideal" that references a widely acknowledged supernatural model (2004:65). Iconographic and hieroglyphic evidence allows for more focused connections to be identified between Late Classic court members and their otherworldly counterparts. We turn now to the cosmological metaphor, which, at the opposite end of the spectrum, casts elites as connected to profound and holy processes.

It is already well known that the ruler—the *k'uhul ajaw* ("holy lord")—derived his mandate for authority from twin sources of power that were both earthly and divine in nature (Houston and Stuart 1996:306–309). A powerful and effective ruler would have acted as a mediator between earthly and divine realms, calling upon access that would not have been available to the common person. Both iconographic and glyphic evidence indicates that contact with gods and cosmological places was not limited to the ruler, however, and points to courtly officers' place in divine contexts as well.

Iconographic depictions demonstrate the confluence of elite offices and certain cosmological roles or counterparts. One recurring visual trope that illuminates the role of courtly elites through a cosmological metaphor is the link established between *pauahtun*s and earthly individuals, especially supporters (literal and metaphorical) of the ruler (Fash 1989:70, 1991:78; Houston 1998:352–56). *Pauahtuns* were divine entities of which there were four. They were located at the corners of the world and were in charge of holding up the sky (Miller and Taube 1993:132). Their positions are thus spatially organized and represent concepts related to the division and organization of the world. They are often equated with *bacab*s (Miller and Taube 1993:155; Schele and Miller 1986:54), whose duties are represented as the separation of earth from sky (Foster and Wren 1996:261).[2] Their role in this type of primordial division may echo the role of court members in defining basic differential identities between elites and nonelites. Maca has argued that concepts of spatial/social organization and replication of power may be writ large on the landscape through the figures of *bacab*s or atlantean figures, as seen in the urban layout of Copán during the Late Classic period (2006:151–52).

*Pauahtun*s, and the courtly officials who are understood as being connected to them, shouldered important responsibilities in supporting and holding up cosmological and political structures. An example of this structural role is seen at Copán, where large sculpted *pauahtun* heads at the corners of Temple 11 support the roof. Schele and Miller argue that this created a cosmologically defined space in which the ruler would have been positioned (1986:113); this is an instance in which conceptions of cosmological and political supporters become conflated, as has also been noted by others (e.g., Fash 1991:78; Houston 1998:352–56). Certainly, in multiple Mesoamerican contexts, *pauahtun*s or related atlantean figures are associated with the buttressing of rulership and the bearing of the burden of office (Miller and Taube 1993:155).

The connection between *pauahtun*s as supporters of a divine realm and courtly officers as related to their rulers is one that is substantiated in both image and text. Lintel 4 from Laxtunich, a satellite site of Yaxchilán, may provide one of the most obvious examples. On this monument, a ruler converses with a courtly elite (a *sajal*); both individuals are seated on a horizontal plane hovering in the middle of the image (figure 36). This plane is held up by the extended arms of two other figures, both of whom are named in their captions as *pauahtun*s. Additionally, one is named as a *baah sajal* ("head *sajal*"), while the other has the designation of "captor." The overlap between official courtly positions and the divine supportive functions of *pauahtun*s is clear. This particular monument also documents an intriguing distinction between different *sajal*s, with one interacting directly with the ruler, handing him an object, and the other acting as a support. As discussed in chapter 2, internal

2. Some sources suggest a need to differentiate between *bacab*s, separating sky from earth, and *pauahtun*s, separating earth from the underworld (Schele and Miller 1986:61).

Figure 36. Lintel 4, Laxtunich. Courtly elites also play the role of *pauahtuns*, holding up the surface on which the ruler and another *sajal* are seated. Photograph courtesy of www.mayavase.com.

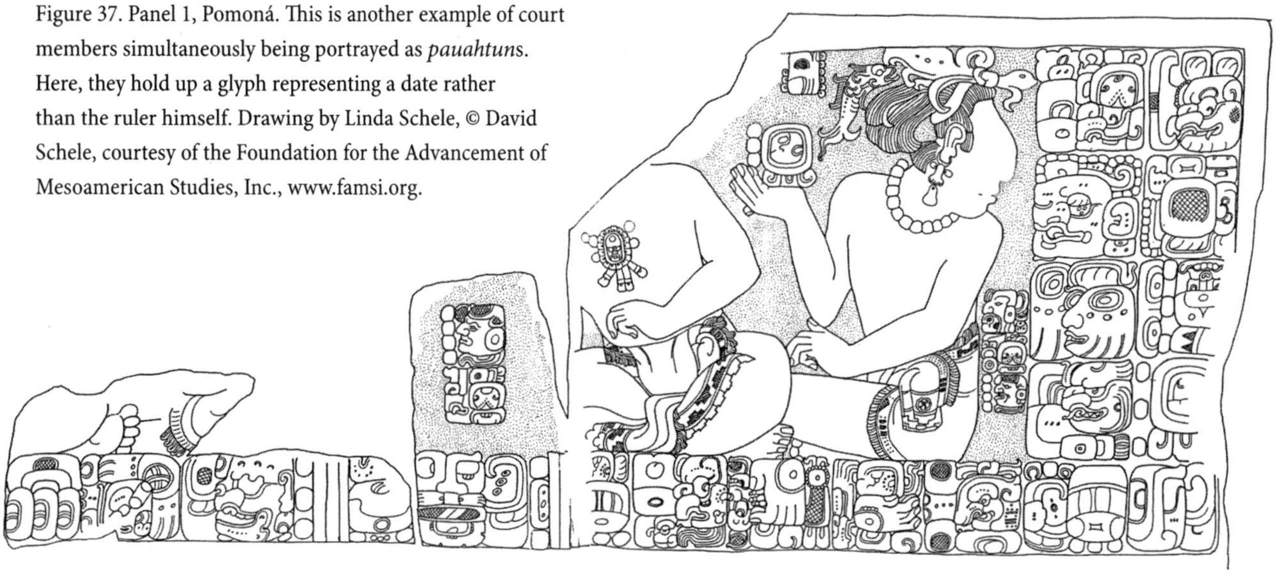

Figure 37. Panel 1, Pomoná. This is another example of court members simultaneously being portrayed as *pauahtuns*. Here, they hold up a glyph representing a date rather than the ruler himself. Drawing by Linda Schele, © David Schele, courtesy of the Foundation for the Advancement of Mesoamerican Studies, Inc., www.famsi.org.

hierarchies among courtly elites, and within particular types of offices, are known. In this case, the higher-ranking official (*baah sajal*) plays the supportive role, suggesting that the *pauahtun* roles were of particular importance and high status.

Pomoná Panel 1 similarly shows individuals who are simultaneously named with political titles and designations as *pauahtuns*. In addition to being *pauahtuns*, one is a *ti'sakhuun*, and the other is both a *ti'sakhuun* and a *sajal* (figure 37); a separate fragment that seems also to be from this panel includes an *ajk'uhuun* glyph. The panel is broken, and it appears that originally there would have been four individuals pictured, appropriate for the *pauahtun* designation, though apparently not critical, as observed on Laxtunich Lintel 4. In this case, the *pauahtuns*/courtly officials, in what remains of the image, are not shown directly holding up a ruler or his seat of power. Rather, the only complete figure (the right-most individual) supports a glyph representing a date. This might be interpreted as a more abstract support of power, the upholding of a key date—possibly an event or anniversary—as a stand-in for the ruler himself. The image makes explicit the dual roles that courtly officials played as named members of the court and as embodiments of named cosmological entities. The understanding that they provided critical support for the ruler is implicit here, indicating the role of support moving beyond a visual device in which court officers are "below" the ruler. Instead, the idea of structural support was, in fact, an inherent aspect of their courtly identity.

A record of a courtly officer on one of the supports of the Del Río Throne from Palenque (figure 38) leads to a further level of abstraction in understanding court members acting as key supports for the ruler himself. On this narrow carved support, the term *pauahtun* is not even recorded. Instead, there is mention of an *ajk'uhuun*, whose textual positioning on a bench support is a more oblique suggestion of the part he played in supporting the ruler. This reference places the courtly player not under the ruler (as on Laxtunich Lintel 4) but rather under his literal "seat of power"—the throne or bench from which he would have ruled, and which served as a key symbol for his governance. Just as the stone bench supports are structurally integral to the stability of this central kingly seat, so are courtly elites understood as fundamental to the political hierarchy. Courtly work involved the shouldering of heavy burdens, in a show of structural support (Houston and Inomata 2009:182).

Figure 38. Edge of Del Río Throne support, Palenque. A more abstract rendering of a court member supporting the ruler (here an *ajk'uhuun*—title highlighted). In this instance the courtier appears in the text on the leg of the ruler's throne. Drawing by Stephen Houston, inked by the author. Courtesy of Stephen Houston.

In sum, examples in which the roles of *pauahtuns* are related to those of courtly officials place elites in the position of assisting earthly rulers. Simultaneously, these parallels cast political hierarchy into a divine light by suggesting that the ruler is on an elevated plane, supported by celestial entities/courtiers. This is one way in which courtly elites are metaphorically understood as playing otherworldly roles. This recasting of Late Classic political systems in divine terms indicates that privileges that have long been associated with the ruler himself—such as access to religious spaces or religious power—were in fact extended to other members of the court in this era. Extending royal prerogatives in this way provides support for the idea of strategic power sharing in the Late Classic and suggests some specific ways it might have happened.

Hieroglyphic evidence also indicates another form that elite-cosmological connections might have taken, one that bypasses the *k'uhul ajaw* as a mediator or linchpin between the two worlds. At Toniná, Monument 165 provides some striking data for understanding direct elite relationships with divine entities (see figure 14). This round altar is the death monument of Kelen Hix (whom we already know well), and as such it lists the titles—*ti'huun* and *ajk'uhuun*—with which he was named during his lifetime. Two notable aspects characterize the use of the well-known title *ti'huun* on this monument. First, this title is modified with the adjective *k'uhul*, meaning "holy." This is an unusual usage. Typically, only the ruler's title of *ajaw* is modified by the *k'uhul* prefix; here a courtly elite is allowed the privilege. Additionally, instead of "belonging" to a ruler—as is frequently seen, through the possessed form of a title—Kelen Hix, the *k'uhul ti'huun* ("holy *ti'huun*"), belonged to (that is, was grammatically possessed by) the paddler gods. This is a remarkable record, as it suggests that, at least in his role as *ti'huun*, Kelen Hix's primary articulated allegiance may have been to deities rather than to an earthly ruler. This represents an intriguing intersection with evidence from chapter 2 that suggests that the cycle of accession into courtly positions operated outside of the rotation of particular rulers and further supports a measure of independence from a particular ruler for those in the courtly hierarchy. The use of the "holy" modifier similarly suggests that this position was operating in a different sphere, outside of the typical political hierarchy. Thus, strong cosmological connections for this particular elite person, at least, defined his roles in the court as recorded in his final reckoning. Part of Kelen Hix's privilege as a courtly official included direct relationships with other-worldly beings in ways that were apparently independent of the ruler.

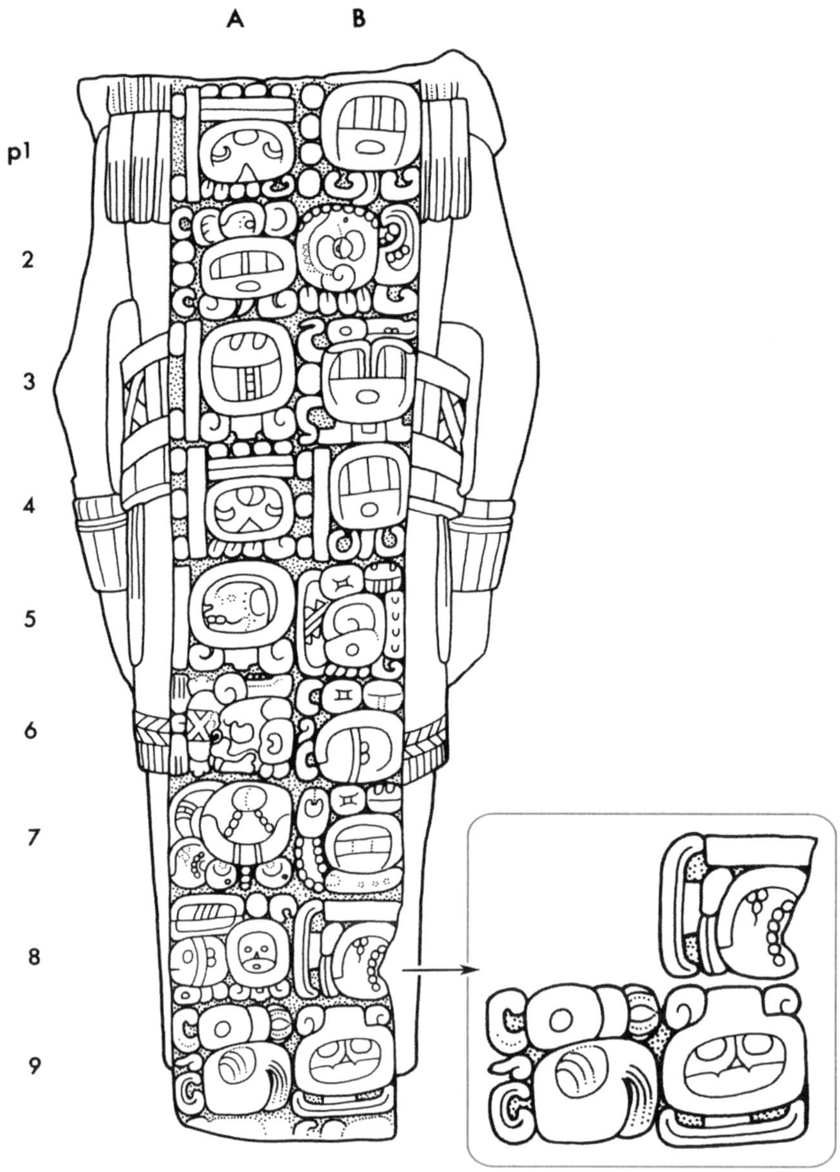

Figure 39. Monument 134, Toniná. In connection with Monument 140, one of the texts from Toniná that may indicate a parallel between courtiers at the site and the paddler gods (text highlighted that mentions paddlers). Drawing by Ian Graham, Courtesy of the Corpus of Maya Hieroglyphic Inscriptions, Peabody Museum of Archaeology and Ethnology, © President and Fellows of Harvard College, 2004.15.6.16.22.

More circumstantially, Monuments 134 (figure 39) and 140 (figure 40) at Toniná may set up a parallel between two elites named on Monument 140, a stela base, and two paddlers discussed on Monument 134, a stela.[3] On Monument 140 two elite individuals are described as witnessing a period-ending celebration that took place under the auspices of Ruler 3 of Toniná. These elites, Kelen Hix and Aj Chaanah, are known from a variety of other Late Classic monuments at the site. On Monument 140 Aj Chaanah is named as an *ajk'uhuun* and *yajaw k'ahk'*, and Kelen Hix is named

3. The connection of these two monuments has been hypothesized by David Stuart (personal communication).

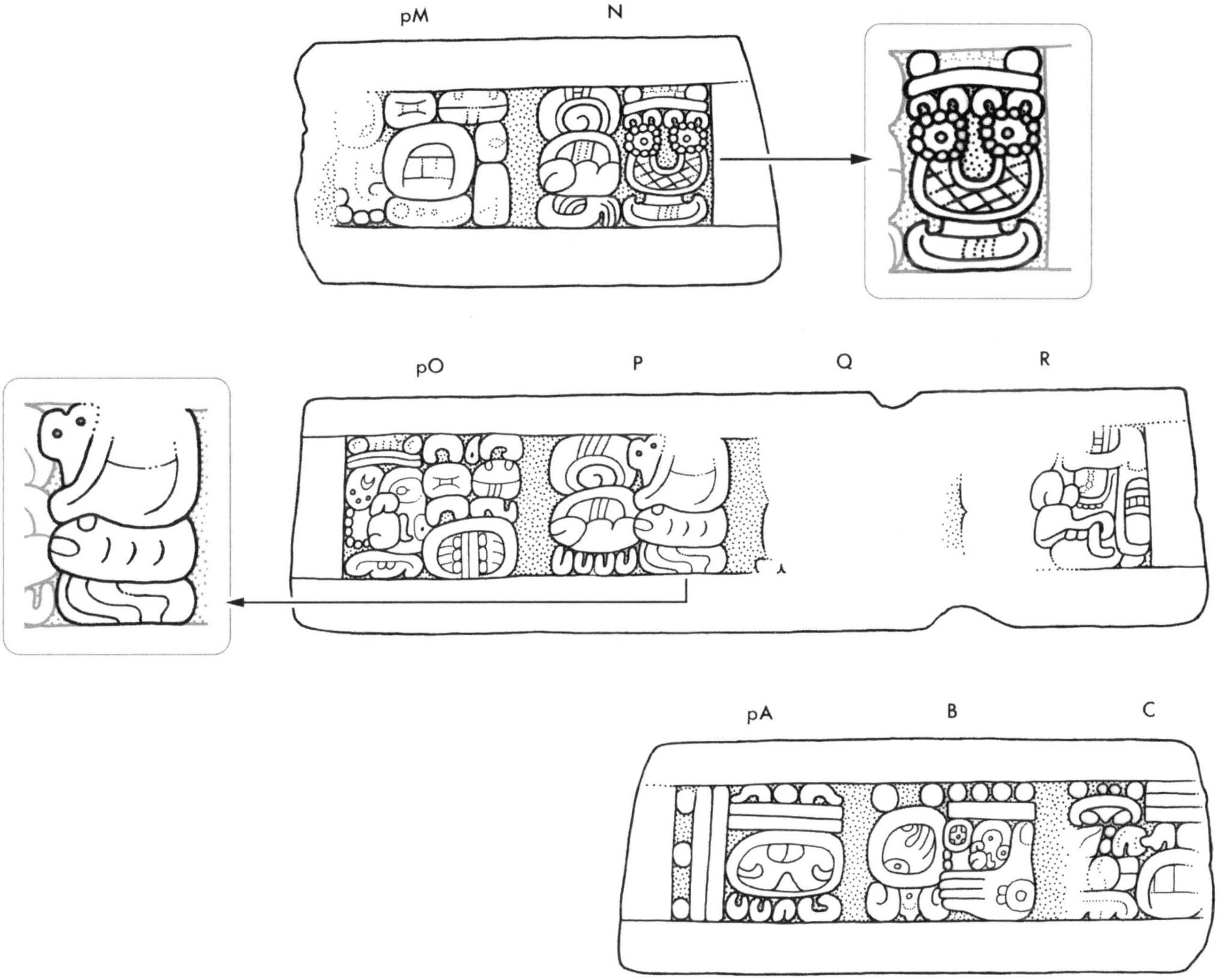

Figure 40. Monument 140, Toniná. In connection with Monument 134, one of the texts from Toniná that may indicate a parallel between certain courtiers at the site and the paddler gods (highlighted text mentions Kelen Hix [at P] and Aj Chaanah [at N]—two of Toniná's titled courtiers). Drawing by Ian Graham, Courtesy of the Corpus of Maya Hieroglyphic Inscriptions, Peabody Museum of Archaeology and Ethnology, © President and Fellows of Harvard College, 2004.15.6.16.30.

Figure 41. Hieroglyphic Stairway 2, Step X, Yaxchilán. A *sajal* (title highlighted at C1) personifying a wind god (A2). Drawing by Ian Graham, Courtesy of the Corpus of Maya Hieroglyphic Inscriptions, Peabody Museum of Archaeology and Ethnology, © President and Fellows of Harvard College, 2004.15.6.7.24.

with two partially effaced titles, one of which is unreadable and one of which is either *ti'huun* or *ti'sakhuun*. (On Monument 165, discussed above, Kelen Hix is named as an *ajk'uhuun*, which may also have been the second title recorded on Monument 140.) In the main text on the stela back of Monument 134, there is a discussion of two paddlers, who are described as "bathing" (or celebrating) the period ending. Potentially echoing the connection between Kelen Hix and the paddlers on Monument 165, these courtly officers and paddlers seem to be set up in a parallel in which human agents act as the earthly manifestations or ambassadors of the paddlers, or aid the paddlers in the performance of duties at this period-ending rite.

This example—admittedly sketchier in detail—similarly suggests loyalties of courtly elites to divine entities. Like the *pauahtun* examples explored above, it indicates parallels between courtly positions and functional roles in the celestial realm. These examples are both rare and limited in distribution. Nonetheless, the vagaries of recording that allowed these examples to be set down may give us access to ways of conceptualizing courtly roles that were not frequently articulated in stone.

Finally, cosmological connections with elites are seen through the practice of impersonation. Episodes of impersonation should not be understood as simple masquerades. Rather, ideas of concurrence seem to have underlain these moments, with divine and human identities actually coinciding within a particular body (Houston et al. 2006:270). Analogous to the known pattern of rulers taking on the identities of various gods (Houston and Stuart 1996:297–300; Houston et al. 2006:270–73; Stone 1991:194–95), other elites also appear as supernaturally associated entities (Houston and Stuart 1996:299–300; Houston et al. 2006:273).

Examples of impersonations by court members show them transforming themselves in ways analogous to what is experienced by rulers. For instance, *sajals* become wind gods in examples from the Yaxchilán Hieroglyphic Stairway 2, Step X

Figure 42. Lintel 2, Laxtunich. Another instance in which a *sajal* (title highlighted) impersonates a wind god (at D1). Drawing by Peter Mathews. Courtesy of Peter Mathews.

(figure 41), and on Laxtunich Lintel 2 (figure 42). An unknown deer figure is personified by *ajk'uhuun*s on the Cleveland incised shell (figure 43) and on an unprovenienced incised travertine pot (figure 44). In these instances, certain impersonations seem to be connected with particular titles or offices.

These are lower-level impersonations than the ruler's adoption of, for example, the Maize God as an alter ego. Nonetheless, the profound nature of concurrent identities represents direct connections between court members and otherworldly entities. Stone argues convincingly that effective use of impersonation is a critical aspect of

Figure 43. Incised shell (Cleveland Museum of Art). An image in which an *ajk'uhuun* (title highlighted) impersonates an unknown deer figure. (Shell with seated noble. Mexico or Central America, Maya style [250–900], 600–900. Conch shell, 16.6 x 7.9 x 3.5 cm. The Cleveland Museum of Art. The Norweb Collection 1965.550.) © The Cleveland Museum of Art.

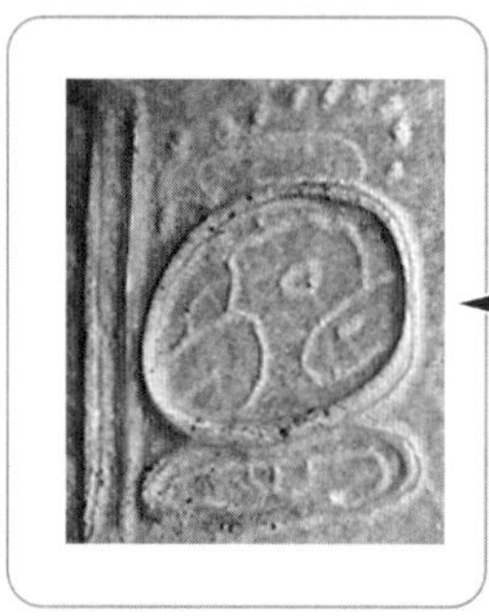

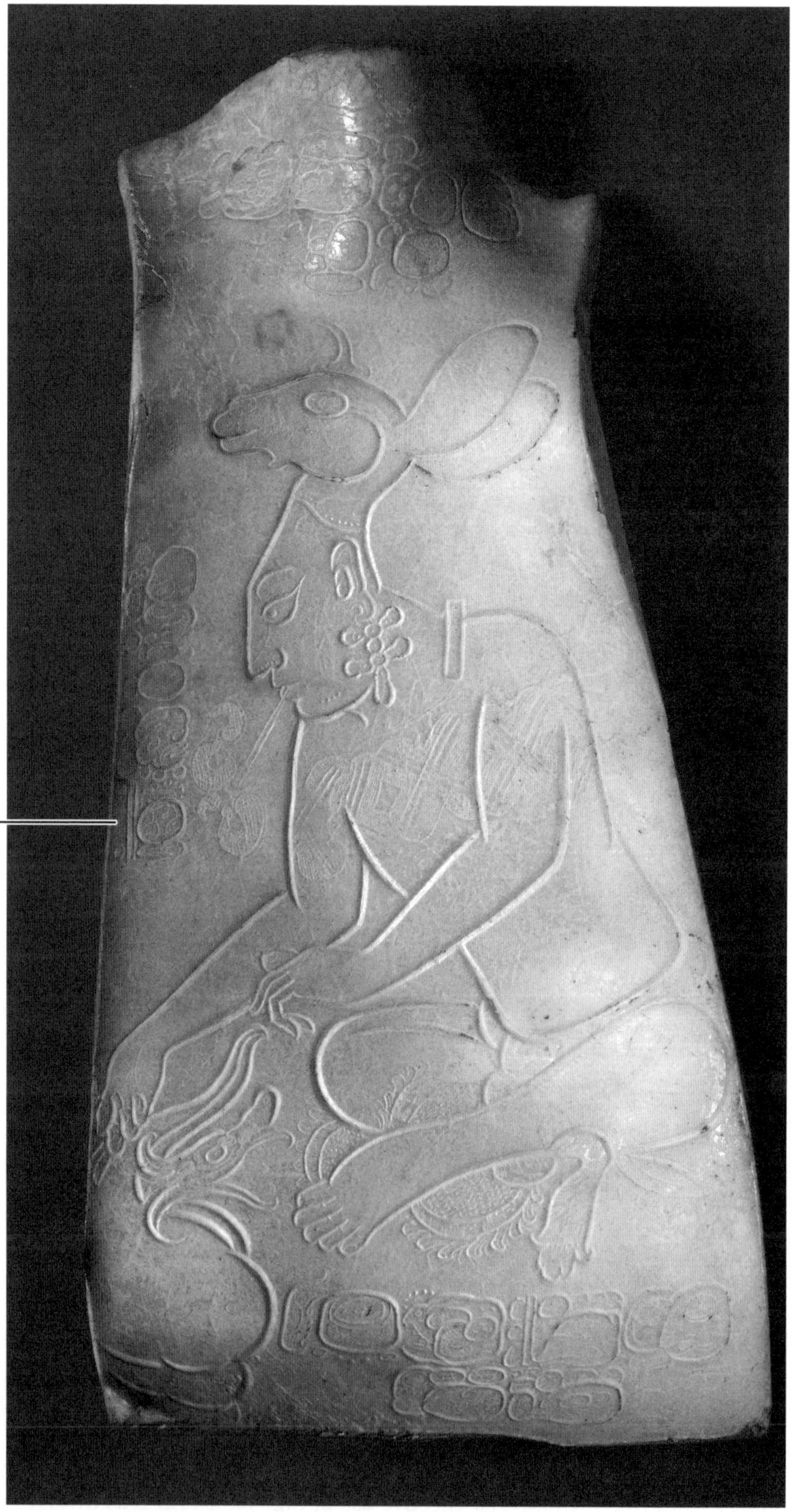

Figure 44. Travertine pot. Another example of an *ajk'uhuun* (highlighted) impersonating a deer figure. Photograph © Justin Kerr, K1606.

the success of political systems that combine divine and terrestrial sources of power (1991:194–95). Like the examples from Toniná above in which courtiers parallel the role of the paddler gods, these representations of impersonation suggest a parallel between real-life hierarchical structures and rankings in the realm of the other world (Houston and Stuart 1996:300). The examples also further suggest identities and roles for courtly elites that extend beyond their status as functionaries in the earthly institution of the court.

In opposition to the quotidian and fundamental concordances set up between elites, governance, and agricultural production that were discussed in the previous section, the metaphors suggested here involve much loftier roles. The texts and iconography discussed indicate that the court was not only a special place in an earthly, political sense but that it was also seen as a vital point of connection between this realm and the otherworld. The existence of a supernatural version of the royal court is documented, particularly on painted ceramic vessels (figure 45) (Jackson 2009:77–78). Imagery of courts that follow familiar tropes of depiction but that are populated by nonhumans makes clear that these institutions operated on multiple levels that at times intersected, whether through "mixed courts" where humans and gods interacted (Jackson 2009:77) or through the invocation of the upper, divine layer by human court members impersonating otherworldly counterparts. This sense of contact was not limited to the person of the *k'uhul ajaw*. It implicated other courtly members and perhaps the concept of courtly hierarchy itself. Through these supernatural connections, courtiers may have had a semi-independent source of status and means of access to the otherworld. Additionally, courtly organization within this metaphor is justified not only by its connections to the daily round of agricultural practice but also through the echoing of the very organization of the cosmos, implying a holy mandate for hierarchical structuring and an essential place for courtiers within Maya political structures.

Figure 45. A rollout image from a painted ceramic vessel of an otherwordly court. This image shows the visual parallels drawn between earthly and supernatural courtly communities. Drawing by Diane Griffiths Peck. Courtesy of Diane Griffiths Peck.

The Oppositions and Tensions of the Court: Reflections on These Metaphors

Earlier I proposed two conceptual metaphors, distilling the specific manifestations of the agricultural and cosmological metaphors discussed above. I provisionally proposed equivalences of rule and agriculture, and status and godliness. The agricultural metaphor proved to have multiple parts, with rulers and their assistants both playing the role of agriculturalists and showing affinity with plants themselves. The cosmological metaphor provided a mapping of certain types of hierarchy onto others and hinted at independent elite access to otherworldly forces. While I hope I have demonstrated compelling evidence for the presence of Classic-era conceptual metaphors that are at least related to the ones that I have proposed, we still have to consider the significance of these metaphors.

The agricultural metaphor calls upon deep-seated themes—subsistence-related and religious—in Mesoamerican life, in which the agricultural process, the life cycle of the maize plant, and the importance of maize as a creative, culturally loaded, and religious substance take center stage. By implicating elites and governance in this process, the political life of the Late Classic is naturalized, literally made organic. It is seen as involving a profoundly understandable type of work, comprehensible to individuals at a variety of status levels. In this metaphor, difference—such as the distinction between the plant and the planter—is seen as a matter of differing roles, predetermined by difference in substance, much as different statuses of Maya or Mesoamerican individuals are supposed to have divergent origins. In this way hierarchy is framed, not as a ranking in which some are more powerful than others, but rather as a reflection of profound and inherent dissimilarities between different entities (plants and farmers, or commoners and elites). The agricultural metaphor also provides a way of understanding change by suggesting that the ebb and flow of seasonal changes—determined by factors outside the control of human agents, and cyclical in form—may also describe the kinds of political changes experienced within or between polities.

The cosmological metaphor aligns two different spaces—the earthly and otherworldly realms of elites and of gods. This metaphor is not a stretch. The gods themselves are often shown arranged in spaces that seem courtly in form (see figure 45) (Jackson 2009:77–78; Miller and Martin 2004:58–59). Such imagery suggests that the idea of a court is one shared by elites and by gods, thereby setting up a parallel between exemplary, divine beings and the elites who served within the court. In addition to an indication of importance, even holiness, in this metaphor, there is again an element of justification for the emergence, or presence, of a system of hierarchy that is founded upon inequality. In this case, courtly elites are presented as foundational, key to supporting the ruler and even the cosmos itself.

I have suggested that metaphors may at times be manipulated or molded for certain ends. Certainly the agricultural and cosmological metaphors would have been advantageous to elites in justifying their elevated position as well as the influence they held over people of lower status. As indicated in earlier chapters, the Late Classic was a period in which elites worked to actively and strategically respond to sociopolitical changes. Nonetheless, it is difficult to determine to what extent these metaphors were consciously created, or to what extent they simply grew out of long-held beliefs in Maya thought. I suspect that it is a combination of the two, and that such a combination represents the only way in which strategic metaphors could be truly effective—that is, if they represent a variation on metaphors that were already utilized in a culture.

In considering these metaphors as strategically deployed, we should be aware of the roles that metaphor can play in intentional concealment and in shepherding change. Clearly, metaphors can illuminate culturally meaningful associations between different things. Metaphors may also be used strategically to hide things (Lakoff and Johnson 1980:10–13). In the process of alignment between the two entities implicated in a metaphor, there typically exist some recognizable similarities, as well as some suggested similarities that are newly illuminated by the use of the metaphor. However, the lining up of the two parts of the metaphor also serves to hide or deemphasize other things, due to the lack of actual or articulated correspondence between aspects of the first entity and its comparative partner. This is intriguing in terms of the power of metaphor to sway perception or experience. In considering Maya metaphors for understanding the roles of courtly elites and the nature of hierarchy, one can imagine that the careful cultivation of certain correspondences would also help to deemphasize less likable aspects of pronounced social difference.

Not only can metaphors be manipulated or strategically developed, but—like all forms of cultural practice—they are also susceptible to change. Lakoff and Johnson indicate the influence of such change in saying that "new metaphors have the power to create a new reality" (1980:145). One imagines that new types of metaphor-derived comprehension might be encouraged through the strategic, even propagandistic, use of text and image supporting a particular way of seeing things. Attributing major cultural shifts, such as the Late Classic changes associated with the royal court, to the implementation of metaphor takes these ideas further than is tenable. Nonetheless, metaphor *matters*. Rather than a simple turn of phrase, metaphor is both profoundly revealing and capable of inspiring action.

The agricultural and cosmological metaphors both illuminate Maya conceptions of the court and provide justifications for the operation of the political hierarchy. Are there meaningful connections between these two sets of metaphors? The most striking parallel between the categories of cosmological metaphor (especially in the case of the *pauahtun*s) and agricultural metaphor is the fact that elite roles are integral to the system represented. They are connected—on scales both grandiose and common—with celestial pillars and living roots; they are not parts that can be excised while leaving a functional whole. These representations, though metaphorical, assert that courtly elites were not an extra, added-on, or optional aspect of the court but rather formed a critical part of that institution. While they were not the head of that system, they were absolutely necessary for the positioning and functioning of that head, or ruler.

Strikingly, several of the correspondences discussed in this chapter center on the body and connect human bodies to other entities or realms. Human bodies correspond with, or replicate, lowly plants while also serving to structure the universe itself (Marcos 2006:65). While metaphors can bring together any two entities, humans' egocentric perspective on the world makes comparisons based in our own corporeal experience particularly powerful, and effective, in describing and organizing the world around us. As Lakoff and Johnson argue, "[w]e can only form concepts through the body, " resulting in a body-centered conceptual framework for all aspects of the world (1999:555). Referring to Aztec contexts, López Austin argues compellingly for the body as an important stage for social differentiation (1988:385–406). In particular, differential qualities, abilities, and prerogatives of bodies form the basis of a more abstract hierarchical order; he points out that these differences are frequently framed with metaphor describing the differences between commoner and elite bodies (López Austin 1988:389–93). Both of the courtly metaphors discussed in this chapter use elite bodies as templates for associations that throw into relief the identity and roles of court members by linking their physical selves with other entities.

These two sets of metaphorical understandings—the cosmological and the agricultural—do not exist in isolation; rather, they shed light on each other in intriguing ways. In addition to the ways in which both metaphors depict elites, the metaphors are also complementary. They signify frames of reference for the Classic Maya that were microcosmic (the farmer's field) and macrocosmic (the heavens and cosmos), representing the most humble and the most exalted touchstones in the daily lives of many, and in this way serve to juxtapose the quotidian and the sublime. By situating itself between such opposite ends of the spectrum, the historical court bound itself together with paired, profound threads.

In some ways, one could not have two metaphors that are further apart. There exists, thus, a certain tension between them in portraying elites and governance in such different ways. This is a productive and powerful tension, and one that is omnipresent in the hierarchically marked space of the court (Inomata 2006:205–12).

Hanks talks about this type of tension between "meaningful oppositions" occurring in the space of ritual activity (1999:246). He notes that in ritual contexts, transformations, dissolution of borders, and the seemingly contradictory presence of distant people and places are all typically observed (1999:236–37). One begins to wonder if the court—the space that the agricultural and cosmological metaphors describe, and from which they emanate—takes on some of the functions of a ritual space by providing a locus for such a marked "dynamic field."

The oppositions or tensions within the space of the court are exhibited in other ways, beyond the metaphors considered in this chapter. The court was a space that operated as a fundamentally separate location, with both behaviors and materials marking the fact that it was a different and exclusive world from that which operated outside. Yet, at the same time, the performances of this profoundly private space served to articulate and activate a shared cultural identity, unifying those who viewed such performances at the same moment that they would have been acutely aware of their outsider status. These are simultaneous processes of exclusion and integration (Baines and Yoffee 1998:236–38; Triadan 2006:160–61). As part of this display, elites demonstrated their fluency in specialized knowledge even while this information was visually shared with observers.

Such apparently oppositional forces were not necessarily contradictory to the Maya. These examples indicate the utilization of a productive tension between accessibility and inaccessibility, or inward and outward turning, in order to make the court relevant. The court as a dynamic field possessed a vibrant, complete quality through the incorporation of these different forces. It served as the embodiment of the complementary opposites that were so important to the Maya worldview. When examined together, and contextualized as powerful, influential, and instructive, the courtly metaphors provide significant perspectives on how the institution of the court was conceptualized by Classic period individuals. Beyond the agricultural and cosmological frames that were notably important, the pairing of these two metaphors reveals the court as a place in which opposing forces, ideas, and tropes (even people) were housed, yielding a space that was dynamic, creative, powerful, and even potentially dangerous.

CHAPTER SIX

Leaving the Court

A Trip along the Usumacinta

Sometime in the eighth century, a stone carver likely stepped into a canoe bobbing along the banks of the Usumacinta. He would have carried with him a sack containing his tools, used for creating stone monuments for the elite individuals who hired him. This person would have been known for his prowess at interpreting images and recording the texts that adorned the walls of buildings throughout cities up and down the river.

We know from textual evidence that this carver—a historical figure—worked on, and signed, Stela 15 at Piedras Negras. The same individual also worked on the wall panel now in the New Orleans Museum of Art, which records the death of a *sajal*. The panel is from the Usumacinta region, but its precise original provenience is unknown. If it was from an Usumacinta satellite site, like El Cayo, we can start to imagine the movement of people such as this carver between sites, carrying ideas and observations about the courts and its impact with him.

If this stone carver rode in a canoe from El Cayo to Piedras Negras, in order to work on a new commission, what might he and the person paddling the canoe have discussed? The paddler might have been curious to hear what the glamorous court was like, up close; the carver might have described his appreciation for the *ajaws*' elaborate costumes and the visions that he had witnessed in the smoke during ceremonies. These two men might have had quite different experiences of such courtly events: the paddler with an emotional appreciation of standing shoulder to shoulder with his kinsmen in the plaza but without a detailed interpretation of the events that unfolded, whereas the carver—despite not being royalty himself—was located adjacent to the action and could more ably have read the symbolism and meanings of particular ceremonies.

The carver and the paddler might have continued to talk, about the interpretations and reinterpretations of courtly events and the constructions and reconstructions of meaning that occurred outside of the court but nonetheless under its influence. Perhaps the paddler's sons and their friends discussed courtly public events for days afterward, debating and disagreeing on how to understand what occurred and what it meant. Perhaps the carver described travels he might have taken to carve personal texts for local lineage heads in the hinterlands, commenting that these lords had distinctive and different interpretations of how to conduct political and religious events. The men might have ended their conversation agreeing that it seemed that everyone—even the gods themselves—was talking about and imitating the court of Ruler 7 of Piedras Negras.

This passage is speculative, though it uses as a starting point historical information about a particular stone carver who worked on multiple monuments, likely at multiple sites in the Usumacinta area. I have imagined the stone carver on the move, one of the many vectors helping to disseminate mores emanating from the court. I indulge in this brief speculative reconstruction in order to think about the movements of people and ideas along the Usumacinta and beyond, as part of the waves of influence and meaning originating from various courts of this era.

Courtly ideals were imitated, manipulated, and reconfigured in many contexts. Such processes locate the esoteric and elite space of the court within a much more inclusive spectrum of society, one that would have engaged with the ideas of the court. The exploration of how these iterations and reiterations of courtly lore and behaviors unrolled outside of the court and across the Maya world lies beyond the scope of the present book. Nonetheless, it is important to remember that a close reading of the court is only a first step in illuminating the interlocking relationships and processes of reproduction that characterized the hierarchy and organization of Late Classic Maya society.

Furthermore, given my emphasis on textual sources in this book, it seems appropriate to finish our courtly reflections with an awareness of the complexity of the construction of narratives about the court, whether the multiple processes of storytelling at work in the past or the scholarly vision of Classic Maya courts that I have reconstructed. As is seen in the passage at the beginning of this chapter, and as I have emphasized throughout the book, individual agents play active roles in lively processes of meaning making. While my primary goal in this work is to leave the reader enlightened about Classic-era political institutions and their significance, I also end with an invitation to reflect about the multiple levels of retelling and reinterpretation inherently involved with text and stories.

Politics and Identities in the Court

In the meantime, what have we learned from inside the court? To return to my initial question, what was the nature of the Classic Maya political community? In thinking carefully about the membership and significance of the institution of the Late Classic Maya royal court, several interpretive lenses have been employed in this text: a consideration of individual titled court members and their construction of courtly identity and status; a focus on variation and change within the court, how they occurred, and how they were understood; and an investigation of the conceptual metaphors that framed the court, in order to extract remnants of cultural systems of thought and understanding. We are left with a picture of a vibrant political institution, populated and shaped by people of the Late Classic era—an opportunity to unite considerations of individuals and of institutions. Allow me to briefly revisit the major topics and themes that the preceding chapters have addressed, while pointing to the connections and significance of these subjects.

Denizens of the Court

In approaching the Classic Maya royal court through a hieroglyphic lens, we have been privileged to both meet individual courtly players of the Late Classic period and adopt a composite view of courtly structures across time and space. The ability to understand the court and its members allows for a close reading of courtly identity and the mechanics of this Late Classic political institution. The evidence that remains about the officials of the court reveals that they can be characterized through a series of official positions that they held, as well as through performances and practices that they undertook.

The consideration of courtly elites undertaken in this book engaged with ideas related to status—both the sources from which it was derived and the ways in which it was marked. I approached "eliteness" as a dynamic identity that was enacted through lived practices, by which individuals and groups connected with, and differentiated themselves from, one another. While not denying the role that sumptuous display played within the theater of the Maya court, my examination of this topic attempted to connect status differences with access to behaviors and ways of being that were performed by elites, on stages big and small. These performances of difference served to articulate identities, while enacting simultaneous strategies of cohesion with the fellow members of their courtly communities and differentiation from those without similar privileges of access and prerogative.

Material objects participated in these processes, as active players in mediating lived realities and as the detritus available to archaeologists to study as we attempt to piece together past realities. The emergent conception of status differentiation discussed in this book suggests, however, that we must be attuned to subtleties of how material goods that are candidates for markers of status (e.g., jade, polychrome ceramics, elaborate architecture) acted within ancient polities. Such extant material markers were only a part of the suite of objects (including perishable ones), ideas, and behaviors that distinguished elites from others in the Classic world. It is in this way that we must understand the material goods that are excavated archaeologically as part of a larger system involving substances that are not directly recoverable. These ephemeral substances must nonetheless be acknowledged if we are to make sense of the elements of that system that are still available or able to be reconstructed. In the case of the court, hieroglyphic texts can be read closely in order to identify or infer the factors that were emphasized as important markers of difference.

Hieroglyphic records of courtly activity also highlight the extent to which we are now reconstructing Maya *history*, with all of the implications of that sister discipline to archaeology and anthropology. The stories of elite lives that were told in chapter 2 transform our perspectives of this era by reminding us of individual experience, and they make accessible the fine-grained perspective of particular voices. These stories are ultimately exceptional and idiosyncratic. Yet they force us, as modern interpreters, to engage with the variable and contingent ways in which societal institutions are negotiated and modified to respond to the local constraints under which they operate. With the available data on courtly elites, we no longer just speculate about these processes. We actually witness them unfolding for particular people. This sense of the individual-in-history also modifies and expands our story of the

Classic era by extending our narrative beyond the personage of the ruler. While we still deal with documentation that is undoubtedly framed and filtered, we can read against the grain of the text to understand aspects of the experience of court members. Textual records are unlikely to extend this inclusivity further, to illuminate the experience of more humble members of Classic Maya communities; thus, we are challenged to creatively read material evidence in an analogous way in order to include the voices (even when indirectly recorded) and perspectives of a greater variety of Classic Maya individuals.

Dynamic Courts

This book has examined the royal court and its members on multiple levels. The excitement of engaging with stories of ancient individuals is complemented by the wider perspective offered by looking at data on court members in aggregate—a view that illuminates trends and patterns beyond the level of particular people. Change and variation emerge as ubiquitous processes characterizing courts across the Maya world. The hieroglyphic evidence considered in the preceding chapters indicates a period characterized by flux, seen here through the institution of the court. I was especially interested in thinking about how Late Classic organizational changes were framed, in order to illuminate the culturally informed meanings associated with processes that we might otherwise read in a distinctively Western and twenty-first-century way. I argued that what appears to us, the modern observers, as change may not always have been experienced as such: a significant level of cultural variation was couched within an overall experience of continuity. In fact, it seems that Maya concepts of cyclicality and continuity were drawn upon strategically by Late Classic rulers in order to bolster a waning power structure and respond to other uncertainties of the period. These changes were rendered acceptable and effective by conforming to culturally legible expectations.

The Late Classic changes embodied by the court involved an increasing inclusivity, marked by the growing size of the court and the expansion in usage of formalized titular positions within that institution. Simultaneously, however, the exclusivity marked by distinctly elite behaviors and markers was performed aggressively as part of the expansion of the court and served to emphasize not a royal/nonroyal distinction but rather an elite/non-elite one. Previously, the *k'uhul ajaw* alone was set apart through his politico-religious authority—a distinction that continued, perhaps attenuated, in the Late Classic. The widening use of prerogatives during this period, ranging from access to the cosmological otherworld to use and display of hieroglyphic texts, meant that a larger community of individuals—the court—claimed power within the polity. This set them apart from the still greater masses that lived within and beyond the city.

Late Classic courts were also dynamic in terms of their composition. As we have seen through both courtly anecdotes and more comprehensive information about the distribution of titles across the lowland landscape, Maya courts did not take a single form. Even as they drew upon a common and mutually acknowledged set of courtly elements, each polity built a governing institution that suited their particular situation. The structure of the court was flexible over space and across time; its lack of fixity was counterbalanced by the shared and limited set of official positions that could comprise it. Like other apparent oppositions that characterized the court (inwardly turned/outwardly turned; informed by precedent/newly conceived; rooted in agriculture/oriented toward the divine), its very makeup was trickily malleable. It satisfied the need for a widely legible governing structure within polities that were mutually aware and frequently interactive. At the same time, the changeable court honored the independence and distinct strategies employed by rulers within their independent polities.

Courtly Framings

The court was similarly dynamic in terms of the meanings and frameworks attached to it. The court must have been an esoteric space to many Classic Maya individuals, imagined from afar but never experienced directly. One wonders whether it exerted a pull on the lower-class inhabitants of a Maya polity or whether it felt remote and irrelevant to their immediate, daily concerns. In thinking about conceptual metaphors related to the court, hieroglyphic and iconographic evidence—as well as ethnohistoric data—provides important clues to how the court was framed. It was described and discussed in ways that attempted to situate it in spheres that felt relevant to many. The double metaphor of the court as reflecting both cosmic and agricultural spaces served both to elevate and to ground this political institution.

I argue that such frameworks represented not merely pretty descriptors or flowery language but rather were powerful and evocative in ways that reflected and reinforced the perception of certain realities. Use of textual, iconographic, and performance-based cues to activate these metaphors would have made them accessible through multiple pathways and dramatically compelling, both to audiences and to those who enacted them.

We must consider how persuasive or accepted these metaphors were to those outside of the court and to what extent such frameworks represented political agendas. Even if the metaphors represent propagandistic strategies, I have argued that they grew out of and drew upon long-held, accepted tropes in Maya culture. The data on courtly metaphors are particularly interesting in that they provide language for talking about the meaning and significance of the court and its members beyond imposed modern categorization (e.g., "political power"). The individuals whose stories are pieced together and retold throughout this book were political figures within the Classic Maya world, but they were also ritual specialists, performers, mediators, cosmic travelers, symbolic agriculturalists, even figurative plants. As we continue to better understand these concurrent roles, the changes afoot in this period—ones that ultimately led to massive reconfigurations of Maya culture in the era of the Collapse—become contextualized through refined understandings of the individuals involved and their own perspectives on their place in the world around them.

Together, these ideas reveal a courtly institution that was a stage for the expressed ideals of the Late Classic world and court members who were active participants in the reconfigurations of power structures during this period. The members of the court were not the only agents of note in this era. Those out working in their milpas, or conducting any number of other necessary economic and social tasks, were also implicated in the dissemination and reworking of these ideas. While I argue that courtly members may have led the dance of power, the footwork of both elites and nonelites impacted the others' sequence of steps. It is my hope that examining a locus of power like the court provides critical information for understanding noncourtly contexts. This is not because influence flowed unidirectionally, or because elites controlled all others. Rather, the signal strength of cultural messages is most powerful, and most easily read, in a documented context like the court. Information on the court provides a starting point for thinking about places and people characterized by less extensive or explicit evidence by recognizing how these different groups acted as foils for each other. While drawing upon the same cultural system, these groups also constructed difference through marked oppositions, useful to modern investigators as we attempt to see multiple parts of society.

Another Meditation on a Monument

Just as we entered the court and oriented ourselves within the Maya world in chapter 1, we now begin the process of leaving the court and returning our awareness to modern contexts and the intersections between ancient and modern power structures. I began this book with a meditation on a monument: the hieroglyphic bench from Structure 9N-82 at Copán, a sculpture that helped set in motion ideas and questions that led me to write the chapters of this book. I end with another monument, one of my favorites: Piedras Negras Panel 3 (figure 46). I have brought up this sculpture already in chapter 2, emphasizing its rich information about the populated and lively court of Ruler 4, but I have not commented on what an evocative piece I find it, personally. I frequently show a slide of this panel in lectures, accompanied by enthusiastic commentary on reconstructing the Late Classic court. I have to check myself when I remember that, to many viewers, this sculpture is less immediately appealing. With the heads of the figures defaced, it appears as a badly eroded and strangely incomplete scene. I understand the ancient individuals who rubbed out the identities of those portrayed. This scene has its own power, and the vivacity and interaction of the courtly space leaps from the medium as in few other Classic-era depictions. This stone may have been deactivated in the practices of the ancients, but the extant texts have allowed the original message to be articulated clearly and powerfully even over a thousand years later.

The panel now resides in the Museo Nacional de Arqueología y Etnología in Guatemala City, located on a wall not far from the open central courtyard of the museum. I like to visit this monument when I am in town and see it at different times of day, in different lights, with different colleagues and friends accompanying me. Often I am in the museum in July during the annual week-long Simposio de Investigaciones Arqueológicas en Guatemala, a conference that brings together scholars, foreign and local, working on archaeological projects in Guatemala to share the information and ideas emerging from their work. At these times the museum is far fuller than on an ordinary afternoon. Groups of students and professors linger and chat, or they sit near the ancient stelae arranged around the courtyard. Amplified voices of those giving presentations are audible from outside the two auditoriums, as the latest interpretations are shared—all in Spanish.

Figure 46. Piedras Negras Panel 3, mounted on the wall in the Museo Nacional de Arqueología y Etnología de Guatemala. Photo by Megan E. O'Neil. Courtesy of Megan E. O'Neil and the Ministerio de Cultura y Deportes de Guatemala and the Museo Nacional de Arqueología y Etnología de Guatemala.

It is a good conference. It reminds us all of the importance of the place in which knowledge is constructed and the dynamics that occur as that knowledge moves further from that place of origin and is reconfigured or used in different ways. It brings together scholars, students, and friends who may be more used to seeing each other in field gear or who may not have caught up since the previous year's meeting. Its location in the museum is a special one, allowing for a prolonged visit with particular objects, or simply offering a reminder of the future of our excavated materials and the importance of caring for the past on behalf of generations yet to come. There are children's school groups in the museum, even during the conference. While their ringing voices may occasionally break the train of thought of one of the presenters, they belong here, too, learning more about one reading of the history of their country. We are situated within larger, and multiple, processes of narrative construction in this museum. Looking around, one realizes that these artifacts are not old objects but objects whose stories continue with their place in this modern space.

This place, this museum, is a place of power production, too. The dynamics at the conference are collegial and complex. Information is shared (or withheld), language differences are negotiated, project plans are made through collaboration or modified due to political or financial constraints. We think about publishing our results, forming new questions, presenting our information to the public or to local, indigenous populations. We strive to do responsible and ethical archaeology and to be reflexive. How can we understand our role in the construction of knowledge and in the power systems that surround our research? How do our own identities impact the investigations we each conduct?

Understanding culture change and the construction of difference is not only a topic for our conference presentations. The newly detailed understandings of the Late Classic court explored in this text shed light on the political landscape of the ancient world but also spur further thought as we return to our modern setting. Affiliations, the voiced (and unvoiced), strategic assertions and shifts, and the political mobilization of identity groups are themes that relate to both ancient and modern cultural contexts. Our work is used and relevant in ways that are both expected and wholly unexpected. It is complicated and changing. In the museum, Ruler 4 leans forward with his hand on the edge of the throne, about to tell a story.

APPENDIX

Occurrences of Courtly Titles

The table that follows lists occurrences I compiled of the five courtly titles that are the focus of the book, as found recorded across the Maya lowlands, and here organized by site. Here I simply provide the basic form of the title (and note if it was a female version of the title), the site from which the courtier came, and the monument or object on which the title hieroglyph was recorded. (See chapter 1 for an explanation of the data set.) Greater descriptive detail of all of these titles may be found in chapter 4 of Jackson 2005. This information is provided to help the interested reader get a sense of the scope of the data used in this book and to allow him or her to follow up on examples of particular interest. I also hope this will enable future scholars to add to this list with further examples. This version of the table does not include all of the detailed contextual information I recorded for each titular record (including modifiers for titles beyond the feminine *ix*), nor does it include instances I compiled of known titled elites who were recorded in other textual contexts without their titles. I only include citations below for objects or monuments that may not be easily recognizable to the reader via their name and that have been published; some examples that would benefit from such clarification have not been published, however, so cannot be referenced in this way.

	Title	Site	Monument/Object
	ajk'uhuun	Bonampak	Lintel 4
	sajal	Bonampak	Room 1, caption 43 (mural)
	sajal	Bonampak	Room 1, caption 45 (mural)
	sajal	Bonampak	Room 2, caption 23 (mural)
ix	sajal	Bonampak	Room 2, caption 36 (mural)
ix	sajal	Bonampak	Stela 2
	ti'huun	Bonampak	Room 1, caption 51 (mural)
ix	ajk'uhuun	Bonampak area	stela (published in Mayer 1991: plate 118)
	sajal	Bonampak area	stela (published in Mayer 1995: plate 104)
	ajk'uhuun	Cancuén	Panel 3
	sajal	Cancuén	Panel 3
	yajaw k'ahk'	Chichén Itzá	Lintel 1, Temple of 4 Lintels
	yajaw k'ahk'	Chichén Itzá	Lintel 1, Temple of 4 Lintels
	yajaw k'ahk'	Chichén Itzá	Lintel 2, Temple of 4 Lintels
	yajaw k'ahk'	Chichén Itzá	Lintel 4, Temple of 4 Lintels
	yajaw k'ahk'	Comalcalco	pendants and spines from funerary urn
	yajaw k'ahk'	Comalcalco	pendants and spines from funerary urn
	ajk'uhuun	Copán	altar fragment (CPN 421)
	ajk'uhuun	Copán	hieroglyphic bench from Structure 9N-82
	ajk'uhuun	Copán	hieroglyphic bench from Structure 9M-18
	sajal	Copán	Altar K
	ajk'uhuun	Copán/Quiriguá	carved ceramic vessel
	"banded bird"	Dos Pilas	Panel 19
	sajal	El Cayo	Lintel 1
	sajal	El Cayo	Lintel 1
	sajal	El Cayo	Lintel 1
	sajal	El Cayo	Lintel 1
	sajal	El Cayo	Altar 4
	sajal	El Cayo area	panel (Cleveland Museum of Art)
	sajal	El Cayo/Piedras Negras area	panel (Dumbarton Oaks)
	sajal	El Cayo/Piedras Negras area	panel (Dumbarton Oaks)
	sajal	El Cayo/Piedras Negras area	panel (Dumbarton Oaks)

	Title	Site	Monument/Object
	sajal	El Cedral	fragment (published in Mayer 1995: plate 172)
	sajal	El Cedral	fragment (published in Mayer 1995: plate 172)
	sajal	El Chicozapote	Lintel 1
	ajk'uhuun	El Señor del Petén	painted ceramic vessel (published in Cortes 1996)
	ajk'uhuun	El Señor del Petén	painted ceramic vessel (published in Cortes 1996)
	ajk'uhuun	Ik' Site	painted ceramic vessel (Kimbell Art Museum)
	ajk'uhuun	Ik' Site	painted ceramic vessel (Kimbell Art Museum)
	ajk'uhuun	Ik' Site	painted ceramic vessel (Kimbell Art Museum)
	ajk'uhuun	Ik' Site	painted ceramic vessel (Kerr 1728)
	ajk'uhuun	Ik' Site	painted ceramic vessel (Kerr 534)
	ajk'uhuun	Jaina area	onyx bowl (Dumbarton Oaks) (Kerr 4340)
	ti'huun	Jonuta	ceramic sherd
	sajal	Lacanha	Kuna-Lacanha Panel 1
	sajal	Lacanha	Kuna-Lacanha Panel 1
	sajal	Lacanha	Kuna-Lacanha Panel 1
ix	sajal	Lacanha	Kuna-Lacanha Panel 1
	ajk'uhuun	La Corona	relief panel (published in Mayer 1995: plate 76)
	ajk'uhuun	La Corona	carved panel (published in Mayer 1980: cat. no. 6)
	sajal	La Mar	Stela 1
	sajal	La Mar	Stela 1
	sajal	La Mar	Stela 2
	sajal	La Pasadita	Lintel 1
	sajal	La Pasadita	Lintel 2
	sajal	La Pasadita	Lintel 4
	sajal	La Pasadita?	panel (Metropolitan Museum of Art) (published in Mayer 1991: plate 93)
	sajal	Laxtunich	Lintel 2
	sajal	Laxtunich	Lintel 3
	sajal	Laxtunich	Lintel 4
	sajal	Laxtunich	Lintel 4
ix	ajk'uhuun	Machaquilá	Stela 11
	sajal	Miraflores	panel fragment (published in Mayer 1991: plate 31)
	sajal	Miraflores	panel fragment (published in Mayer 1991: plate 28)

	Title	Site	Monument/Object
	yajaw k'ahk'	Miraflores	panel fragment (published in Mayer 1991: plate 31)
	ajk'uhuun	Naranjo area	painted ceramic plate (Kerr 4669)
	ajk'uhuun	Naranjo area	painted ceramic vessel (Kerr 7786)
	ajk'uhuun	Nebaj area	Fenton Vase (published in Schele and Miller 1986: plate 54)
	ajk'uhuun	Nebaj area	painted ceramic vessel (Kerr 2352)
	ajk'uhuun	Palenque	Piedras Negras Stela 26
	ajk'uhuun	Palenque	Tablet of the Slaves
	ajk'uhuun	Palenque	incensario stand (from period of K'inich Janab Pakal I)
	ajk'uhuun	Palenque	Temple XIX sculpted pier
	ajk'uhuun	Palenque	Tableritos, Palace South Facade
	ajk'uhuun	Palenque	Pakal's Sarcophagus lid
	ajk'uhuun	Palenque	Pakal's Sarcophagus lid
	ajk'uhuun	Palenque	Pakal's Sarcophagus lid
	ajk'uhuun	Palenque	Pakal's Sarcophagus supports, southwest
	ajk'uhuun	Palenque	Pakal's Sarcophagus supports, southeast
	ajk'uhuun	Palenque	Pakal's Sarcophagus supports, northwest
	ajk'uhuun	Palenque	Blocks reused in Temple IV, North Group
	ajk'uhuun	Palenque	Del Río Throne supports
	"banded bird"	Palenque	Temple XIX sculpted platform, Portrait C
	"banded bird"	Palenque	K'an Tok Panel
	"banded bird"	Palenque	K'an Tok Panel
	"banded bird"	Palenque	K'an Tok Panel
	"banded bird"	Palenque	K'an Tok Panel
	"banded bird"	Palenque	K'an Tok Panel
	"banded bird"	Palenque	K'an Tok Panel
	"banded bird"	Palenque	K'an Tok Panel
	"banded bird"	Palenque	obsidian blade (published in Ruz Lhuillier 1958)
	sajal	Palenque	Group IV incensario stand
	sajal	Palenque	Group IV incensario stand
	sajal	Palenque	Group IV incensario stand
	sajal	Palenque	Tablet of the Slaves
	sajal	Palenque	Pakal's Sarcophagus lid

	Title	Site	Monument/Object
	sajal	Palenque	Pakal's Sarcophagus supports, northwest
	ti'sakhuun	Palenque	Group IV incensario stand
	yajaw k'ahk'	Palenque	Tablet of the Slaves
	yajaw k'ahk'	Palenque	Temple XIX sculpted platform, Portrait E
	yajaw k'ahk'	Palenque	Temple XIX sculpted pier
	yajaw k'ahk'	Palenque	Temple XIX alfarda tablet
	yajaw k'ahk'	Palenque	Group IV incensario stand
	yajaw k'ahk'	Palenque	Blocks reused in Temple IV, North Group
	ajk'uhuun	Piedras Negras	Stela 1
	ajk'uhuun	Piedras Negras	Panel 3
	ajk'uhuun	Piedras Negras	Panel 1 (also called Lintel 1 in Montgomery 1998)
	sajal	Piedras Negras	Palenque Tablet of the Orator
	sajal	Piedras Negras	Panel 3
	sajal	Piedras Negras	Panel 3
	sajal	Piedras Negras	Panel 3
	sajal	Piedras Negras	Altar 1 supports
	sajal	Piedras Negras	Stela 5
	ajk'uhuun	Piedras Negras area	sculpture (published in Houston 1993:134)
	ajk'uhuun	Piedras Negras area	wall plaque (published in Mayer 1995: plate 266)
	sajal	Piedras Negras/ Usumacinta area	panel (New Orleans Museum of Art)
	sajal	Piedras Negras/ Usumacinta area	panel (New Orleans Museum of Art)
	sajal	Piedras Negras/ Usumacinta area	Hellmuth Panel
	sajal	Piedras Negras/ Usumacinta area	Hellmuth Panel
	sajal	Pomoná	La Mar Stela 3
	sajal	Pomoná	Panel 1
	sajal	Pomoná	Piedras Negras Stela 12
	sajal	Pomoná	Piedras Negras Stela 12
	sajal	Pomoná	Piedras Negras Stela 12
	sajal	Pomoná	Piedras Negras Stela 12
ix	sajal	Pomoná	Panel 6

	Title	*Site*	*Monument/Object*
	ti'sakhuun	Pomoná	Panel 1
	ti'sakhuun	Pomoná	Panel 1
	ajk'uhuun	Pomoná area	Yomop Stela
ix	ajk'uhuun	Pomoná area	stela (published in Mayer 1991: plate 143)
	sajal	Sak Tz'i'?	Randel Stela
	sajal	Sak Tz'i'?	Randel Stela
	sajal	Sak Tz'i'?	Randel Stela
	sajal	Sak Tz'i'?	Randel Stela
	"banded bird"	Seibal	Stela 1
	"banded bird"	Seibal	Stela 6
	ajk'uhuun	Site R	Lintel 4
	sajal	Site R	Lintel 1
	sajal	Site R	Lintel 5
	ajk'uhuun	Tikal	painted ceramic vessel (Kerr 2695)
	ajk'uhuun	Toniná	Monument 3 (stela)
	ajk'uhuun	Toniná	Monument 76 (altar)
	ajk'uhuun	Toniná	Monument 110 (altar)
	ajk'uhuun	Toniná	Monument 110 (altar)
	ajk'uhuun	Toniná	Monument 140 (stela base)
	ajk'uhuun	Toniná	Monument 151 (sculpture of captive)
	ajk'uhuun	Toniná	Monument 156 (stela base)
	ajk'uhuun	Toniná	Monument 165 (altar)
	ajk'uhuun	Toniná	Monument 182 (stela base)
	ajk'uhuun	Toniná	Monument 183 (stela)
	ajk'uhuun	Toniná	Fragment 34
	ajk'uhuun	Toniná	undesignated fragment (published in Jackson and Stuart 2001: figure 1, page 218)
	sajal	Toniná	Monument 116 (altar)
	sajal	Toniná	collections, Altar 1
	sajal	Toniná	ceramic sherd (Museo Toniná)
	ti'huun/ti'sakhuun	Toniná	Monument 140 (stela base)
	ti'sakhuun	Toniná	Monument 162 (stela base)
	ti'huun	Toniná	Monument 165 (altar)

	Title	Site	Monument/Object
	ti'sakhuun	Toniná	Monument 182 (stela base)
	yajaw k'ahk'	Toniná	Monument 140 (stela base)
	yajaw k'ahk'	Toniná	Monument 162 (stela base)
	"banded bird"	Tortuguero	carved wooden box (published in Coe 1973a)
	sajal	Usumacinta area	Stendahl Panel
	yajaw k'ahk'	Wa-bird site	Piedras Negras Stela 12
	sajal	Wak'ab' site	Yaxchilán Lintel 16
	sajal	Xcalumkín	Column 1
	sajal	Xcalumkín	Column 2
	sajal	Xcalumkín	Column 3
	sajal	Xcalumkín	Column 6
	sajal	Xcalumkín	Jamb 1
	sajal	Xcalumkín	Jamb 2
	sajal	Xcalumkín	Jamb 7
	sajal	Xcalumkín	jamb? (Puebla—Museo Amparo, published in Mayer 1995: plate 233)
	sajal	Xcalumkín	Panel 5
	sajal	Xcalumkín	Miscellaneous 5 (jamb/lintel)
	sajal	Xcocha	capital (Campeche Museum)
	sajal	Xcombec	carved pillar (published in Mayer 1991: plate 100)
ix	ajk'uhuun	Yaxchilán	Lintel 28
ix	ajk'uhuun	Yaxchilán	Lintel 53
ix	ajk'uhuun	Yaxchilán	Stela 11
ix	ajk'uhuun	Yaxchilán	Stela 11
	sajal	Yaxchilán	Piedras Negras Stela 8
	sajal	Yaxchilán	Lintel 3
	sajal	Yaxchilán	Lintel 6
	sajal	Yaxchilán	Lintel 8
	sajal	Yaxchilán	Lintel 14
	sajal	Yaxchilán	Lintel 42
	sajal	Yaxchilán	Hieroglyphic Stair 2, Step X
	sajal	Yaxchilán	Hieroglyphic Stair 3, Step IV
ix	sajal	Yaxchilán	Lintel 13

	Title	Site	Monument/Object
ix	sajal	Yaxchilán	Lintel 14
ix	sajal	Yaxchilán	Lintel 54
ix	sajal	Yaxchilán	Lintel 57
	sajal	Yucatán (Xcombec?)	fragment (published in Mayer 1984: plate 106)
	sajal	Yucatán area	column (Museo del Camino Real, Hecelchakan) (published in Mayer 1991: plate 101)
	sajal	Yucatán area	capital (Museo del Camino Real, Hecelchakán) (published in Mayer 1995: plate 115)
	ajk'uhuun	unprovenienced	incised shell pendant (Princeton) (published in Graham 1971)
	ajk'uhuun	unprovenienced	incised shell (Cleveland Museum of Art)
	ajk'uhuun	unprovenienced	incised travertine vessel (Kerr 1606)
	sajal	unprovenienced	carved fragment (Mayer 1995: plate 149)

Bibliography

Acuña, R. 1993. *Bocabulario de maya than: Codex Vindobonensis N. S. 3833: facsímil y transcripción crítica anotada*. Universidad Nacional Autónoma de México, México.

Adams, R. E. W. 1970. Suggested Classic Period Occupational Specialization in the Southern Maya Lowlands. In *Papers of the Peabody Museum of Archaeology and Ethnology, Harvard University,* vol. 61, pp. 487–502. Peabody Museum of Archaeology and Ethnology, Harvard University, Cambridge, Mass.

Aldana, G. 2007. *The Apotheosis of Janaab' Pakal: Science, History, and Religion at Classic Maya Palenque*. University Press of Colorado, Boulder.

Anaya Hernandez, A., S. P. Guenter, and M. U. Zender. 2003. Sak Tz'i', a Classic Maya Center: A Locational Model Based on GIS and Epigraphy. *Latin American Antiquity* 14 (2): 179–92.

Ara, D. de, and M. Humberto Ruz. 1986. *Vocabulario de lengua tzeldal según el orden de Copanabastla*. Universidad Nacional Autónoma de México, México.

Austin, J. L. 1962. *How to Do Things with Words*. Harvard University Press, Cambridge, Mass.

Baines, J., and N. Yoffee. 1998. Order, Legitimacy, and Wealth in Ancient Egypt and Mesopotamia. In *Archaic States*, edited by G. M. Feinman and J. Marcus, pp. 199–260. School of American Research Press, Santa Fe, N.Mex.

Barrett, J. C. 1994. *Fragments from Antiquity: An Archaeology of Social Life in Britain, 2900–1200 BC*. Blackwell, Oxford.

Barth, F. 1969. Introduction. In *Ethnic Groups and Boundaries: The Social Organization of Cultural Difference*, edited by F. Barth, pp. 9–38. Waveland Press, Prospect Heights, Ill.

Bauer, B. S. 1996. Legitimization of the State in Inca Myth and Ritual. *American Anthropologist* 98 (2): 327–73.

Becquelin, P., M.-C. Arnauld, E. Taladoire, and D. Michelet. 1994. Proyecto Arqueológico 'Xcalumkín, en su trayectoria cronológica': Segunda temporada (enero-marzo de 1993). *Mexicon* 16 (5): 93–99.

Becquelin, P., and D. Michelet. 1992. Proyecto 'Xcalumkín en su trayectoria cronológica': La temporada (1992). *Mexicon* 14 (6): 113–18.

Becquelin, P., D. Michelet, L. Lopez Lujan, and R. Avila. 1996. Proyecto arqueológico 'Xcalumkín, en su trayectoria cronológica': Tercera temporada (1994). *Mexicon* 18 (4): 65–67.

Beeman, W. O. 1993. The Anthropology of Theater and Spectacle. *Annual Review of Anthropology* 22:369–93.

Benson, E. P. 1974. Gestures and Offerings. In *Primera Mesa Redonda de Palenque, Part 1, 1973*, edited by M. Greene Robertson, pp. 109–20. Pre-Columbian Art Research, Robert Louis Stevenson School, Pebble Beach, Calif.

Bernal Romero, G. 2002. Analisis epigrafico del Tablero de K'an Tok, Palenque, Chiapas. In *La organización social entre los mayas: Memoria de la Tercera Mesa Redonda de Palenque*, I, edited by V. Tiesler Blos, R. Cobos, and M. Greene Robertson, pp. 401–24. INAH, México.

Bloch, M. 1987. The Person of the King. In *Rituals of Royalty*, edited by D. Cannadine and S. Price, pp. 271–97. Cambridge University Press, Cambridge.

Borhegyi, S. F. de. 1956. Development of Folk and Complex Cultures in the Southern Maya Area. *American Antiquity* 21:343–56.

Bourdieu, P. 1977. *Outline of a Theory of Practice*, translated by R. Nice. Cambridge Studies in Social Anthropology 16. Cambridge University Press, Cambridge.

———. 1984. *Distinction: A Social Critique of the Judgment of Taste*, translated by R. Nice. Harvard University Press, Cambridge, Mass.

Bricker, V. R. 1981. *The Indian Christ, the Indian King: The Historical Substrate of Maya Myth and Ritual*. University of Texas Press, Austin.

———. 2007. Literary Continuities across the Transformation from Maya Hieroglyphic to Alphabetic Writing. *Proceedings of the American Philosophical Society* 151 (1): 27–42.

Carlsen, R. S. 1997. *The War for the Heart and Soul of a Highland Maya Town*. University of Texas Press, Austin.

Carmack, R. M. 1981. *The Quiché Mayas of Utatlán: The Evolution of a Highland Guatemala Kingdom*. University of Oklahoma Press, Norman.

Carrasco, D. 1990. *Religions of Mesoamerica: Cosmovision and Ceremonial Centers*. Harper and Row, San Francisco.

Carrasco, M. 2010. From Field to Hearth: An Earthly Interpretation of Maya and Other Mesoamerican Creation Myths. In *Pre-Columbian Foodways: Interdisciplinary Approaches to Food, Culture, and Markets in Ancient Mesoamerica*, edited by J. E. Staller and M. Carrasco, pp. 601–34. Springer, New York.

Chase, A. F. 1992. Elites and the Changing Organization of Classic Maya Society. In *Mesoamerican Elites: An Archaeological Assessment*, edited by D. Z. Chase and A. F. Chase, pp. 30–49. University of Oklahoma Press, Norman.

Chase, A. F., and D. Z. Chase. 1992. Mesoamerican Elites: Assumptions, Definitions, and Models. In *Mesoamerican Elites: An Archaeological Assessment*, edited by D. Z. Chase and A. F. Chase, pp. 3–17. University of Oklahoma Press, Norman.

Chinchilla, O. M., and S. D. Houston. 1993. Historia política de la zona de Piedras Negras: Las inscripciones de El Cayo. In *VI Simposio de investigaciones arqueológicas en Guatemala*, edited by J. P. Laporte, H. Escobedo, and S. V. de Brady, pp. 63–70. Museo Nacional de Arqueología y Etnología, Guatemala City.

Christenson, A. J. 2010. Maize Was Their Flesh: Ritual Feasting in the Maya Highlands. In *Pre-Columbian Foodways: Interdisciplinary Approaches to Food, Culture, and Markets in Ancient Mesoamerica*, edited by J. E. Staller and M. Carrasco, pp. 577–600. Springer, New York.

Christie, J. J., ed. 2003. *Maya Palaces and Elite Residences*. University of Texas Press, Austin.

Ciudad Real, A. D., and R. Arzápalo Marín. 1995. *Calepino de Motul: diccionario maya-español*. Universidad Nacional Autónoma de México, México.

Coe, M. D. 1973. *The Maya Scribe and His World*. Grolier Club, New York.

———. 1974. A Carved Wooden Box from the Classic Maya Civilization. In *Primera Mesa Redonda de Palenque, Part 2*, edited by M. Greene Robertson, pp. 51–58. Pre-Columbian Art Research, Robert Louis Stevenson School, Pebble Beach, Calif.

———. 1999. *Breaking the Maya Code*. Thames and Hudson, New York.

Coe, M. D., and E. P. Benson. 1966. *Three Maya Relief Panels at Dumbarton Oaks*. Studies in Pre-Columbian Art and Archaeology, no. 2. Dumbarton Oaks, Washington, D.C.

Coe, M. D., and J. Kerr. 1998. *The Art of the Maya Scribe*. Harry N. Abrams, New York.

Coe, M. D., and M. Van Stone. 2001. *Reading the Maya Glyphs*. Thames and Hudson, London.

Cortes de Brasdefer, F. 1996. A Maya Vase from "El Señor del Petén." *Mexicon* 18 (1): 6.

Coto, T. de, and R. Acuña. 1983. *Thesaurus verboru[m]: vocabulario de la lengua cakchiquel u [el] guatemalteca: nuevamente hecho y recopilado con summo estudio, travajo y erudición*. Universidad Nacional Autónoma de México, México.

Culbert, T. P. 1974. *The Lost Civilization: The Story of the Classic Maya*. Harper and Row, New York.

D'Altroy, T. N. 2002. *The Incas*. Blackwell, Malden, Mass.

Donnan, C. B. 1990. An Assessment of the Validity of the Naymlap Dynasty. In *The Northern Dynasties: Kingship and Statecraft in Chimor*, edited by M. E. Moseley and A. Cordy-Collins. Dumbarton Oaks, Washington, D.C.

Eberl, M., and T. Inomata. 2001. Maya Royal Headband (Sak Hunal) from Aguateca. *Mexicon* 23 (6): 134–35.

Edmonson, M. S. 1965. *Quiché-English Dictionary*. Middle American Research Institute, Publication 30. Middle American Research Institute, Tulane University, New Orleans.

Evans, S. T. 2001. Aztec Noble Courts: Men, Women, and Children of the Palace. In Inomata and Houston, *Royal Courts of the Ancient Maya*, vol. 1: *Theory, Comparison, and Synthesis*, pp. 237–73.

Evans, S. T., and J. Pillsbury, eds. 2004. *Palaces of the Ancient New World*. Dumbarton Oaks, Washington, D.C.

Farriss, N. M. 1984. *Maya Society under Colonial Rule: The Collective Enterprise of Survival*. Princeton University Press, Princeton, N.J.

Fash, B., W. Fash, S. Lane, R. Larios, L. Schele, J. Stomper, and D. Stuart. 1992. Investigations of a Classic Maya Council House at Copán, Honduras. *Journal of Field Archaeology* 19 (4): 419–42.

Fash, W. L. 1983. Maya State Formation: A Case Study and Its Implications. Ph.D. dissertation, Harvard University.

———. 1988. A New Look at Maya Statecraft from Copan, Honduras. *Antiquity* 62:157–69.

———. 1989. The Sculptural Facade of Structure 9N-82: Content, Form, and Significance. In Webster, *House of the Bacabs, Copán, Honduras*, pp. 41–72.

———. 1991. Lineage Patrons and Ancestor Worship among the Classic Maya Nobility: The Case of Copán Structure 9N-82. In *Sixth Palenque Round Table, 1986*, edited by M. Greene Robertson and V. M. Fields, pp. 68–80. University of Oklahoma Press, Norman.

———. 2005. Toward a Social History of the Copán Valley. In *Copán: The History of an Ancient Maya Kingdom*, edited by E. W. Andrews and W. L. Fash, pp. 73–102. School of American Research Press, Santa Fe.

Fash, W. L., and D. S. Stuart. 1991. Dynastic History and Cultural Evolution at Copan, Honduras. In *Classic Maya Political History: Hieroglyphic and Archaeological Evidence*, edited by T. P. Culbert, pp. 147–79. Cambridge University Press, Cambridge.

Fischer, E. F. 2001. *Cultural Logics and Global Economies: Maya Identity in Thought and Practice*. University of Texas Press, Austin.

Foster, L., and L. Wren. 1996. World Creator and World Sustainer: God N at Chichén Itzá. In *Eighth Palenque Round Table, 1993*, edited by M. J. Macri, J. McHargue, and M. Greene Robertson, pp. 259–69. Pre-Columbian Art Research Institute, San Francisco.

Freidel, D. A., L. Schele, and J. Parker. 1993. *Maya Cosmos: Three Thousand Years on the Shaman's Path*. W. Morrow, New York.

Geertz, C. 1980. *Negara: The Theatre State in Nineteenth-century Bali*. Princeton University Press, Princeton, N.J.

Giddens, A. 1979. *Central Problems in Social Theory: Action, Structure, and Contradiction in Social Analysis*. University of California Press, Berkeley.

———. 1984. *The Constitution of Society: Outline of the Theory of Structuration*. University of California Press, Berkeley.

Gillespie, S. D. 2000. Maya "Nested Houses": The Ritual Construction of Place. In Joyce and Gillespie, *Beyond Kinship: Social and Material Reproduction in House Societies*, pp. 135–60.

Goffman, E. 1974. *Frame Analysis: An Essay on the Organization of Experience*. Harvard University Press, Cambridge, Mass.

Golden, C. 2003. The Politics of Warfare in the Usumacinta Basin: La Pasadita and the Realm of Bird Jaguar. In *Ancient Mesoamerican Warfare*, edited by M. K. Brown and T. W. Stanton, pp. 31–48. AltaMira Press, Walnut Creek, Calif.

———. 2010. Frayed at the Edges: Collective Memory and History on the Borders of Classic Maya Polities. *Ancient Mesoamerica* 21:373–84.

Graham, I. 1979. *Corpus of Maya Hieroglyphic Inscriptions*, vol. 3, pt. 2: *Yaxchilan*. Peabody Museum of Archaeology and Ethnology, Harvard University, Cambridge, Mass.

———. 1982. *Corpus of Maya Hieroglyphic Inscriptions*, vol. 3, pt. 3, *Yaxchilan*. Peabody Museum of Archaeology and Ethnology, Harvard University, Cambridge, Mass.

Graham, I., and P. Mathews. 1999. *Corpus of Maya Hieroglyphic Inscriptions*, vol. 6, pt. 3: *Tonina*. Peabody Museum of Archaeology and Ethnology, Harvard University, Cambridge, Mass.

Graham, I., and E. Von Euw. 1977. *Corpus of Maya Hieroglyphic Inscriptions*, vol. 3, pt. 1: *Yaxchilan*. Peabody Museum of Archaeology and Ethnology, Harvard University, Cambridge, Mass.

———. 1992. *Corpus of Maya Hieroglyphic Inscriptions*, vol. 4, pt. 3: *Uxmal, Xcalumkin*. Peabody Museum of Archaeology and Ethnology, Harvard University, Cambridge, Mass.

Graham, J. A. 1971. *A Maya Hieroglyph Incised on Shell*. Archaeological Research Facility, University of California, Berkeley.

Greene Robertson, M. 1983. *The Sculpture of Palenque*. Princeton University Press, Princeton, N.J.

Grube, N., and W. Nahm. 1991. Signs with the Phonetic Value *Sa*. Unpublished letter.

Hammond, N. 1982. *Ancient Maya Civilization*. Cambridge University Press, Cambridge.

Hanks, W. F. 1990. *Referential Practice: Language and Lived Space among the Maya*. University of Chicago Press, Chicago.

———. 1999. Copresence and Alterity in Maya Ritual Practice. In *Intertexts: Writings on Language, Utterance, and Context*, pp. 221–48. Rowman and Littlefield, Lanham, Md.

Houston, S. D. 1989. *Maya Glyphs*. University of California Press, Berkeley.

———. 1993. *Hieroglyphs and History at Dos Pilas: Dynastic Politics of the Classic Maya*. University of Texas Press, Austin.

———. 1994. Literacy among the Pre-Columbian Maya: A Comparative Perspective. In *Writing Without Words: Alternative Literacies in Mesoamerica and the Andes*, edited by E. H. Boone and W. D. Mignolo, pp. 27–49. Duke University Press, Durham, N.C.

———. 1998. Classic Maya Depictions of the Built Environment. In *Function and Meaning in Classic Maya Architecture*, pp. 333–72. Dumbarton Oaks, Washington, D.C.

———. 2001. Decorous Bodies and Disordered Passions: Representations of Emotion among the Classic Maya. *World Archaeology* 33 (2): 206–19.

———. 2006. Impersonation, Dance, and the Problem of Spectacle among the Classic Maya. In Inomata and Coben, *Archaeology of Performance*, pp. 135–58.

———. 2009. A Splendid Predicament: Young Men in Classic Maya Society. *Cambridge Archaeological Journal* 19 (2): 149–78.

Houston, S., and T. Cummins. 2004. Body, Presence, and Space in Andean and Mesoamerican Rulership. In Evans and Pillsbury, *Palaces of the Ancient New World*, pp. 359–98.

Houston, S. D., and T. Inomata. 2009. *The Classic Maya*. Cambridge University Press, New York.

Houston, S. D., and P. McAnany. 2003. Bodies and Blood: Critiquing Social Construction in Maya Archaeology. *Journal of Anthropological Archaeology* 22 (1): 26–41.

Houston, S. D., Robertson, J., and D. Stuart. 2000. The Language of Classic Maya Inscriptions. *Current Anthropology* 41 (3): 321–56.

Houston, S. D., and D. Stuart. 1989. *The Way Glyph: Evidence for Co-essences among the Classic Maya*. Research Reports on Ancient Maya Writing 30. Center for Maya Research, Washington, D.C.

———. 1996. Of Gods, Glyphs and Kings: Divinity and Rulership among the Classic Maya. *Antiquity* 70 (268): 289–312.

———. 1998. The Ancient Maya Self: Personhood and Portraiture in the Classic Period. *Res* 33:73–101.

———. 2001. Peopling the Classic Maya Court. In Inomata and Houston, *Theory, Comparison, and Synthesis*, vol. 1 of *Royal Courts of the Ancient Maya*, pp. 54–83.

Houston, S. D., Stuart, D., and K. A. Taube. 1989. Folk Classification of Classic Maya Pottery. *American Anthropologist* 91 (3): 720–26.

———. 2006. *The Memory of Bones: Body, Being, and Experience among the Classic Maya*. University of Texas Press, Austin.

Houston, S. D., O. W. Chinchilla Mazariegos, and D. Stuart, eds. 2001. *The Decipherment of Ancient Maya Writing*. University of Oklahoma Press, Norman.

Innes, M. 2003. "A Place of Discipline": Carolingian Courts and Aristocratic Youth. In *Court Culture in the Early Middle Ages*, edited by C. Cubitt, pp. 59–76. Brepols, Turnhout, Belgium.

Inomata, T. 2001a. King's People: Classic Maya Courtiers in a Comparative Perspective. In Inomata and Houston, *Theory, Comparison, and Synthesis*, vol. 1 of *Royal Courts of the Ancient Maya*, pp. 27–53.

———. 2001b. Power and Ideology of Artistic Creation: Elite Craft Specialists in Classic Maya Society. *Current Anthropology* 42 (3): 321–49.

———. 2006. Politics and Theatricality in Mayan Society. In Inomata and Coben, *Archaeology of Performance*, pp. 187–222.

———. 2008. *Warfare and the Fall of a Fortified Center: Archaeological Investigations at Aguateca*. Vanderbilt University Press, Nashville.

Inomata, T., and L. S. Coben, eds. 2006. *Archaeology of Performance: Theaters of Power, Community, and Politics*. AltaMira Press, Oxford.

Inomata, T., and S. Houston, eds. 2001a. *Royal Courts of the Ancient Maya*, vol. 1: *Theory, Comparison, and Synthesis*. Westview Press, Boulder.

———2001b. *Royal Courts of the Ancient Maya*, vol. 2: *Data and Case Studies*. Westview Press, Boulder.

Inomata, T., D. Triadan, E. Ponciano, E. Pinto, R. E. Terry and M. Eberl. 2002. Domestic and Political Lives of Classic Maya Elites: The Excavation of Rapidly Abandoned Structures at Aguateca, Guatemala. *Latin American Antiquity* 13 (3): 305–30.

Jackson, S. E. 2005. Deciphering Classic Maya Political Hierarchy: Epigraphic, Archaeological, and Ethnohistoric Perspectives on the Courtly Elite. Ph.D. dissertation, Harvard University.

———. 2009. Imagining Courtly Communities: An Exploration of Classic Maya Experiences of Status and Identity through Painted Ceramic Vessels. *Ancient Mesoamerica* 20 (1): 71–85

———. 2011. Continuity and Change in Early Colonial Maya Community Governance: A Lexical Perspective. *Ethnohistory* 58 (4): 683–726.

Jackson, S. E., and D. Stuart. 2001. The Aj K'uhun Title: Deciphering a Classic Maya Term of Rank. *Ancient Mesoamerica* 12 (2): 217–28.

Jones, S. 1997. *The Archaeology of Ethnicity: Constructing Identities in the Past and Present*. Routledge, London.

Josserand, J. K. 2002. Women in Classic Maya Hieroglyphic Texts. In *Ancient Maya Women*, edited by T. Ardren, pp. 114–51. AltaMira Press, Walnut Creek, Calif.

Joyce, R. A., and S. D. Gillespie, eds. 2000. *Beyond Kinship: Social and Material Reproduction in House Societies*. University of Pennsylvania Press, Philadelphia.

Kidder, A. V. 1950. Introduction. In *Uaxactun, Guatemala*, edited by A. L. Smith. Carnegie Institution of Washington, Washington, D.C.

King, A. 2000. Thinking with Bourdieu against Bourdieu: A 'Practical' Critique of the Habitus. *Sociological Theory* 18 (3): 417–33.

Knorosov, Y. 1956. New Data on the Maya Written Language. *Journal de la Société des Américanistes de Paris* 45:209–17.

Kovacevich, B., H. Neff, and R. L. Bishop. 2005. Laser Ablation-ICP-MS Chemical Characterization of Jade from a Jade Workshop at Cancuen, Guatemala. In *Laser Ablation ICP-MS in Archaeological Research*, edited by R. J. Speakman and H. Neff, pp. 39–57. University of New Mexico Press, Albuquerque.

Kurjack, E. B. 1974. *Prehistoric Lowland Maya Community and Social Organization: A Case Study at Dzibilchaltun, Yucatan, Mexico.* Middle American Research Institute, Publication no. 38. Middle American Research Institute, Tulane University, New Orleans.

Lacadena, A. 1996. A New Proposal for the Transcription of the A-k'u-na/A-k'u-HUN-na Title. *Mayab* 10:46–49.

Lakoff, G., and M. Johnson. 1980. *Metaphors We Live By*. University of Chicago Press, Chicago.

Lamb, D., and G. Lamb. 1951. *Quest for the Lost City*. Harper, New York.

Laughlin, R. M., and J. B. Haviland. 1988. *The Great Tzotzil Dictionary of Santo Domingo Zinacantán: With Grammatical Analysis and Historical Commentary*. Smithsonian Contributions to Anthropology, no. 31. Smithsonian Institution Press, Washington, D.C.

Leventhal, R. M. 1979. Settlement Patterns at Copan, Honduras. Ph.D. dissertation, Harvard University.

Lévi-Strauss, C. 1984. *Paroles données*. Plon, Paris.

López Austin, A. 1961. *La constitución real de México-Tenochtitlan*. Universidad Nacional Autónoma de México, México.

———. 1988. *The Human Body and Ideology: Concepts of the Ancient Nahuas*, translated by T. Ortiz de Montellano and B. R. Ortiz de Montellano. University of Utah Press, Salt Lake City.

———. 1997. *Tamoanchan, Tlalocan: Places of Mist*, translated by B. R. Ortiz de Montellano and T. Ortiz de Montellano. University Press of Colorado, Niwot.

Maca, A.L. 2006. Body, Boundaries, and "Lived" Urban Space: A Research Model for the Eighth Century City at Copan, Honduras. In *Space and Spatial Analysis in Archaeology*, edited by E. C. Robertson, J. D. Seibert, D. C. Fernandez, and M. U. Zender, pp. 143–56. University of Calgary Press, Calgary.

MacLeod, B. 1990. Deciphering the Primary Standard Sequence. Ph.D. dissertation, University of Texas, Austin.

Marcos, S. 2006. *Taken from the Lips: Gender and Eros in Mesoamerican Religions*. Brill, Leiden, Netherlands.

Marcus, J. 1976. The Origins of Mesoamerican Writing. *Annual Review of Anthropology* 5:35–67.

———. 1992. Royal Families, Royal Texts: Examples from the Zapotec and Maya. In *Mesoamerican Elites: An Archaeological Assessment*, edited by D. Z. Chase and A. F. Chase, pp. 221–41. University of Oklahoma Press, Norman.

———. 1993. Ancient Maya Political Organization. In *Lowland Maya Civilization in the Eighth Century A.D.*, edited by J. A. Sabloff and J. S. Henderson, pp. 111–84. Dumbarton Oaks, Washington, D.C.

Marken, D. B., and K. D. Straight. 2007. Conclusion: Reconceptualizing the Palenque Polity. In *Palenque: Recent Investigations at the Classic Maya Center*, edited by D. B. Marken, pp. 279–324. AltaMira Press, Lanham, Md.

Markman, P. T., and R. H. Markman. 1989. *Masks of the Spirit: Image and Metaphor in Mesoamerica*. University of California Press, Berkeley.

Martin, S. 2006. Cacao in Ancient Maya Religion: First Fruit from the Maize Tree and Other Tales from the Underworld. In *Chocolate in Mesoamerica: A Cultural History of Cacao*, edited by C. L. McNeil, pp. 154–83. University Press of Florida, Gainesville.

Martin, S., and N. Grube. 2000. *Chronicle of the Maya Kings and Queens: Deciphering the Dynasties of the Ancient Maya*. Thames and Hudson, London.

Mathews, P. 1988. The Sculpture of Yaxchilan. Ph.D. dissertation, Yale University.

Mathews, P., and M. Aliphat Fernández. 1997. *Informe de la temporada de campo 1993, Proyecto El Cayo*. Report presented to the Consejo de Arqueología del Instituto Nacional de Antropología e Historia.

Maxwell, J. M., and C. A. Hanson. 1992. *Of the Manners of Speaking That the Old Ones Had: The Metaphors of Andrés de Olmos in the TULAL Manuscript*. University of Utah Press, Salt Lake City.

Mayer, K. H. 1980. *Maya Monuments: Sculptures of Unknown Provenance in the United States*. Acoma Books, Ramona, California.

———. 1984. *Maya Monuments: Sculptures of Unknown Provenance in Middle America*. K.-F. von Flemming, Berlin.

———. 1991. *Maya Monuments: Sculptures of Unknown Provenance*, suppl. 3. Verlag von Flemming, Graz, Austria.

———. 1995. *Maya Monuments: Sculptures of Unknown Provenance*, suppl. 4. Academic Publishers, Graz, Austria.

McAnany, P. A. 1993. The Economics of Social Power and Wealth among Eighth-Century Maya Households. In *Lowland Maya Civilization in the Eighth Century A.D.*, edited by J. A. Sabloff and J. S. Henderson, pp. 65–90. Dumbarton Oaks, Washington, D.C.

———. 1995. *Living with the Ancestors: Kinship and Kingship in Ancient Maya Society*. University of Texas Press, Austin.

Miller, M., and S. Martin. 2004. *Courtly Art of the Ancient Maya*. Thames and Hudson, San Francisco.

Miller, M., and M. Samayoa. 1998. Where Maize May Grow: Jade, Chacmools, and the Maize God. *Res* 33:54–72.

Miller, M., and K. A. Taube. 1993. *The Gods and Symbols of Ancient Mexico and the Maya: An Illustrated Dictionary of Mesoamerican Religion*. Thames and Hudson, New York.

Monaghan, J. 1998. The Person, Destiny, and the Construction of Difference in Mesoamerica. *Res* 33:137–46.

Mondloch, J. L. 1980. K'E?S: Quiché Naming. *Journal of Mayan Linguistics* 2:9–25.

Montgomery, J. 1998. Monuments of the Middle Usumacinta River Valley. Unpublished manuscript.

Moore, J. D. 1996. *Architecture and Power in the Ancient Andes: The Archaeology of Public Buildings*. Cambridge University Press, Cambridge.

Morán, F., and W. Gates. 1935. *Arte y Diccionario en Lengua Choltí: A Manuscript Copied from the Libro Grande of Fr. Pedro [i.e. Francisco] Morán of About 1625: In Facsimile*. Maya Society, Publication no. 9. Maya Society, Baltimore.

Morley, S. G. 1947. *The Ancient Maya*. Stanford University Press, Stanford, Calif.

Moseley, M. E. 2001. *The Incas and Their Ancestors: The Archaeology of Peru*. Thames and Hudson, London.

Nelson, J. L. 2003. Was Charlemagne's Court a Courtly Society? In *Court Culture in the Early Middle Ages*, edited by C. Cubitt, pp. 39–58. Brepols, Turnhout, Belgium.

Ong, W. J. 1982. *Orality and Literacy*. Routledge, London.

Palka, J. W. 1995. Classic Maya Social Inequality and the Collapse at Dos Pilas, Peten, Guatemala. Ph.D. dissertation, Vanderbilt University.

———. 2005. *Unconquered Lacandon Maya: Ethnohistory and Archaeology of Indigenous Culture Change*. University Press of Florida, Gainesville.

Pérez, J. P., and O. Michelon. 1976. *Diccionario de San Francisco*. Akademische Druck- u. Verlagsanstalt, Graz, Austria.

Pérez Martinez, V., F. Garcia, F. Martinez, and J. Lopez. 1996. *Diccionario del idioma ch'orti'*. Proyecto Lingüístico Franscisco Marroquín, Antigua, Guatemala.

Pollock, H. E. D. 1980. *The Puuc: An Architectural Survey of the Hill Country of Yucatan and Northern Campeche, Mexico.* Memoirs of the Peabody Museum, vol. 19. Peabody Museum of Archaeology and Ethnology, Harvard University, Cambridge, Mass.

Proskouriakoff, T. 1960. Historical Implications of a Pattern of Dates at Piedras Negras, Guatemala. *American Antiquity* 25 (4): 454–75.

———. 1963. Historical Data in the Inscriptions of Yaxchilan, pt. I. *Estudios de Cultura Maya* 3:149–67.

Rands, B. C., and R. L. Rands. 1961. Excavations in a Cemetery at Palenque. *Estudios de Cultura Maya* 1:87–106.

Recinos, A., D. J. Chonay, and D. Goetz, trans. 1953. *The Annals of the Cakchiquels / Title of the Lords of Totonicapán*. University of Oklahoma Press, Norman.

Reents-Budet, D. 2001. Classic Maya Concepts of the Royal Court: An Analysis of Renderings on Pictorial Ceramics. In Inomata and Houston, *Theory, Comparison, and Synthesis*, vol. 1 of *Royal Courts of the Ancient Maya*, pp. 195–233.

Restall, M. 1997. *The Maya World: Yucatec Culture and Society, 1550–1850*. Stanford University Press, Stanford, Calif.

Rice, P. 2008. Time, Power, and the Maya. *Latin American Antiquity* 19 (3): 275–98.

Ringle, W. M. 1988. Of Mice and Monkeys: The Value and Meaning of T1016, the God C Hieroglyph. *Research Reports on Ancient Maya Writing*, no. 18. Center for Maya Research, Washington, D.C.

Ruz Lhuillier, A. 1952. *Exploraciones en Palenque*: 1950. *Anales del Instituto Nacional de Antropología e Historia* 3:25–45.

———. 1958. *Exploraciones en Palenque: 1955 anales del Instituto Nacional de Antropología e Historia* 10 (39):185–240.

Sáenz de Santa María, C. 1940. *Diccionario cakchiquel-español*. Tipografía nacional, Guatemala.

Sanders, W. T. 1986. *Excavaciones en el área urbana de Copán*. Secretaria de Cultura y Turismo, Instituto Hondureño de Antropología e Historia, Tegucigalpa.

———. 1989. Household, Lineage, and State at Eighth-Century Copán, Honduras. In Webster, *House of the Bacabs, Copán, Honduras*, pp. 89–105.

Sanders, W. T., and B. J. Price. 1968. *Mesoamerica: The Evolution of a Civilization*. Random House, New York.

Sandstrom, A. 1991. *Corn Is Our Blood: Culture and Ethnic Identity in a Contemporary Aztec Indian Village*. University of Oklahoma Press, Norman.

Saturno, W. A., D. Stuart, and B. Beltrán. 2006. Early Maya Writing at San Bartolo, Guatemala. *Science* 311 (5765): 1281–83.

Schele, L. 1989. A House Dedication on the Harvard Bench at Copán. *Copán Note 51*. Art Department, University of Texas, Austin.

———. 1991a. Demotion of Chac-Zutz': Lineage Compounds and Subsidiary Lords at Palenque. In *Sixth Palenque Round Table, 1986*, edited by M. Greene Robertson and V. M. Fields, pp. 6–11. University of Oklahoma Press, Norman.

———. 1991b. An Epigraphic History of the Western Maya Region. In *Classic Maya Political History: Hieroglyphic and Archaeological Evidence*, edited by T. P. Culbert, pp. 72–101. Cambridge University Press, New York.

———. 1992. *Notebook for the XVIth Maya Hieroglyphic Workshop at Texas*. University of Texas Press, Austin.

Schele, L., and D. A. Freidel. 1990. *A Forest of Kings: The Untold Story of the Ancient Maya*. Morrow, New York.

Schele, L., N. Grube, and S. Martin. 1998. *Notebook for the XXIInd Maya Hieroglyphic Forum at Texas*. University of Texas Press, Austin.

Schele, L., and P. Mathews. 1979. *The Bodega of Palenque, Chiapas, Mexico*. Dumbarton Oaks, Washington, D.C.

———. 1991. Royal Visits and Other Intersite Relationships among the Classic Maya. In *Classic Maya Political History: Hieroglyphic and Archaeological Evidence*, edited by T. P. Culbert, p. 226–52. Cambridge University Press, Cambridge.

———. 1998. *The Code of Kings*. Scribner, New York.

Schele, L., and M. E. Miller. 1986. *The Blood of Kings: Dynasty and Ritual in Maya Art*. Braziller, New York.

Scholes, F. V., and R. L. Roys. 1968. *The Maya Chontal Indians of Acalan-Tixchel: A Contribution to the History and Ethnography of the Yucatan Peninsula*. University of Oklahoma Press, Norman.

Sharer, R. J. 1993. Social Organization of the Late Classic Maya: Problems of Definition and Approaches. In *Lowland Maya Civilization in the Eighth Century A.D.*, edited by J. A. Sabloff and J. S. Henderson, pp. 91–109. Dumbarton Oaks, Washington, D.C.

Smailus, O. 1975. *El maya-chontal de Acalán: análisis lingüístico de un documento de los años 1610–12*. Centro de Estudios Mayas, Cuaderno 9. Universidad Nacional Autónoma de México, Coordinación de Humanidades, México.

Stone, A. 1991. Aspects of Impersonation in Classic Maya Art. In *Sixth Palenque Round Table, 1986*, edited by M. Greene Robertson and V. M. Fields, pp. 68–80. University of Oklahoma Press, Norman.

Stross, B. 2006. Maize in Word and Image in Southeast Mesoamerica. In *Histories of Maize: Multidisciplinary Approaches to the Prehistory, Linguistics, Biogeography, Domestication and Evolution of Maize*, edited by J. E. Staller, R. H. Tykot, and B. F. Benz, pp. 577–98. Elsevier Academic Press, Amsterdam.

Stuart, D. 1985a. The "Count-of-Captives" Epithet in Classic Maya Writing. In *Fifth Palenque Round Table, 1983*, edited by M. Greene Robertson and V. M. Fields, pp. 97–101. Pre-Columbian Art Research Institute, San Francisco.

———. 1985b. New Epigraphic Evidence of Late Classic Maya Political Organization. Unpublished manuscript.

———. 1987. *Ten Phonetic Syllables*. Research Reports on Ancient Maya Writing, no. 14. Center for Maya Research, Washington, D.C.

———. 1989a. Hieroglyphs on Maya Vessels. In *Maya Vase Book: A Corpus of Rollout Photographs of Maya Vases*, vol. 1, edited by J. Kerr, pp. 149–60. Kerr Associates, New York.

———. 1989b. The Maya Artist: An Iconographic and Epigraphic Study. Senior honors thesis, Princeton University.

———. 1992. Hieroglyphs and Archaeology at Copan. *Ancient Mesoamerica* 3 (1): 169–84.

———. 1993. Historical Inscriptions and the Maya Collapse. In *Lowland Maya Civilization in the Eighth Century A.D.*, edited by J. A. Sabloff and J. S. Henderson, pp. 321–54. Dumbarton Oaks, Washington, D.C.

———. 1995. A Study of Maya Inscriptions. Ph.D. dissertation, Vanderbilt University.

———. 1996. Kings of Stone: A Consideration of Stelae in Ancient Maya Ritual and Representation. *Res* 29:148–71.

———. 1997a. The Hills Are Alive: Sacred Mountains in the Maya Cosmos. *Symbols* (Spring):13–17.

———. 1997b. Kinship Terms in Maya Inscriptions. In *The Language of Maya Hieroglyphs*, edited by M. Macri and A. Ford, pp. 1–11. Pre-Columbian Art Research Institute, San Francisco.

———. 2003. Longer Live the King: The Questionable Demise of K'inich K'an Joy Chitam of Palenque. *PARI Journal* 4 (1): 1–4.

———. 2004. The Paw Stone: The Place Name of Piedras Negras, Guatemala. *PARI Journal* 4 (3): 1–6.

———. 2005a. Ideology and Classic Maya Kingship. In *A Catalyst for Ideas: Anthropological Archaeology and the Legacy of Douglas W. Schwartz*, edited by V. L Scarborough, pp. 257–86. School of American Research Press, Santa Fe.

———. 2005b. *The Inscriptions from Temple XIX at Palenque: A Commentary*. The Pre-Columbian Art Research Institute, San Francisco.

———. 2007. Gods and Histories: Mythology and Dynastic Succession at Temples XIX and XXI at Palenque. In *Palenque: Recent Investigations at the Classic Maya Center*, edited by D. B. Marken, pp. 207–32. AltaMira Press, Lanham, Md.

Stuart, D., and I. Graham. 2003. *Corpus of Maya Hieroglyphic Inscriptions*, vol. 9, pt. 1: *Piedras Negras*. Peabody Museum of Archaeology and Ethnology, Harvard University, Cambridge., Mass.

Stuart, D., and G. Stuart. 2008. *Palenque: Eternal City of the Maya*. Thames and Hudson, London.

Stuart, D., S. Houston, and J. Robertson. 1999. *Notebook for the 1999 Maya Hieroglyphic Forum at Texas*. University of Texas, Austin.

Taube, K. 1985. The Classic Maya Maize God: A Reappraisal. In *Fifth Palenque Round Table, 1983*, edited by M. Greene Robertson and V. M. Fields, pp. 171–81. The Pre-Columbian Art Research Institute, San Francisco.

———. 1993. *Aztec and Maya Myths*. University of Texas Press, Austin.

———. 1994. The Birth Vase: Natal Imagery in Ancient Maya Myth and Ritual. In *The Maya Vase Book: A Corpus of Rollout Photographs of Maya Vases*, vol. 4, edited by J. Kerr, pp. 650–85. Kerr Associates, New York.

Tedlock, B. 1982. *Time and the Highland Maya*. University of New Mexico Press, Albuquerque.

Tedlock, D. 1996. *Popol Vuh: The Mayan Book of the Dawn of Life*. Simon and Schuster, New York.

Thompson, J. E. S. 1954. *The Rise and Fall of Maya Civilization*. University of Oklahoma Press, Norman.

Triadan, D. 2006. Dancing Gods: Ritual, Performance, and Political Organization in the Prehistoric Southwest. In Inomata and Coben, *Archaeology of Performance*, pp. 159–86.

Turner, V. 1969. *The Ritual Process: Structure and Anti-Structure*. Aldine de Gruyter, New York.

Vico, D. de, and W. Gates. 1913. *Vocabulario Cakchiquel*. Reproduction by W. E. Gates.

Villela, K. D. 1993. The Classic Maya Secondary Tier: Power and Prestige at Three Polities. M.A. thesis, University of Texas, Austin.

Vogt, E. Z. 1969. *Zinacantan: A Maya Community in the Highlands of Chiapas*. Belknap Press, Cambridge, Mass.

Watanabe, J. M. 2004. Some Models in a Muddle: Lineage and House in Classic Maya Social Organization. *Ancient Mesoamerica* 15 (1): 159–66.

Webster, D. 1989a. The House of the Bacabs: Its Social Context. In Webster, *House of the Bacabs, Copán, Honduras*, pp. 5–40.

———, ed. 1989b. *The House of the Bacabs, Copán, Honduras*. Dumbarton Oaks, Washington, D.C.

Willey, G. R., R. M. Leventhal, and W. L. Fash. 1978. Maya Settlement in the Copan Valley. *Archaeology* 31 (4): 32–43.

Willey, G. R., and R. M. Leventhal. 1979. Prehistoric Settlement at Copan. In *Maya Archaeology and Ethnohistory*, edited by N. Hammond and G. R. Willey, pp. 75–102. University of Texas Press, Austin.

Zender, M. 2002. The Toponyms of El Cayo, Piedras Negras, and La Mar. In *Heart of Creation: The Mesoamerican World and the Legacy of Linda Schele*, edited by A. Stone, pp. 166–84. University of Alabama Press, Tuscaloosa.

———. 2004. A Study of Classic Maya Priesthood. Ph.D. dissertation, University of Calgary.

Zorita, A. de. 1994. *Life and Labor in Ancient Mexico: The Brief and Summary Relation of the Lords of New Spain*, translated by B. Keen. University of Oklahoma Press, Norman.

Zuidema, R. T. 1964. *The Ceque System of Cuzco*. Brill, Leiden, Netherlands.

Index

Page numbers in italics refer to illustrations.